light on wood

susan h jones

light on wood

mass timber architecture

Birkhäuser
Basel

"Undertake a pilgrimage of reconciliation with the world that is our home, to help make it more beautiful."

Pope Francis

to Marco, Rogan and Domenica

Foreword

Sylvan Leadership

A decade ago, I attended a workshop for leaders in architecture and design, both practitioners and educators. The participants were asked at the outset to draw an image to represent their understanding of "leadership," as a way to introduce ourselves and as a prompt for further discussion. Reflexively, I drew an image of a forest. While I have never discussed this with my friend and colleague Susan Jones, the author of this book, I suspect that she would have drawn a similar image. More importantly, I believe that she would have drawn hers years ahead of mine, foreseeing the moment in which we now live.

The value of the forest as both an actual and a conceptual construct for education and practice in architecture and design is as a proposition for our vision and imagination, for the wise exercise of human activity within and upon the forest. Yes, for the conversion of the forest to human use, but also for our stewardship of forests for future generations. This is ancient wisdom—that capacity for techne, for the application of imaginative vision to the given world, out of compassion for others and for the further exercise of labor and technique.

Wise students of architecture will know that the ethos of techne is intrinsic to their self-identity, in fact it is embedded in the very term 'archi-tect'. The fundamental proposition here is that the imaginative vision is, in part at least, rooted in a vision of the forest. Implicit in the assertion of techne and its origins in the forest is also the understanding that that forest-centered vision is focused on more than immediate needs or desires. Implicit is the proposition that those who exercise techne do so responsibly, with foresight, on behalf of those others we may never meet, know or share the world with.

Historically, the forest has been central to the human understanding of the world in both sacred and utilitarian terms. To live and work within the conceptual forest as an architect, designer, and educator, is to live and work as well within the ethical landscape of our society and our natural world, and to know deeply, with foresight and insight, the far-reaching responsibilities and the compassionate qualities intrinsic to our roles and work.

In *Light on Wood*, Susan Jones positions us in this metaphorical forest, and as importantly, in the actual forest. Her narrative is rooted in the deeply personal story of her life; of this, she writes with unabashed emotion, sensitivity, and care. But her narrative is just as expressive of professional responsibility, constructional technologies, evidence-based research, and the hard work of bureaucratic policymaking. The synthesis of these life experiences is a compelling study in "sylvan leadership." *Light on Wood* is at once an autobiography of a remarkable design leader, a report on the state of essential code-focused research, an analysis of low-carbon futures in architecture and design, and a call to positive, optimistic action in a world of ever-growing environmental challenges.

Susan and I share many mutual friendships in this cause, in this forest of leadership, but chief among them is that with the Finnish architect and educator Juhani Pallasmaa. More prescient than either of us, and with a bracing imperative tone, he declared in 1993 that,

"...(T)oday, however, I cannot imagine any other desirable view of the future than an ecologically adapted form of life where (contemporary) architecture returns to its early, biologically-derived ideals ... this view implies a paradoxical task for architecture: to become more primitive and more refined at the same time. More primitive, in terms of meeting the most fundamental human needs with an economy of expression and meditating our relation to the world in an equally fundamental and literal way, and more sophisticated, in the sense of adapting to the cyclic systems of nature, in terms of both matter and energy. Ecological architecture also implies a view of building more as a process than a product."

Reading *Light on Wood* entails engagement with a process rather than obtaining a product. Encountering Susan Jones in these pages is to meet her in the forest, to understand her ecology and its relevance to our own lives, and to hear her own encouragements to become both more primitive and refined—to become authentic leaders.

Peter B. MacKeith
August 28, 2025

Introduction

This book has awoken me in the quietest hours of the night. I found myself writing it the summer of 2024, during writing retreats, three to four days at a time. But it kept demanding more days, stealing more time from my beloved practice and team at atelierjones.

Despite the best choreographed outline, I would sit down to write a section and find myself writing different words, on different tangents that would take me down deep paths of memory, very far from the beginning of my telling. Inevitably, gaps occurred between the starts and the finishes. My ever-patient copyeditor, bewildered, would ask me to explain the gaps, and then the next bout of writing would take off. Again and again, this book directed itself, implacably.

How else to tell the story of everything it means to practice an *Architecture of the Present?*

Architecture is an intensely personal and passionate endeavor, and it makes deep demands of the intellect, the hand, and the heart. How to tell the interweaving of design burning like fire to be realized with the need to use our deeply technical brains in parallel? We use our loose and creative sketching hands, in one moment moving soft grainy charcoal pencils, the next harnessing crisp technological machines and their software. Our brains, our hands, and our voices reflect and communicate multiple realities, over and over, decade after decade, as we refine our talents to build spaces and buildings of meaning. We are both humanists and technocrats, spiritual and entrepreneurial, and weave every fiber of our being into bringing space into life, from a vision in our heads to reality.

Outwardly, we present an authentic personal self over and over. To potential clients, sometimes in the throes of difficult financial and design decisions they have never faced before. To personal, political, and public leaders who have their own dedicated paths of service to honor and build for. To a larger public who knows little of what we do or offer the world.

As design leaders, we direct teams of the young and ardent and teams of brilliant but weary souls who have confronted every line in the ever-changing volumes of codes. With technology, our design teams have grown even more complex, demanding teams of different leaders, each using wildly different and continuously evolving software platforms, each exploring different questions at different stages of each project. The constant need for collaboration requires evolving ingenious leadership, balancing the demanding honesty of young colleagues, with working within constraining realities, including codes, costs and constructability.

Collaboration between different engineering and design disciplines, each with their own language—from structural, civil, mechanical and electrical engineering to more recent areas of focus and expertise, including acoustics, fire-protection, and envelope consulting, just to name a few—becomes part of the architect's domain. Along with technological changes, the profession of architecture has become richly embedded with external and broad societal values based in community, walkability, health, accessibility, and many others through detailed and complex regulatory language and lengthy public processes.

Practicing architecture today, reflecting the present urgency of climate change, presents an even deeper ethical imperative. What do we do in the face of our building industry's damning 40% contribution to global carbon emissions? Attempting to answer or address such an enormous question requires phenomenal vision guided by deep, exacting research.

Light on Wood describes the arduous path of an architect who instinctually understood that the same rich, synthetic complexities required of architecture could also serve a larger arena of impact.

Light on Wood opens with a personal story, of being a child, walking along a trail, observing the natural environment, especially the space of a forest. This trail—where deep grief, curiosity, peace and fortitude are entwined—is the path of becoming more human and becoming an architect dedicated to delving into broader natural, technocratic and spiritual worlds to try to create impactful change.

Light on Wood is both a journey back into the most primordial human experiences of the forest, and also by seeing the forest in all of its many manifestations, about an architect's path forward, towards designing light on wood, designing to bring light into the woods, and designing lightly with wood.

Light on Wood sheds light on the myriad ways we can all engage with our forests and our homes and cities. From understanding differently, to living differently and building our cities differently. Using both less wood and more wood, in the right places, in ways that reflect the true value of carbon, transparently.

Light on Wood is also a journey forward into the urgency that this book ends on: an intense scherzo of fire. As architects, this challenges us to extend our thinking, not only to embrace the scale of buildings, but also the scale of landscape itself. This demands we change the way we approach projects as architects, calling us to take a leadership role in adapting to continental-scale environmental disaster.

Light on Wood describes atelierjones' multivalent work to confront these challenges. This work has required research and design, crossing disciplinary boundaries, and embracing risk to build prototypes at multiple scales. It also describes my most disruptive venture—both to my personal practice, but also to our entire 20th-century way of delivering carbon-intensive buildings—reaching outside our discipline entirely, and into new collaborative modes of leadership: applying designer-led research to create new data-driven national policies.

Light on Wood discusses a new depth and urgency of practice. Shifting at scale from 20th-century concrete and steel design typologies to the use of bio-based materials in order to create lower-carbon architecture has become the driving motivation of my practice, atelierjones. But building with timber, even from well-managed and regulated forests, entails an imperative to help understand and ensure the health of the forest. The devastating danger that our forests are experiencing under ever-intensifying fires, with their immense stores of carbon being released into our already-overcarbonated atmospheres and oceans, requires investigating paths previously unknown to the realm of architecture. Architects have a unique capacity to create impact on a world that desperately needs leadership during the crisis of climate change.

Seeing the forest for the trees, bringing light on wood is the foundation of this book, opening up pathways for how architecture to engage with the present in order to design for the future.

Ultimately, *Light on Wood* is about expanding the territories of architecture to deepen our collective knowledge of how and why we build. These expanded territories help us understand the systems in which our buildings are built and their impacts; the origins and sources of their materials, the carbon impacts of their construction, and their ability to be reused, repurposed, or disassembled, once their designed life has ended. They challenge us to imagine new material sources, including our ever-growing, collective streams of waste.

Expanding into these extra-architectural realms means collaborating with visionary communities of policymakers, life-cycle scientists, foresters, wood scientists, global economists, real estate professionals, and clients of all types. These explorations mine existing methodologies from these fields and apply them to architecture, creating new methodologies for design. It has been a foundational practice of atelierjones' work since its inception in 2003.

This focused transdisciplinarity, grounded in a voracious curiosity and love of learning, requires an essential, deep humility. This entails knowing when one's resources, intellectual and otherwise, have been reached, and one must stretch a hand across the aisle to ask for help in understanding the next unknown. It is an invitation to all of us to reach out and collaborate, to walk into darkness together in search of new light beyond.

Light on Wood encapsulates atelierjones' vision of how design and research can work systemically together to make beautiful, meaningful, and impactful architecture.

Light on Wood brings light to a new way of systemic thinking to address the urgent questions of the 21st century and impact people's lives on direct, everyday levels.

I.

"For as far as two leagues the cedars shivered when Enkidu felled Humbaba, the guardian of the forest"

The Epic of Gilgamesh

f o r e s t

A Constructed Forest

When I give a talk about our work, whether in Tokyo, New York, or Bordeaux, I invariably present a picture of a forest. Often it is a lush, memory-laden photo from the Mt. Baker National Forest in Washington State, which, like its other Pacific Northwest cousins, is held fast within the knots of state regulation. These best management practices are rooted in the contentious history of the Pacific Northwest's forest regulations, especially the Timber Wars of the 1990s that were resolved in tense and complex court cases. To urbanites, outsiders with eyes unaccustomed to the subtle language of forestry, it is simply a forest.

If I want to train their eyes, I add another image. This I call *Waste Ecologies*. It is gray, not the green fairy-tale forest. It is crowded with leaning stalks, 4 inches around or smaller, reaching up into the sky they themselves obscure. One can just make out the gray dirt, cluttered with fallen tree detritus, and crowded with small, excruciatingly long gray trunks of 20-year-old hemlock trees that started life in packed, bushy green stands.

The foresters call these young western hemlocks *doghair*. At five years old, they stand straight up, still pliant, each confident they will reach the sky first. But even as they grow, they are diminished, their root area confined into a small, crowded ball below the gray dirt, pushing out against the others. When you pull one out by the flimsy, quarter-inch trunk, you often pull another one or two, their meager roots entangled.

Some 20 or 30 years later, these optimistic patches of doghair become a forest, of sorts. The survivors have fought one another for the light and air, so plentiful in the dog days, but as they grow taller and taller, up to 40 feet, they create a closed ground plane where no light falls. They remain tiny, thin, and almost dead, excepting a small fluffy branch or two at the top. Most of them do not survive. They choke themselves out, creating a world that is inconducive to life. They close in the forest, close out the light, and create their own pockets of death.

Waste Ecologies 2013

I do not use such emotional language in the urban talks. Instead of death, I call it *waste. Waste Ecologies.* To frame these forests systemically and leave room for possible solutions. Human solutions to human-created problems. After all, an *unmanaged* forest is not the same as a *natural* forest.

Indeed, little if any of our forest land in the United States exists outside of the prolonged influence of humankind. Even before European settlers began the large-scale exploitation of the bounteous, tree-covered continent, indigenous peoples had long been clearing, harvesting, and tending the forests themselves, albeit with a better understanding of how to do so sustainably.

My photo was taken on my family's forest land, bought by my grandfather near the summit of Mt. Constitution, on Orcas Island in the Puget Sound. Even this remote mountainous island, far north on the west coast, has been logged at least twice. We see this from the huge Douglas fir stumps, approximately 8 feet in diameter, scattered some 50 feet from one another all throughout our property. Under a careful eye, the softly degrading beds of old logging roads emerge, often shrouded in moss. We estimate that the first logging was done around 1910, around the time that Seattle mayor Robert Moran was logging the land that would become his eponymous State Park.

My memories of my grandfather, walking me through what looked like a wasteland in the early 1960s, recall that the land was also cut for logs shortly before he purchased it from previous owners, in the 1950s or so. Twice clearcut, the land was bare and open to the sun, and the fast-growing western hemlock flourished. The ancient forest ecosystem had been fundamentally changed by the touch of humans.

An unmanaged forest is not a natural forest, I say again, as we gaze at the image of deathly clutter.

But then, I point out a different shade. More brown than gray, and deeply rutted with black ridges. To the trained eye, this healthy Douglas fir bark is immediately familiar, and stands out among the broken and scattered hemlocks. A tree that was planted by my grandfather. After buying the property, he planted thousands of Douglas firs and western white pines, trying to restock the starkly cleared land. There is a picture of me standing in front of a little seedling in the fall of 1963. Both of us are three years old, standing the same height. We seem to recognize each other.

Gradually the story becomes clearer. I explain that this Douglas fir in the picture, healthy and huge, is a survivor. I call her my sister.

She was planted by hand the year I was born on my grandfather's land. Planted in light. For the first two or three years, she grew well, stretching out roots into the mycelium. For the next few years as she grew, green with nubile needles each May, she became a springtime delicacy for the hungry deer. Somehow, she survived the mastication

Susan Jones at Mt. Constitution, 1963

of these predators, or she was simply lucky and was missed. Later, the western hemlocks shot past her, crowding her root structure, and she fell under a soft fringe of hemlock darkness, night and day.

Somehow, she fought her way through the hemlock doghair. It took her years. Most of her sister Douglas firs did not survive, falling victim to deer or darkness. Some of her sisters made it taller, only to befall the same fate as the western hemlocks. At 30 feet tall but only 3 inches around, with a truncated 12 inch root structure, you are likely to fall, an Icarus growing too tall, too fast, to reach the sun. Fallen Douglas firs abound in the photo, along with the hundreds of fallen western hemlocks. But this sister did not fall.

She grew and grew her own green growth of high overstory. Not quite normal, mind you. She leans to the right in this picture, straining for light. The marks of these trials remain.

Still, in the understory of this overstocked forest, the gray truncated waste of the hemlock doghair ecology supports no Douglas fir-green either. Were it not for the healthy, deep brown and black ridges rippling around the trunk, 24 inches in diameter at breast height, you might never know that this Douglas fir has lived some 60 years now. She spreads her majestic, needled branches high only in the upper third of her green canopy into the sky, some 60 feet above the gray dirt and hemlocks, absorbing the light and CO_2, turning it into green rings of growth.

This photo I call Waste Ecologies shows six decades of the evolution of a young forest, both accelerated by human clearcutting and slowed down by ecological reaction to the sudden abundance of light and air on the forest floor. At 60, this forest is mired in waste. Rhythms have been interrupted, under- and overstories ripped apart.

Yet today, we only see this moment. My sister will keep on growing, as will her Douglas fir and larger western hemlock sisters that have also survived. Some are robust and strong. And over time, the Waste Ecology of the gray understory will rot, releasing its carbon. Over decades, the dying and dead western hemlocks could turn to soil themselves, becoming, after a century or so, the soft, healthy understory of the first image, thick with rich, green detritus.

The middle story will clear, below the waistlines of the survivors. Light again will emerge, falling softly to the ground, and moss and sword ferns will shyly start sprouting through the soil. But after 60 years of human intervention, we have interrupted those cycles, perhaps irrevocably, and now time is precious. This forest is anything but natural.

In 2014, after many years, I came back to the forest. I looked for the small friendly trees I remembered, just my height. They were not there. Instead, they towered above. How could I forget time, forget that over 60 years had elapsed since I was three, and the trees were three?

Our human construction of time is so radically different than a forest's. A tree's lifespan stretches out ten times longer than our own. They are patient and, if we let them, they will become ancient forests again. The trees will keep growing. Nature will outlive us all, there is no doubt.

But my title remains: *Waste Ecologies*. How, I asked myself, could we intersect this waste to accelerate the process of healing? Once constructed, always constructed. Could we enter lightly and help return light to the understory, while turning the waste into something of value?

Could this process, starting at the scale of a tiny, three-year-old seedling, help not only heal the forest, but also heal another broken, human-constructed and wasted ecosystem: our carbon-intensive cities of concrete and steel?

I began to look more closely at the forest.

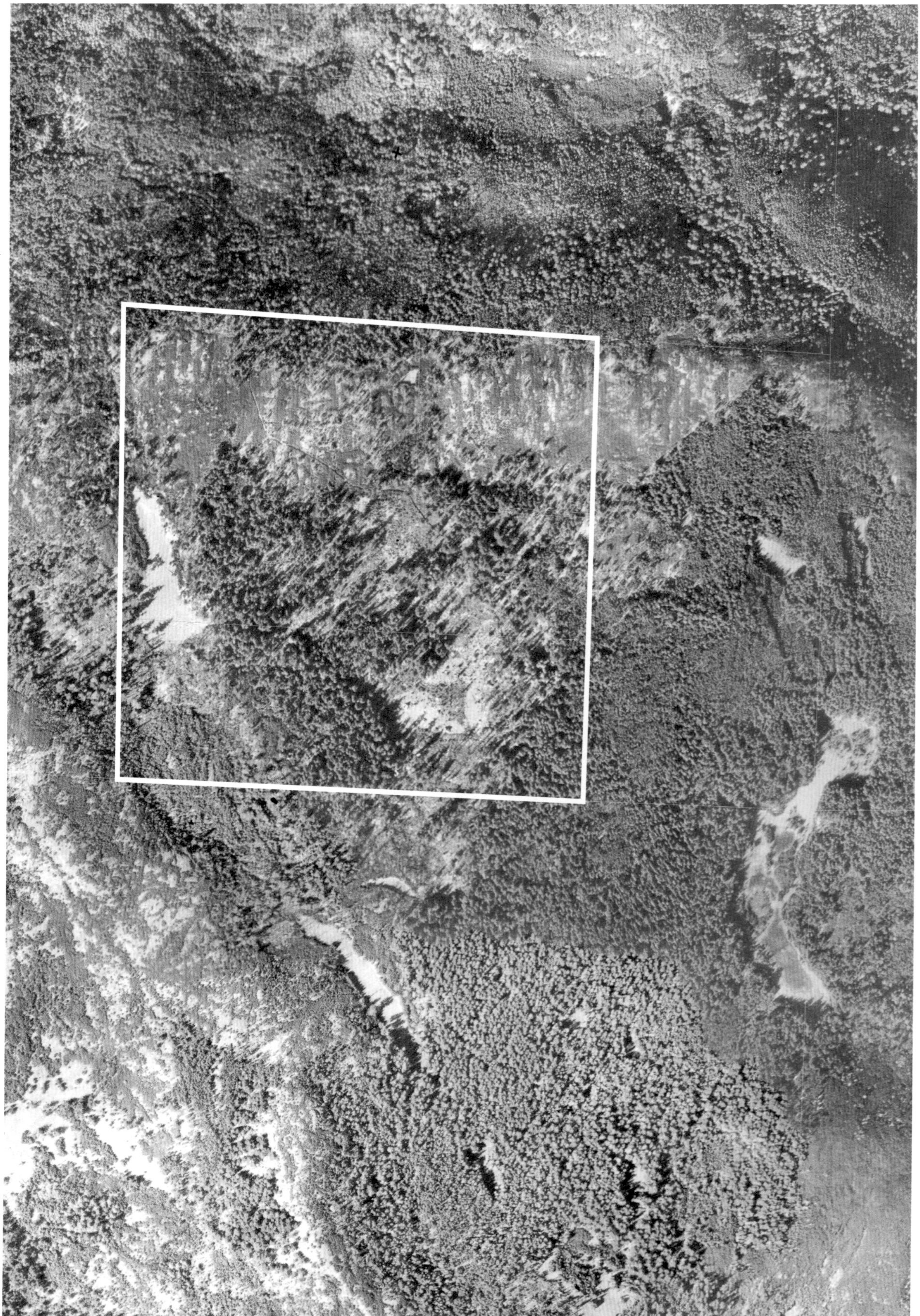

1932 Canadian Royal Air Force photo of future Jones property, showing clearcuts and second-growth forest

Forest Care

The decision to care for our family's forest was a generational one. It reached back in time, addressing the three interventions the forest had endured over the last 120 years: two clearcuts and my grandfather's decision to plant thousands of native trees without a plan to manage them. It reaches forward into the future, accelerating the centuries it would take for the forest to naturally heal. Rectifying the past and shaping the future is not lightly undertaken. Like raising a child, care involves commitments of time and resources.

But as deep as I felt a generational imperative, it was overshadowed by the urgency of the present. On our warming planet, fires are becoming larger and more common every year. Our tangled and overgrown forest was a real threat to the small island community, where an out-of-control fire could quickly become a human and ecological disaster.

I had to figure out what to do. So, guided by our ecologist's Forest Management Plan, and inspired by deep, clean breaths in the mountaintop forests, I committed to caring for the forest, aided by my family and a large circle of enthusiastic friends and colleagues. Weekend by weekend we began to let light down into the forest.

The process is multifaceted. Each stand gets multiple treatments. Every forest, in every region, has its own management strategies. Creating a healthy forest is always a unique process. In overstocked Pacific Northwest conifer forests, it involves reducing the forest canopy to allow more light down to the forest floor, creating both a healthy understory and a healthier overstory in the green branches above the trunks. The balance between the fullness of the canopy and the light coming down to the forest floor is important. In our forest, we have developed, intuitively, five forest treatments that we apply to every stand as we slowly work our way around the property.

We use hand tools, or sometimes just hands. Some of us use a 12-inch electric chain saw or Boy's Axe. My tools of choice are simply a hardhat and gloves, to yank out or push over the western hemlocks that choke out the sporadic Douglas firs, spruces, and western white pines.

Our land is typically overstocked with 400 to 550 of these weedy hemlocks per acre, which rarely grow bigger than 4 inches in diameter. A healthy stand would contain approximately 200 trees. We have many to remove.

We are not scientific in our selection. One develops an eye for the unhealthiest, and more than half are already dead standing. We are often just moving the dead to the ground, hoping to absorb some of their already-releasing carbon into the soil, and open up the forest to the light. Doing so also relieves the tension within the fragile overstory. During winter winds and snows, these trees—or often only their top halves—fall, catching against others and causing stress in the high overstory or crashing to the ground and blocking carefully tended dirt roads and potentially causing danger to those below.

I was kept awake for some nights one week after reading about the importance of dead, standing snags, just after we had cleared a large section of them. But, of course, there are still hundreds and hundreds of dead trees that we have not yet taken down, and now when we come across a larger standing snag, we leave it as a habitat for insects and birds.

The second treatment is managing the fallen biomass of the thinned trees. As the trunks fall, we cut them first into manageable lengths to move and stack in piles, then array them across the soil, allowing their decaying trunks to add to their carbon to the soil, building more depth and rich nutrients. Others we drag or toss, harpoon-like, to the softly curved edges of the mossy clearings that mark the

property's historic logging roads. Once cleared of their dog-hair growth, these rich green avenues suddenly appear in the dark brown forest floor and become the pathways we use to traverse the woods. We call them superhighways of moss.

We cut the long, thin, arcing branches, strongly curved toward what little light they sense above. Growing towards the light, the branches often have as much biomass as the tiny trunks that support them. We stack the branches in piles, parallel woody arcs in deep, historic hollows. Many of these remain from the clearcuts from the 1950s, where dirt was moved to accommodate a truck or, earlier, in the 1900s, a horse-drawn skid to get the big trees out. Sometimes natural hollows have been created by a larger tree falling from wind, their 20- to 30-foot-diameter root masses upended above our heads, slowly releasing their root carbon to the atmosphere.

During the second treatment we also remove any human debris we find as we walk the forest. One year we hired a local contractor to bring up a dump truck to our forest stand. With dear friends, we removed an entire truck load of old outhouse toilets, rusted 1920s' woodstoves, old metal bed springs and bedframes, countless beer and liquor bottles from the 1930s to the 1990s, dozens of rusting gas tanks—many still with propane in them—and yards of plastic hoses and pipes. We humans have often treated these forests with low regard over our two centuries of contact and used them as dumps.

The third treatment gathers the smaller wood waste, branches and limbs from the forest floor into bio-habitat piles. This allows still more light to hit the soil, sparking new green growth. I call this *"beautifying the area,"* riffing off an old saying my father would repeat. My husband Marco warns me not to fall in love with any one area with so much acreage left to treat. Of course, he is right, but there is tremendous satisfaction to pulling the trees to construct larger piles, and to clearing the mossy patches and mossy roads of light trapping woody debris, to opening the light onto the forest floor.

Sometimes, we burn the piles in the winter months to create biochar. This can be added to the soil to provide nutrients for the growing understory and help hold water through the dry Pacific Northwest summer. Although we have yet to find a system that will let us scale this process while limiting the methane and carbon offgassing, biochar offers an enticing promise for our scrawny, overstocked hemlocks, which otherwise have no commercial value.

The fourth treatment is simply time. Waiting. Silently, the dead wood in the piles decomposes, releasing carbon as the piles start to flatten and compress naturally. Sometimes we accelerate the time required for this long, slow process by chipping the piles, if equipment and labor is available, and spreading the chips across the forest floor. Regardless of the treatment, the carbon from the decaying wood is mostly released into the atmosphere. But the more wood that is in contact with the ground, the more carbon that will be released downward into the earth. By taking the small trees down, we are helping to build soil.

But the most important product of time is growth. With the now-more-open overstory letting light down to the now-more-open understory, plant growth is sparked. Having completed acres and acres of this work since 2018, we can see that this work is effective. The green slowly comes back, first with layers of moss, then small spiral punctures of sword ferns, bracken ferns, and mushrooms, poking through the soft brown soil.

The fifth treatment is active logging. This is what Carson Sprenger, our local ecologist, recommended in his 2013 Forest Management Plan. He suggested two experimental logging plans on small, 3.5-acre stands. For the first, 70% of the trees were logged in a lop-and-scatter method, leaving the downed timber as soil cover to discourage future hemlock growth. No trees were manually replanted; Sprenger preferred to rely only on the slow, natural propagation of new trees.

In the second plan, 90% of the trees were logged and sold, but with extensive replanting of saplings across the stand. Although more labor intensive, this had the potential to create a healthy, variably-aged stand more quickly. Even though our family was excited by the commercial potential of this logging, the difficult logistics of transporting logs from a mountainous island to sell on the mainland meant that we only broke more or less even.

So later, we tried a third approach on a 7-acre stand. Rich Harvey, a fourth-generation forester on the island, did a pre-commercial thin, taking approximately 30% of the trees, mostly crowded hemlocks. After taking out hundreds of these 6- to 12-inch logs, he milled them into firewood to sell to campers at neighboring Moran State Park. By selling the logs locally, even as a lower-value product, Rich was able to earn some income while helping us open up our forest.

Moving forward, we plan to expand our connections to the small local timber industry on the island. In the near future, we intend to actively log some 30% of the acreage that we have thinned by hand, working with small mills on the island to produce and sell lumber locally, supporting both the community and our small forest.

We no longer see logging as a bad thing. The three plots where we have employed active treatments are now some of the healthiest on the property, with venerable large trees still standing and hearty new growth springing up from below. When performed with sensitivity, logging is one of the best means of healing a neglected forest. Waste becomes value.

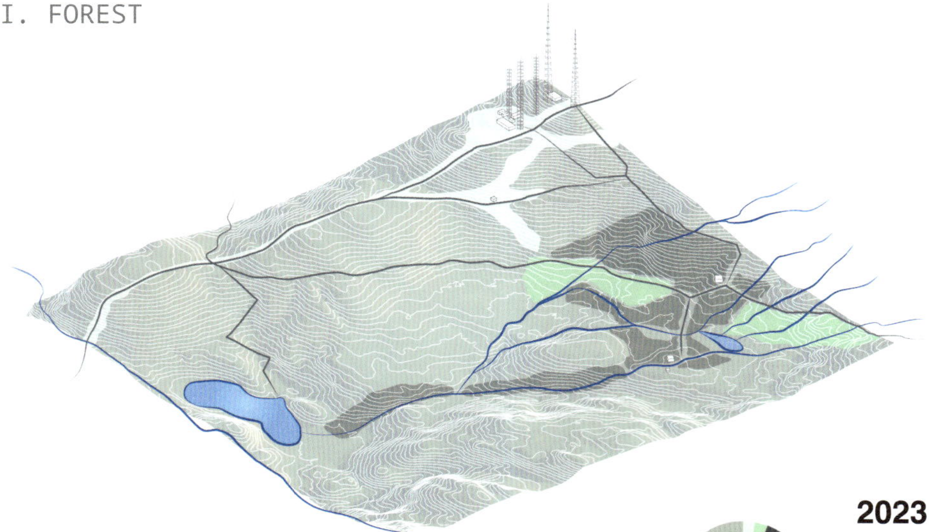

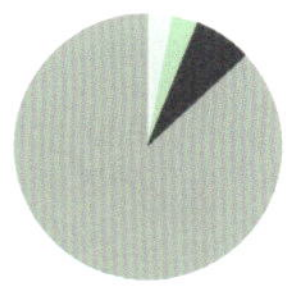

2023
119 acres: forest
15 acres: management (2018–2023)
7 acres: forest management (2013)
3 acres: cleared

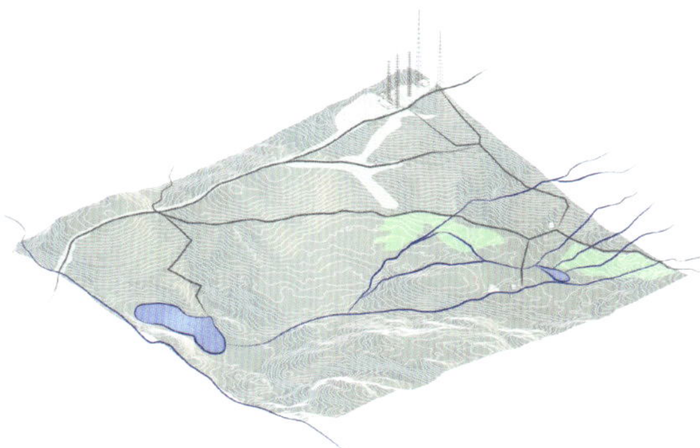

2013
134 acres: forest
2 acres: forest management (2013)
3 acres: cleared

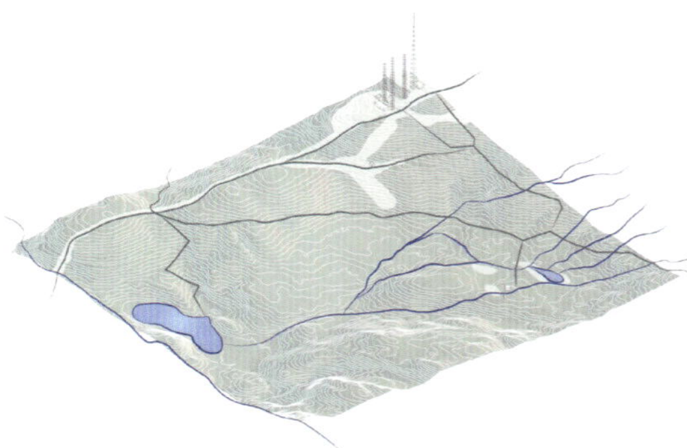

2006
143.6 acres: forest
.4 acres: cleared

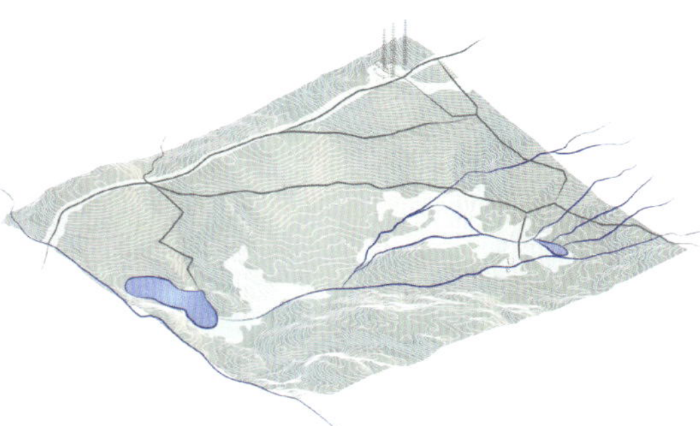

1969
128 acres: forest
16 acres: cleared

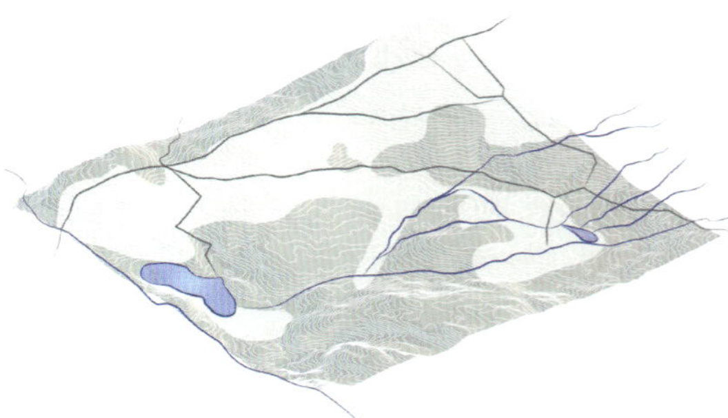

1932
101 acres: forest
43 acres: cleared

Jones Property forest development over time

Seeing the Future

Walking today through the 30-or-so acres that we have worked on, we see more birds flitting about, more insects that thrive on our bio-habitat piles, and more small fingers of green. Gray squirrels and chipmunks dart in and out of these piles, providing food for owls that stunningly call to us in the late afternoons, when we our faces are dripping with sweat in the summer or mist from the winter rains. We imagine the remaining trees growing slowly healthier, with access to more soil nutrients below, and more light from above. Still dense, the remaining 300 or so trees per acre could be thinned again. The once domineering western hemlock has now learned to coexist with the hardy Douglas fir, Sitka spruce, western white pine, and the occasional red alder, spreading its soft gracious leaves, a welcome deciduous tree amongst the conifers. We imagine our 60-year-old forest starting to retain more carbon, as health returns to the remaining trees.

The five stages of forest management, as we practice them above, are highly labor-intensive, acts of love. They allow us urbanites to become absorbed into the rhythms of the forest and its extensions of time, where trees will live out their lives over centuries. Particularly during the COVID-19 pandemic, visiting the forest and breathing in its life became not only an act of self-preservation, but a reminder that these trees will outlive our hyper-anxious and tentative human grasp of what we believe to be civilization.

Over the years, our bodies have become used to the strenuous, physical labor it takes to move 150 trees per acre into manageable piles over a series of months and years. And our vision has become honed to understand nuances of the life of the trees, in all of their stages, species, and the surrounding biodiversity that we have helped spark, as we see the impact of light on the health of the forest.

Collectively, our band of foresters, including family, friends, and partners, have treated some 20% of our land over the past ten years. We are still working to bring light back to the remaining, badly overstocked forest. As I write this, May shines with the misty forest light grazing over the new electric-green moss. Over the summer, we will bring some 30 people up to work and sweat in the forest, as new spatial relationships slowly emerge between marshes, streams, roads, and stands. As the forest slowly heals.

2018–2021
Orcas Island, Washington

atelierjones:
Susan Jones, Lenore Wan

Contractor:
Happy Acres Construction

Photography:
Lara Swimmer

Constitution Shed

Orcas Island, Washington, with Jones property and Constitution Shed

Restoration

During breaks from our intensive forest work on the top of the mountain, we would take walks to explore the property. We had stumbled across The Shed once or twice, but it kept slipping out of sight, until we could finally reliably track the path to it. It was just north of the power lines extending up to the radio and television towers my grandfather had erected at the highest rocky point of the property in the 1960s.

In the 1930s, the WPA constructed power lines to bring electricity to the summit of Mt. Constitution. Once the long, straight easement was clearcut for these lines, a shed was built to support a small water tank to fight forest fires.

Fire was always a danger, as the only route up the mountain was the small two-lane road about half a mile to the east of the property. The Shed was in the northwest corner of the property, where trails led down to the Buck Mountain communities to the north. Aerial photos from the 1930s show the site was then almost fully cleared of trees in its northern half, a reminder of how harvested trees do grow back over time, whether planted or not.

The wooden structure was approximately 8 feet square, standing about 10 feet tall with a 4-foot-high, 6-foot diameter steel tank on top. Water would be added at the beginning of every dry season, standing at the ready for park rangers or firefighters to deploy in the event of a fire. At some point, though, it had been forgotten. Over the years, the walls had begun to weaken and deteriorate, and the back wall had already collapsed when we first discovered it.

Proportionally, it was striking. A tall, narrow thing, with two elemental materials: aged gray boards of Douglas fir, and the rusted brown curves of almost 100-year-old steel, catching the light like a Serra or Judd sculpture. We loved the surprise of coming upon it on our hikes around the property.

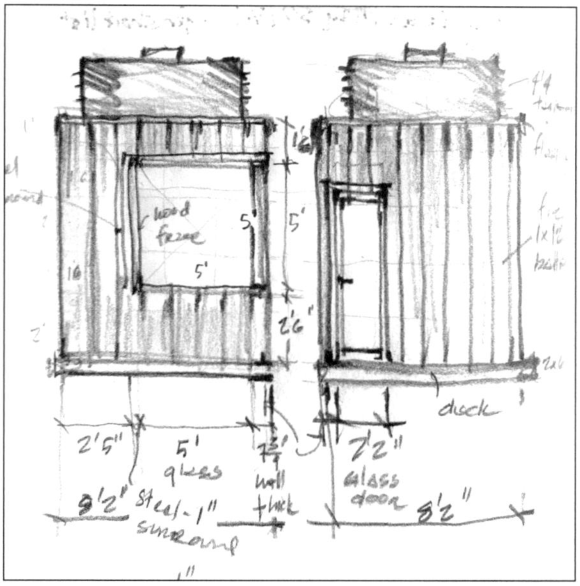

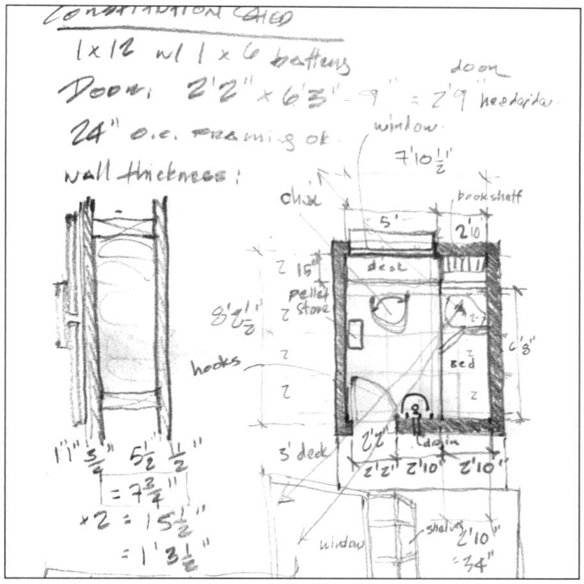

In 2018, I reached out to Rolf Ericksen, a contractor and local friend who helped my family maintain the five radio, television, and cell towers on the mountaintop. Rolf, along with our long-trusted and beloved site manager, Erling Manley, would sometimes hike up to turn on the site's backup generator when deep winter snows closed the narrow, winding road that provides access to the mountain top.

"Any chance we could figure out a way to restore The Shed? What would it take?"

"If I can build a new ski lodge at 4,500 feet on Mt. Baker in one season, I can get a little shed restored and back up to the mountain. But we'll need to move it down. I can have a truck crane up there next week. Would that work for you?" And so the process of restoring the 90-year-old wooden shed began.

The sketches were elemental. Broad-stroked pencil drawings done on the ferries back and forth to the island or on site for Rolf. The exterior form was left unchanged, save for the addition of 6 inches of insulation and a plywood interior for the unconditioned, off-grid space. A door was added for the existing opening, retaining the odd two-foot-two-inch proportion. And a large fiberglass-framed window was inserted on the main approach side.

Although the design was simple, the complexity of working on a decayed 90-year-old structure, on a mountain, on an island, in the middle of a pandemic, turned the 64-square-foot renovation into a three-year-long project.

Rolf observed that the exterior wooden walls were almost entirely rotted through, and that they were not made from commercially available lamstock, instead had likely been milled from existing trees on the site. Fortunately, he had his own mill at his workshop, and, even more fortuitously, he already had several large firs downed from our own property. The logs would provide raw material for the newly milled boards to the same dimensions to replace the 1930s originals.

Deep in the isolation of the COVID pandemic, the process of restoring The Shed brought us closer to the rural island community. We shared stories of our families, entwined through the radio business over three generations, and, with our kids, helped Rolf collect honey from his bee colonies. We met his extended network of island collaborators, who often held multiple jobs at once just to make ends meet.

Finally, in January 2021, we brought the band of trained contractors up to the mountain with a 1940s truck crane to lift the now-fortified and much heavier shed onto its waiting steel pin foundations, sitting on the frozen ground. It was one of the highlights of our time during the pandemic.

Today, the Constitution Shed sits lightly on these foundations, handset between Douglas firs and western hemlocks. Underground, their roots connect with mycelium and intertwine, like those of our urban and rural families brought together by the forest.

One enters the property, through the red and white security gate and down the gravel road, a dense cover of evergreen boughs above. Suddenly, behind the rugged trunk grooves of an old Douglas fir, appears a reflection of the forest. Brilliant patterns of light, filtered through the canopy, fall on the large, triple-paned window, shimmering at the end of the road. Marking a place for our forest community to linger, to share food, to read, to write, to rest.

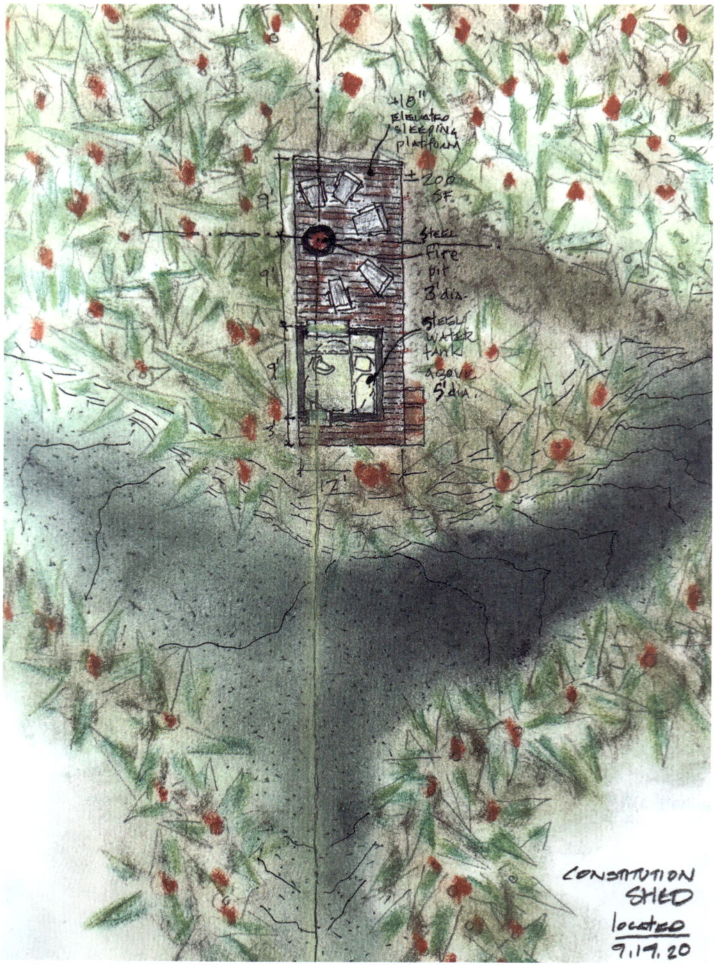
+18"
ELEVATED
SLEEPING
platform
±200
SF.
9'
9'
9'
3'
12'
STEEL
fire
pit
3' dia.
STEEL
WATER
tank
above
5' dia.
CONSTITUTION
SHED
located
9.19.20

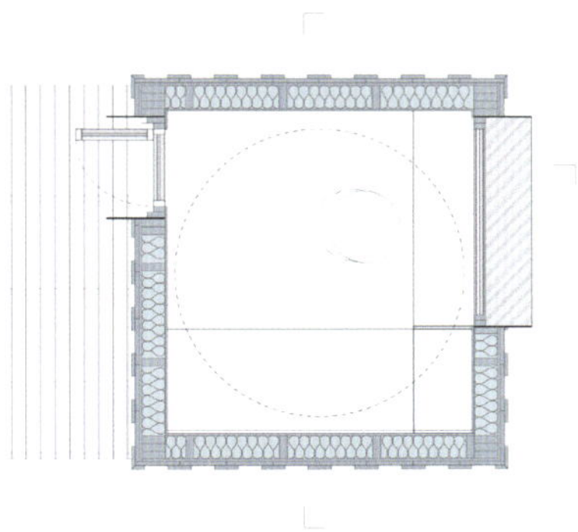

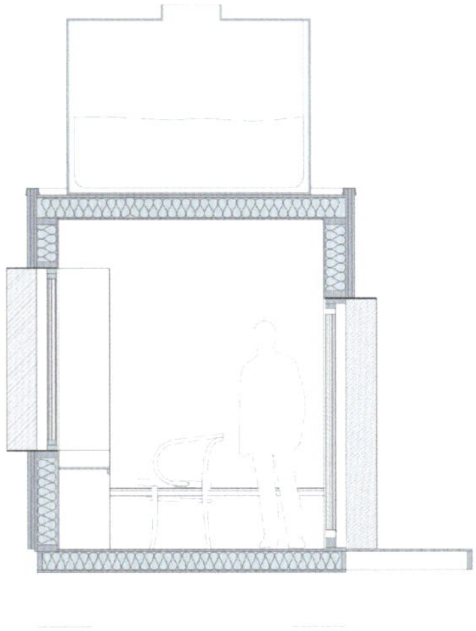

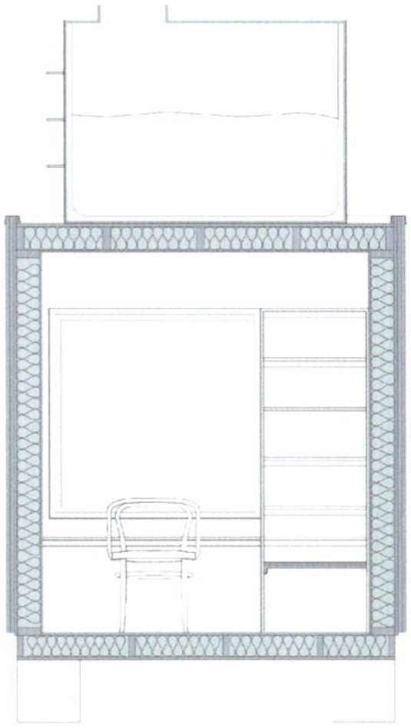

CONSTITUTION SHED
VIEW OUT
3.20.21

II.

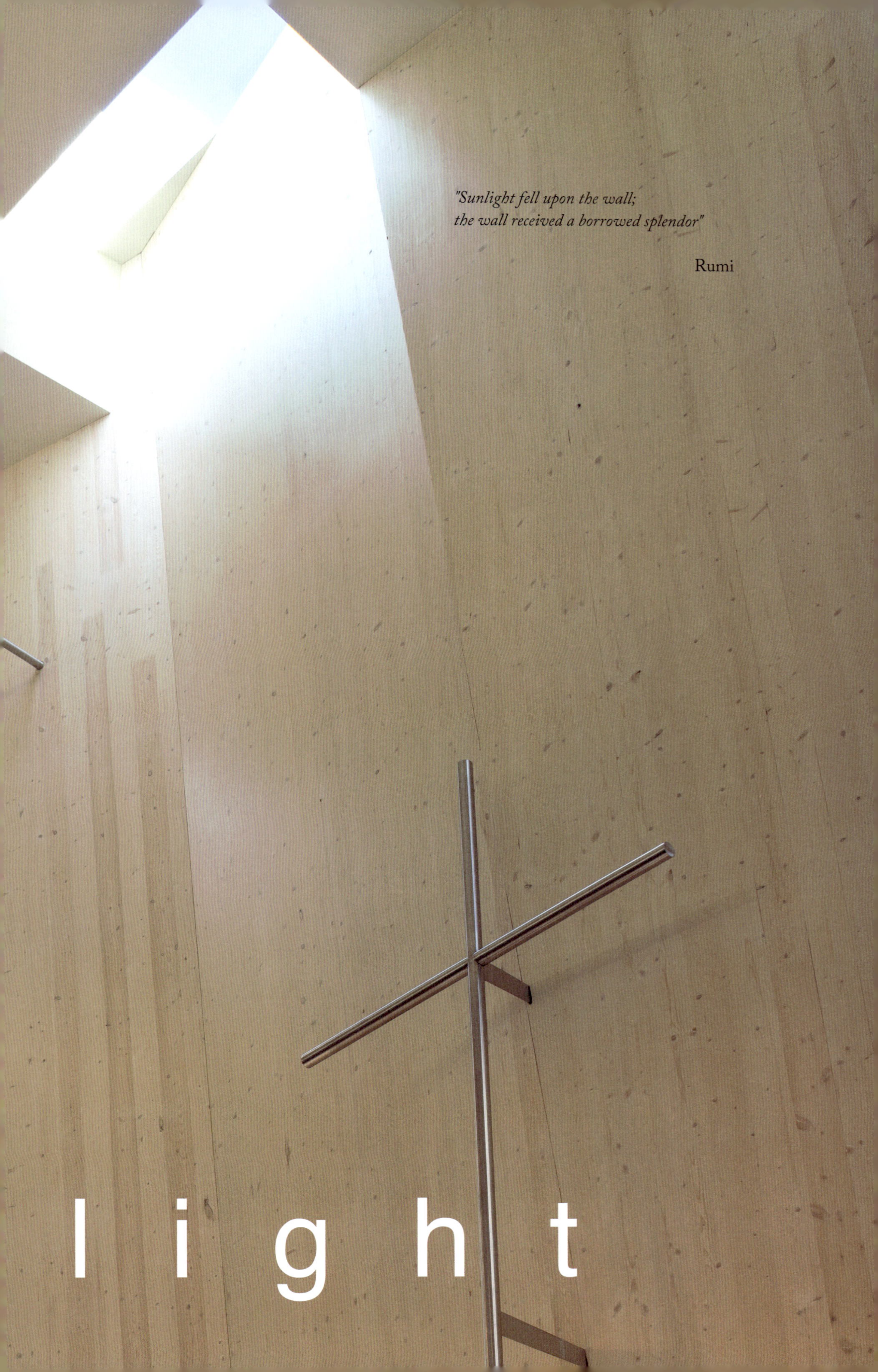

"Sunlight fell upon the wall;
the wall received a borrowed splendor"

Rumi

l i g h t

Emily Carr, "Lone Cedar" 1936

The Light of the Forest

Walking the half mile to the yellow school bus, the sound of footfall from my schoolgirl leather shoe soles was a therapeutic rhythm, momentarily absorbing my grief through the devastating illness of my father at ages 10 and 11, and his death in the spring of my 12th year, five days after his 40th birthday.

Walking alone through *The Trail*, as I named it, became a meditative respite of focus and observation. The elements of The Trail, carved deeply in my memories, still provide a talismanic comfort. I remember the repetitive motions of my body and keen observations of the slowing mutating curvatures of the worn pathway, always varying slighting under my feet, with its changes in rains, ice, baking sun, and soft emerging spring light. Observing over time, for instance, The Rock, with its scattered lichen patterns, counterbalanced against the rhythms of changing mud, ice sheets and cracked dry basin of The Puddle around it, provided a palette for careful intuitive records and rhythms of change.

Seasonal and spatial surprises of the sudden early February magenta vibrance and bracing quinine smell of The Flowering Quince, or the brilliance of the May new growth of electric light-green Douglas fir needles, soft and weepy against my cheek, marked transitions from winter to spring. In the summer, the blazing hot, waving wild grasses of The Field were a prelude to the faded romantic textures of Ocean Spray in late June. And in winter, as The Field decayed into brown stalks, the crisp white pop of snowberries would appear, arcing over the ice sheets that cracked slightly against The Puddle's contours. They all became touchstones of constancy for me as I lived with them through these solitary morning walks, in all seasons, all weathers.

Walking further, The Trail turned to a broad brown flatness, a soft loamy carpet of layers of deep brown fir needles below my feet, stretching under tall dark trunks of second-growth Douglas fir trees. Always, my breathing slowed, my shoulders rested, upon entering the tall darkness of The Forest, with its cool in summer, dry in winter, and, always, its quiet.

The Forest created a tall space, under the tall brown trunks of the young Douglas fir trees, bubbling with sap pockets, with vertical layers and layers of dark brown, light brown, airy, unneedled skeletal lower branches, almost always dry, even in the rainiest of Northwest winters. The Forest formed space, a shelter, dry and quiet, with the trees soaring above to the soft filtered white and golden light from above. The dappled fall of light descended through the light veil of brilliant spring evergreen above, down, filtered more and more, filtered through ever increasing layers of black twigs and stark black branches, onto the soft earth under my feet, creating a stippled, dappled veil of light on the earth, lighting my way through the forest.

My eyes followed the dancing, rippling light across the needled floor, up and down the vertical spaces between the trunks and their branches reaching over The Trail. Forgetting sharp pains of grief, momentarily meditative, focused, entranced. Seeing The Forest.

It was a vision of light within structured darkness. Refracted light fell onto a muted, brown, softly needled dirt trail, opening horizontally out onto bright golden transparent light, with space growing vertically through sharp dark branches, dancing with dappled light.

Walking through the darkness of the forest path, soft step by soft step, each day, I walked towards the light at the end of the path. A sharp, white-green-yellow golden light, a glowing green lacy fringe at the bottom of the dark, crisp black structure of the trees.

This paradigm of the indigenous Pacific Northwest Forest, similar to the Nordic Forest as written about by Christian Norberg-Schulz, would later become the conceptual framework for many projects. Gunnar Asplund's prototypical modernist icon, the Woodland Chapel was an intuitive territory for me, experienced in my later twenties outside Stockholm. Later, during the renovation of St. Paul's Church, I discovered the visionary early-20th-century female painter Emily Carr and her moving paintings of deep northwest forests and contrasting light, a painterly depiction of these childhood walks.

Designing and building *the light of the forest*, has been a constant in my work, from my first work of significance —a small prayer chapel for a large urban Catholic cathedral —to the renovation of a mid-century Episcopal church, to the powerful, muscular shaping of space and light in the Bellevue First Congregational Church, with newly emerging tectonics of the large, ungainly blanks of cross-laminated timber.

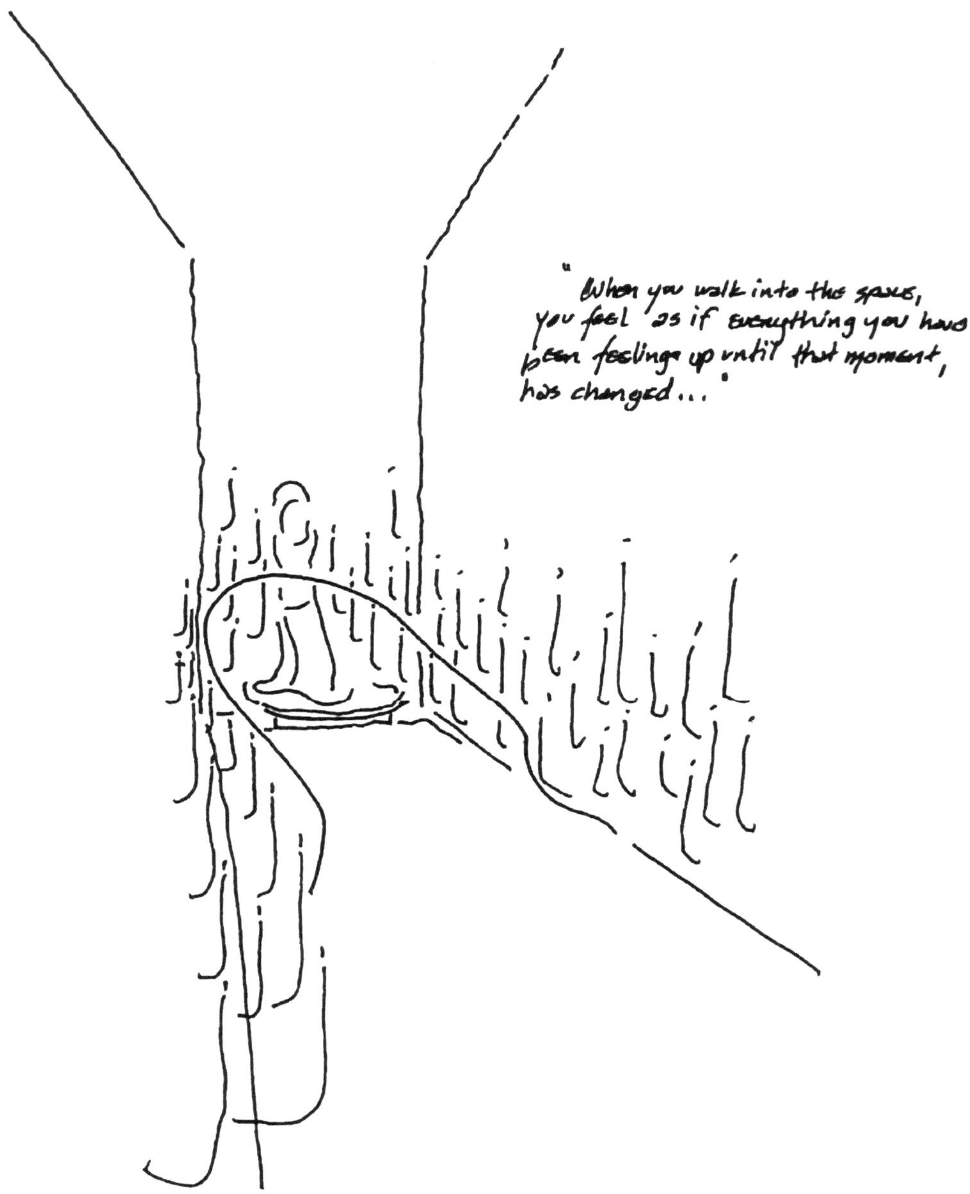
"When you walk into the space,
you feel as if everything you have
been feelings up until that moment,
has changed..."

2009–2012
Seattle, Washington

atelierjones:
Susan Jones, Brian Gerich, Greg Bishop, Kristin Saunders, Audrey Van Horne, Roma Shah

Owner:
St. Paul's Episcopal Church, with particular deep regard for the contributions of Rector Melissa Skelton as well as John and Ellen Hill

Architect (1962):
Steinhart, Theirault & Anderson

Structural Engineering:
Harriott Valentine Engineers

Contractor:
Foushée

Altar, Font, and Tabernacle:
Julie Speidel Studio

Lighting Design:
DePelecyn Studio

Custom Fabrications:
Bill Joy

Photography:
Lara Swimmer

St. Paul's Episcopal Church Renovation

Father John Lockerby with St. Paul's under construction, 1962

A Forest in the City

Located at the base of Queen Anne Hill, in a dense Seattle streetcar neighborhood, St. Paul's Episcopal Church sits just blocks from the site of the 1962 World's Fair. It was parallel with this futurist display that the church rose, built quickly and for a modest budget. The original, thoughtful and adventurous architects, Steinhart, Theirault & Anderson, convinced their clients to create a structure reflective of their faith – and their faith in the future. The power of the building from the exterior, is still evident today.

Upon entering the soaring mid-century modernist church, I was reminded of the forest trail of my youth. Huge soaring glulam (glued laminated timber) columns rose, angling inwards, some 60 feet in the air, dissolving wall and roof, creating an undulating, rippling, tent-like interior. Delicate diamonds of skylights were suspended between the dark, massive, trunk-like curving, angled columns. Light filters slowly down, capturing every nuance of the subtly shaped, supple wood trunks of the structure, falling on a dramatically suspended organ, designed to cast its magnificent tones throughout the wooden vessel to amplify, resonate and reverberate. The experience is intensely interior, held in this wooden vessel and softly nuanced northwest light.

The visionary Pastor Melissa Skelton, former Pastor Ralph Karskadden, patrons John and Ellen Hill, and a passionate and thoughtful group of parishioners had held several years of discernment sessions to determine the future of the church. The structure remained inspiring, but age and accumulated renovations had marred the main space.

Together, we spent the early months of 2009 refining a vision to refresh the space, focusing on a few key goals. First, to open the church out to the street, to become a welcoming, transparent, accessible presence, revealing the power of ancient, collective rituals of baptism and faith. To add a baptismal font, sized for full immersion baptisms that would anchor the new narthex entry. To replace the flimsy plastic and glass single-pane windows with a new insulated art glass wall. To add an accessible restroom to the ground-level, and to replace the altar, altar platform, lighting and finishes. In the midst of the economic recession, a modest project budget was established and strictly adhered to.

Together our collective experiences of the Northwest forest, opening out onto bright, golden, transparent light, became the conceptual framework for the Building Committee and the design team. Emily Carr, the visionary early-20th-century Canadian painter, and her moving paintings of the deep Northwest forests and contrasting light, gave us a guiding reference through which to realize our vision.

An image of the church as *a forest in the city* developed. While the silvan metaphor was boldly realized in the original design, the experience was cloistered and cut off from the surrounding city. It was time for the forest to reach out.

A quirky, heavy canopy was demolished and replaced with a light airy narthex, projecting the spirit of the church outward to the city of Seattle. It was anchored by the new baptismal font—deep, cast, double voluptuous basins of bronze—designed by talented local artist Julie Speidel. The narthex would glow under gray Seattle skies, harvesting volumes of light, animated by the swirling motions of people and bronze, sumptuously overflowing with water. It would draw the curious closer, toward the peaceful solace of the enormous forest inside. It was a bold vision: to throw open the forest to the city.

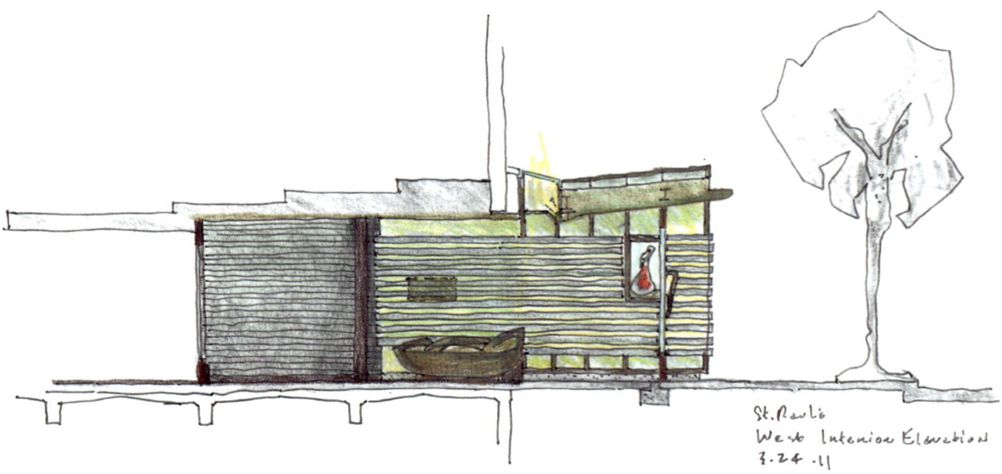

THE
EPISCOPAL CHURCH
WELCOMES YOU
St. Paul's
15 Roy Street
(206) 282-0786

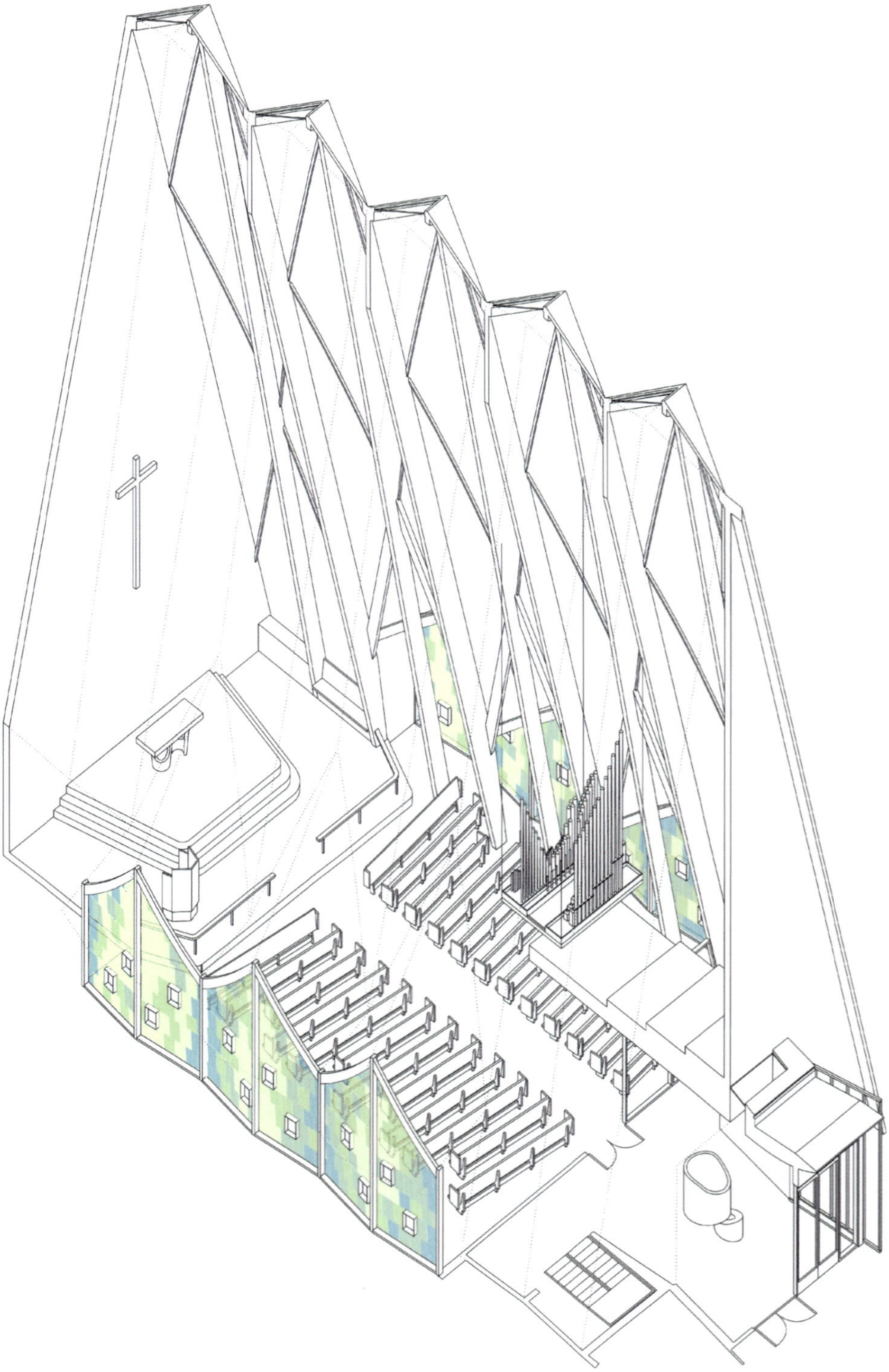

Renewing the clarity of the original vision of the building was a matter of stripping away and returning to the primeval vision of forest. With the soaring glulam timbers as the trunks of great trees, light filtered down through their blue-green canopy. The lower realm of the interior of the church would be a soft, muted warm brown, reflecting the peace of the inner world of the forest. Wherever possible, finishes were stripped back to a single natural color and extraneous materials were removed. The wooden pews, altar, altar rail, and altar platform were refinished with rich, warm browns. The aggregate floor slab was exposed, the mottled gray-brown of the forest floor.

Looking out into the nave, a new wall of gold, green and sky blue glass emerges as a horizon between tree trunks, bringing in dappled light. At the scale of the congregant, light surrounds the viewer. Each of the six small side chapels holds a different, layered set of colored, resin-laminated glass shingles, handset into custom aluminum extrusions. Vertically, bright golds descend to light greens, to deeper, rich blues suggesting the passage of light down the edges of the forest and fringes of light-dappled evergreen needles. Walking from the organ loft towards the altar, the rich blues and greens evolve into a lighter palette of clear bottle green and bright gold. The overlapping shingles provide additional layers of translucency between pieces of glass, the four colors multiplied into a mosaic of changing light.

Behind the art glass, the flimsy, dilapidated plexiglass panels were replaced with a new insulated aluminum window wall, bringing thermal comfort and quiet to the nave for the first time since the church was built. These two layers were carefully orchestrated, studied through extensive physical modeling. Eventually involving craftspeople from four different skilled local subcontractors, the result was a custom aluminum profile extruded through an 8-inch mold. This extrusion was then cut into individual clips to support the overlapping glass shingles, supported by a frame attached back to the window wall. Steel frames interrupt the art glass, opening out to the operable window wall behind, framing views out to the columbarium garden.

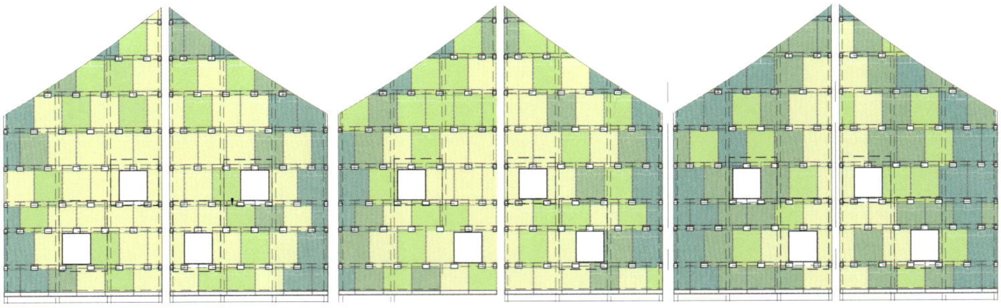

PULP
STUDIO
PULP
STUDIO

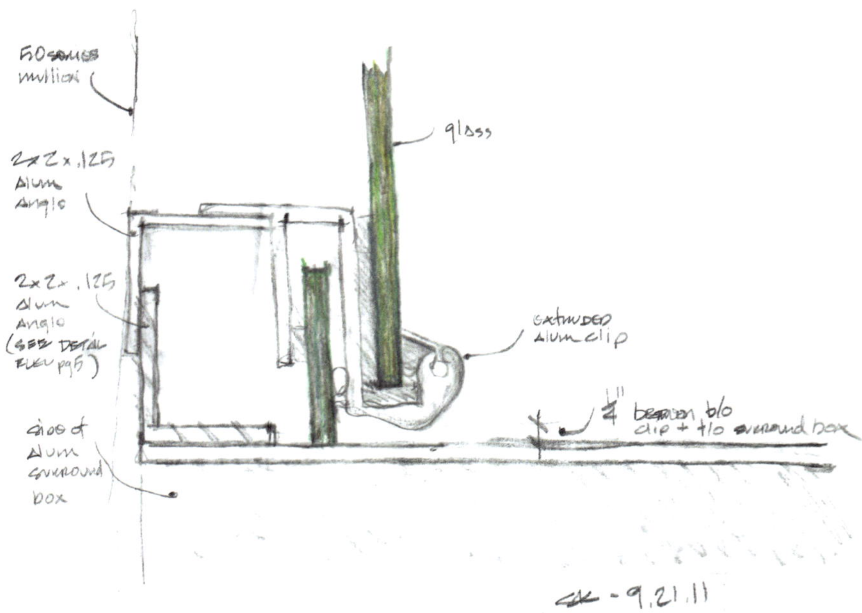
mullion
glass
2x2x.125
Alum
Angle
2x2x.125
Alum
Angle
(SEE DETAIL
ELEV pg5)
extruded
alum clip
1/4" between b/o
clip + t/o surround box
side of
alum
surround
box
9.21.11

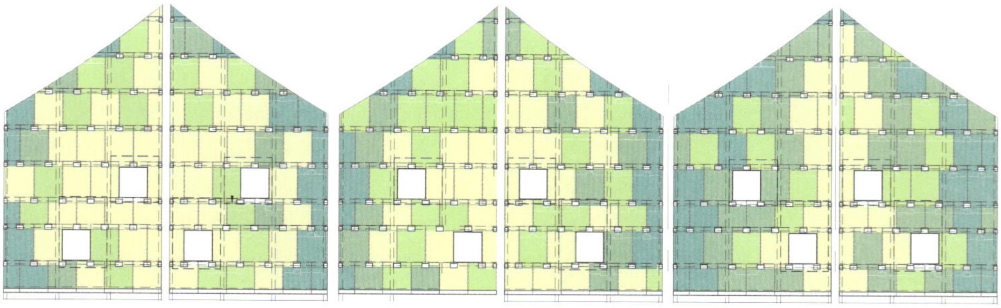

Behind a new altarpiece, a soaring 60-foot wall rises up toward the peak of the canopy. I spent weeks hand-painting in-situ mockups of new paint palettes to test the capture of the glinting light falling softly from 60 feet above. Overnight, our equally passionate client would mark with large swaths of blue painter's tape the acceptance or rejection of the mockups. The result was a soft mélange of bronze and silver metallic paints painted on the wall's handcrafted plaster pattern of triangular boughs. With light falling from above, its surface glows with an understated intensity, an ethereal backdrop for this arboreal sanctuary.

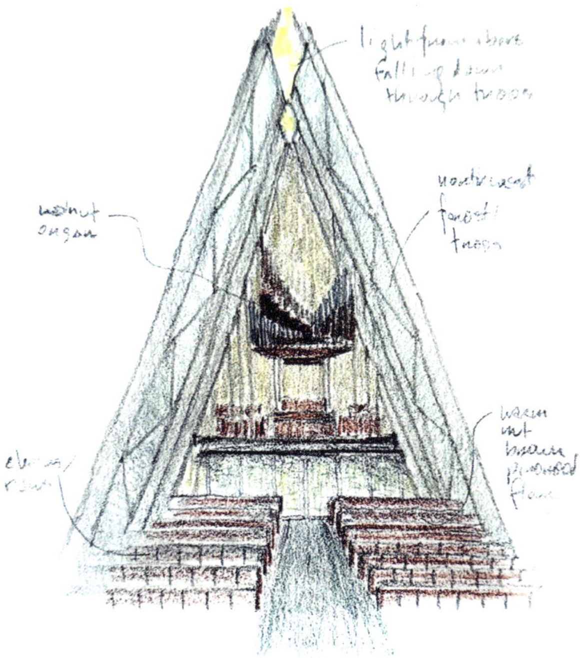

Back above the nave, the suspended organ still hovers as a breathtaking centerpiece in the sanctuary, its acoustic power amplified by the shell of the church. In the original architects' design, the modern, forward-thinking spirit of our region was combined with a much older sense of reverence for our ancient, life-giving forests. This attitude is one that atelierjones still aspires to today, and through this renovation that vision is extended, kept vibrant through the continued presence of the St. Paul's community. The clear, open narthex opens out to the busy street, harvesting volumes of light, and beckoning the patrons of the city to stop, linger, and engage. The bustling city is engaged and invited to come into the quiet of a soaring forest.

1993 – 1994
Seattle, Washington

Susan H Jones, Architect

Owner:
St. James Cathedral of the Catholic Archdiocese of Western Washington

Architect of Record:
Bumgardner Architects

Contractor:
Lease Crutcher Lewis

Photography:
Fred Housel, Elizabeth Deveraux, Eleanor Kinsel, Susan Jones

Marian Chapel

A Room of Light

Fra Angelico, Annunciation, 1430

The structured space and light of the Marian Chapel began with a vision in the night. I awoke suddenly, experiencing the completed space—its flickering candle lights, its tall darkness, and blackened floors. I also awoke knowing what I needed to do. It started with a letter to the Very Reverend Father Ryan, volunteering my time and willingness to meet with him and the architects for the overall renovation of St. James Cathedral.

This had never happened to me before, and never has it occurred again with such stark, driven clarity. The next six months were a whirl of putting the steps into place and drawing what I had seen. The only surprise was that I had to add a 40-foot wall into the cathedral, on the nave side of the chapel's side aisle. The tall, narrow, enclosed proportions had been there in my night vision, but when I met with Father Ryan and the Building Committee on site, the wall was not there. Looking at the arched opening, I was as surprised as anyone to hear the words come out of my mouth: "We have to build a new wall there."

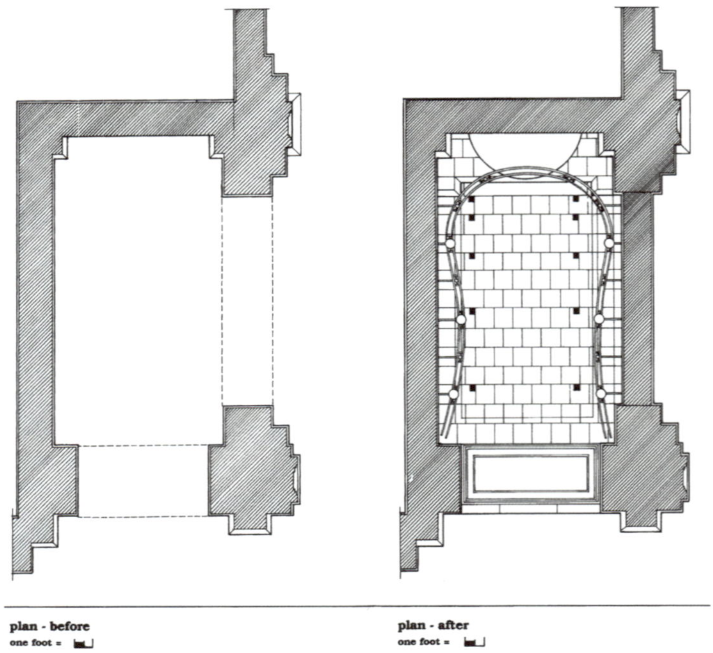

In designing a space as archaic and fundamental as a chapel, there is always a risk of being overly literal. One can quickly be weighed down by metaphor and slip into banality, thereby losing the essence.

Designing a space to evoke transcendence demands a dynamic and muscular architectural language, in the most ancient tradition of spiritual architecture. It must invoke immense and precise dynamism within the section, and through that, invoke a section of the unseen, of that which is beyond the delineated architectural section. What emerged was the urgency of the leaping of light, as I would later call it. *Light leaps.*

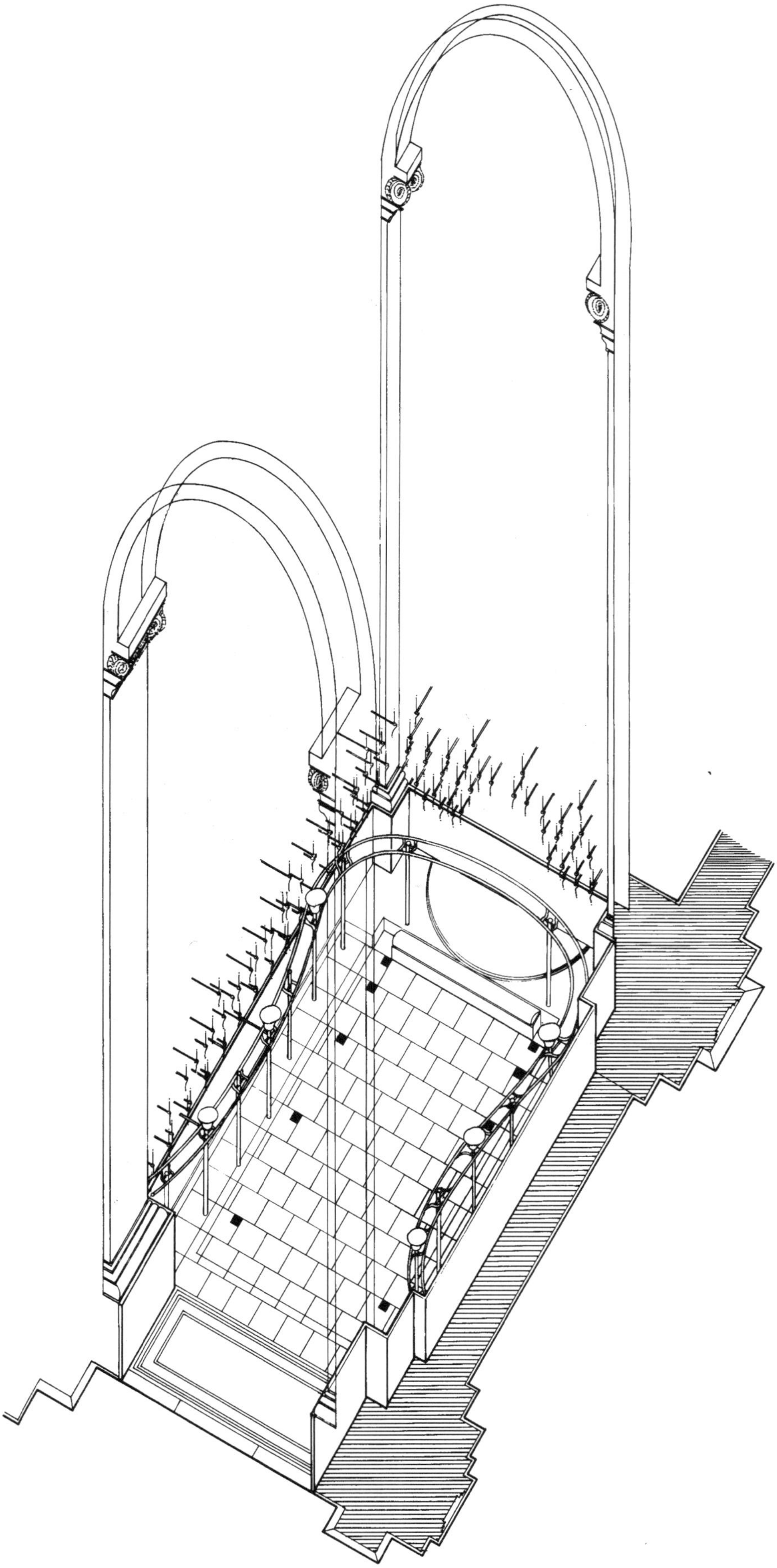

It was the same light that came to me on those childhood walks through the forest, with its towering, cathedral-pier firs and quiet, loamy sanctuaries. An understanding of those vertical, soaring spaces had been etched indelibly into my heart, and now, into that vertical spatial structure of the tall chapel. Height, light, paint, beeswax, candlelight, and silicon bronze would stretch thinly upwards, creating a vertical section that coalesced in enveloping warmth and light around the human experience, around the human body.

At the time, I could not have articulated any of that as the young, barely licensed, female architect trying to describe my vision to a skeptical building committee. But, thankfully, my gestures and small drawings and command of the proportions and vision was enough for them to take that leap with me. With their assent came the constraints and opportunities of the given spaces, materials, and, and, of course, budgets – a modest $35,000 in this case.

One crosses the threshold from the busy urban cathedral nave to the side aisle. Entering the chapel, one feels the quiet darkness. The darkness first encloses, then, as eyes adjust to the light, allows focus on the lit candles. One hundred eighty of them line the walls in bronze votive holders, increasing in tempo as they approach the central figure of Mary. The tall, thin, beeswax candles each have a different relationship to the human body; some at eye level, some at the heart, some a stretch upwards to light with a delicate wooden punk. The bronze candleholders vary in section, in their distance from the walls, so that the highest ones start to stretch out over the body, ever so slightly, creating a warm, human-lit space that subtly envelopes one in darkness.

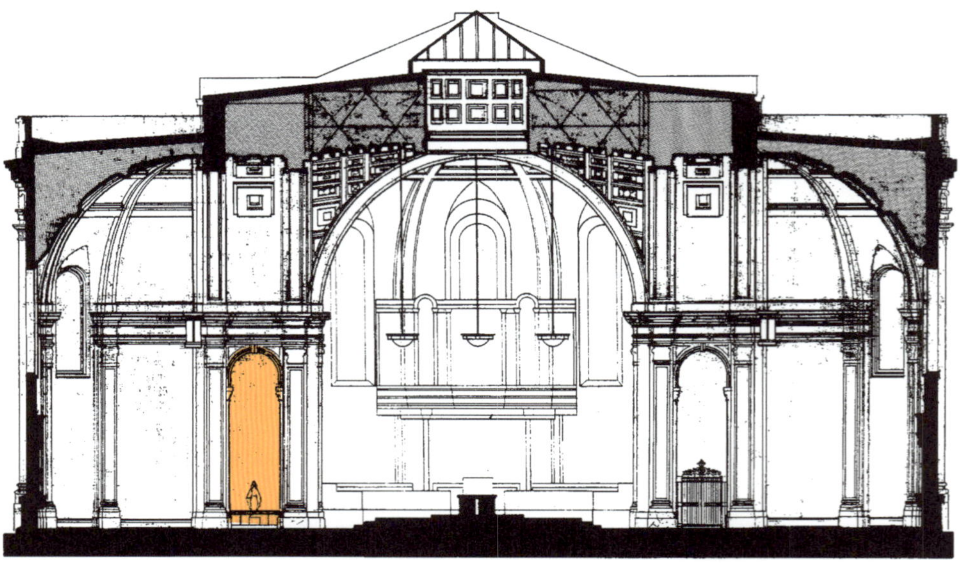

St. James Cathedral section after renovation, Marian Chapel at center left

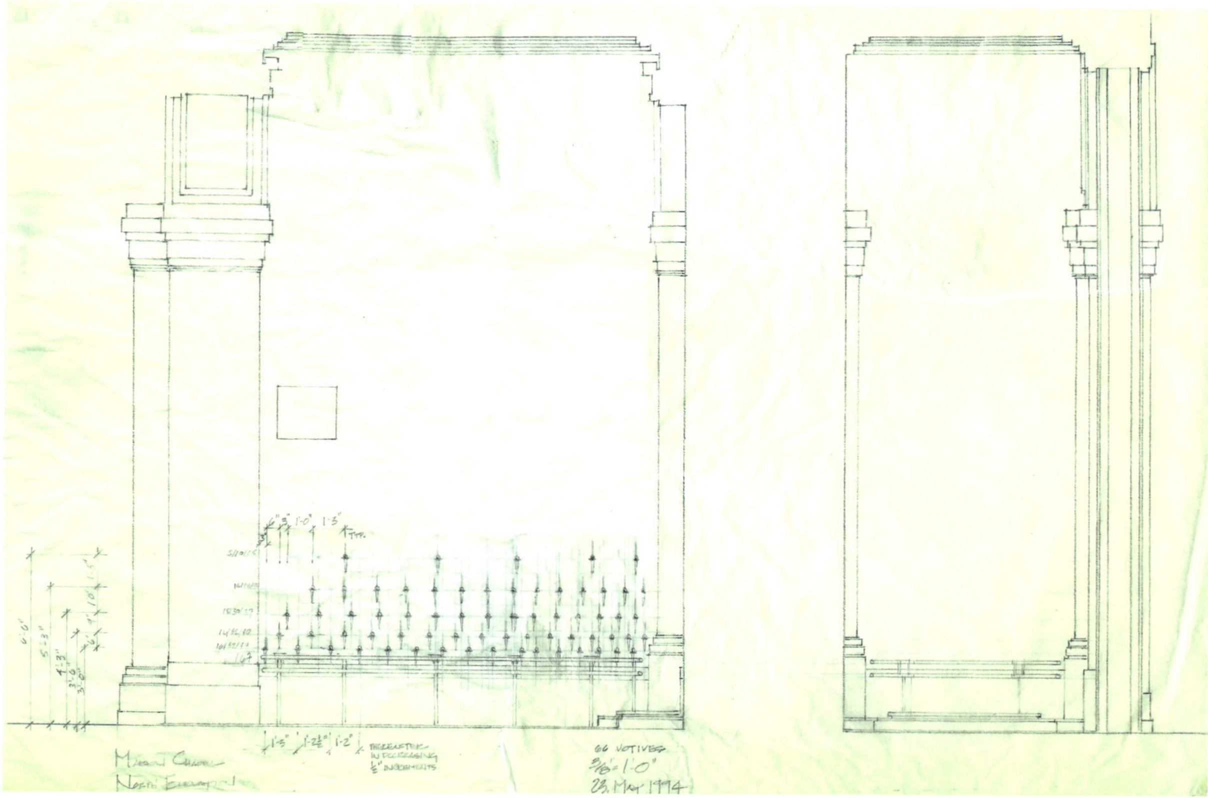
66 VOTIVES
3/8" = 1'-0"
23 May 1994
1'-3"
1'-2½"
1'-2"
THEREAFTER IN DECREASING ½" INCREMENTS

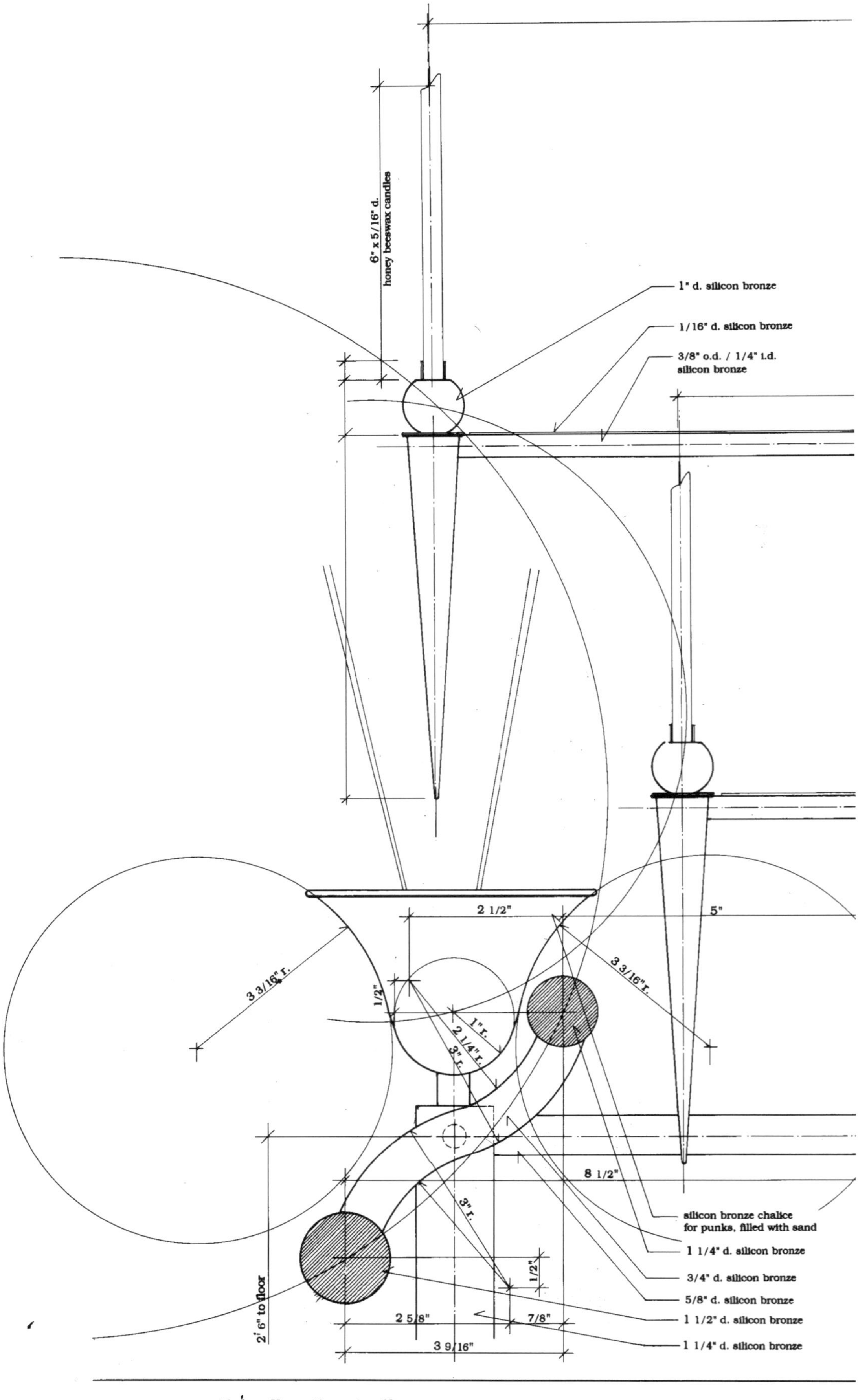

partial wall section at rail
one inch =

The tawny beeswax candles are lit individually, so the experience of light is rarely the same. It flickers and sways with the motion of people's movements, words, tears, or prayers. The light dances everywhere, reflecting again and again, back and forth against the worn sheen of the curved bronzework and the shellacked, honey-colored walls.

Above one's reach upwards is the darkness, below one's feet, the darkness. The subtle dynamism of the forced perspective presses one closer, towards the icon of Mary at the end of the chapel, clear and lit, open, gracious and waiting. Her light is of the human scale, enveloping our bodies. In it is that experienced sanctuary of the forest, with its gifts of memory, safety, and peace, transcending time and grief.

Light Leaps.

Bravest of all humans,

consent
illumined her.

The room filled with its light,

the lily glowed in it,

and the
iridescent wings.

Consent,

courage
unparalleled,

opened her utterly.

Denise Levertov,
Annunciation

2013–2016
Bellevue, Washington

atelierjones:
Susan Jones, Joe Swain, Michelle Kang, Brooks Brainerd, Marisol Foreman, Mesa Sherriff, Dhara Goradia, Brett Holverstott, Megumi Migita

Owner:
Bellevue First Congregational Church, Pastor Lisa Horst Clark

Structural Engineering:
DCI Engineers

Contractor:
Goudy Construction

Mass Timber Supplier/Fabricator:
Structurlam

Lighting Design:
Blanca Lighting

Daylighting:
UW Integrated Design Lab

Acoustic Design:
Arup

Photography:
Lara Swimmer

Bellevue First Congregational Church

Shoulder to Shoulder

The scale of the wooden blanks surprised us all. Their large, ungainly masses with angled edges slanted and stretched along the 40-foot truck bed. The 8-foot-wide panels were lifted gently onto wheeled roller beds and rolled into the church atrium, their anthropomorphic proportions making them look like giants temporarily immobile upon their backs. Goliaths surrendered, surrounded by us Lilliputians.

The installation of these giants was accomplished with the most straightforward of machinations. Ropes and pullies, guided by construction workers on scissors lifts. Simple stuff, but employed with great exertion and care. Each precisely cut panel—fit with custom steel brackets to be bolted to the structure behind—was hoisted, bending and lurching, until it finally stood on its narrow, angled edge. One by one the Goliaths were wedged in against one another, slanting forward, sideways, and outwards as if to peer down at us.

Then silence, as the final bolts were fastened and the ropes released from their pullies, the lifts lowered to the ground. Wood fit against wood, Goliath against Goliath, each one similar yet unique. They stood, waiting to stretch the light along them, down them, over them.

The archaic installation of these giants belied a process that had been anything but archaic. Our clients had asked for a space of *awe*. What does that mean in our casual linguistic culture where every third word is *awesome*? How to make a space that could connect to thought structures, brain pathways,[1] beliefs not of this world? To spaces unseen. The strangeness of the new, an awkward transportation, towards a break of transcendence. Light Leaps. A scale jump, from the human to the otherworldly. A space for light to leap.

1: Julio Bermudez, 2022. *Spirituality in Architectural Education.*

This transcendent space would need to emerge from the substrate of an aging, beige, suburban 1970s office building. To secure the future of their congregation, the church had sold their downtown Bellevue parcel and purchased this more peripheral one, netting a healthy difference. But if they wanted to bring a sense of spirit to this hermetic, dark, and outmoded building, we would have to let the light in.

We studied ways to break open the north wing of this office building and create a new sanctuary, allowing the soft, diffuse light of the Pacific Northwest to permeate its interior. Here, the volume of the building could be extended, announcing the church's presence in the city, reaching upwards to capture light.

But on what would that light fall?

The design of the sanctuary became a way to continue the investigations started in our earliest experiments with cross-laminated timber.

CLT, a transformative material, is made from the most recognizable of elements: the unassuming 2x6-inch planks that one could find at any hardware store in America. The CLTChurch, as I came to call it, became a vigorous design investigation as to how these huge, awkward, 21st-century panels, made from so many small pieces of wood, could be designed into something that would express their transformative hybrid quality. How to make *construction* into *architecture*, the essential into art? Or, as Karl Bötticher phrased it so long ago, *Kernform* into *Kunstform*.[2]

2: Karl Bötticher, 1854. *Die Tektonik der Hellenen.*

The idea began to take shape in my mind to show these raw panels folding against one another—these giant, sublime composites of so many small, unassuming elements—as a backdrop for the gathering space.

We humans are so prosaic, humble and broken. In our own worlds, isolated, we share so many of the same needs, again and again. But then, we come together. We create things much larger than ourselves. Giant pathways to awe. Our collective institutions and communities—be they political, educational, creative or spiritual—carry us forward, sustaining knowledge, vitality and life for the next generation to carry forward again.

CLT panels pressed and ready for CNC cutting

Expressing this individuality into the panels, one by one, was only possible through 21st-century technology. We could move beyond the modernist dream of creating precisely repetitive products, people, ready for systemic deployment. For, from mass production to mass customization, we now have tools at our disposal that millennia of woodworkers could never have dreamed of.

Early in our mass timber journey, I had visited the Structurlam factory in British Columbia, the only CLT factory west of the Mississippi River in North America at the time. I was keenly aware of how the power of prefabrication could be harnessed to shape angles of wood, to make spaces, ready for angles of light. The mechanized, digitally driven cranes, motorized, moving platforms, and 5- and 6-axis Computer Numerical Controlled (CNC) mills could slide over these huge Goliaths, cutting them into uniquely precise angles in ways that humans never could.

21st-century technology on huge awkward panels of ancient wood. *21st-century wood*. Each angle on all four sides of the 17 panels became slightly different, to fit together and create an off-kilter, slightly awkward, uncanny wall, made of strange, new, beautiful, and awe-inspiring wood.

As architects we focused on the light. How to bathe the wall in light? We modeled the box of light, building large physical models to study how light would shed down upon the wooden panels, across the folded community of wooden Goliaths. We drew the light, sketched the light. We studied deeply the precedents of Aalto's churches, particularly the stunning Church of Three Crosses, in Imatra, Finland, where I had made a pilgrimage in 1990. We drew section after section, studying how to illuminate the wood without revealing the light's source.

Sanctuary model at the UW IDL

We brought a scale model of the sanctuary space into the University of Washington (UW) Daylighting Lab, a strange, controlled environment where the real daylight was closed out to study simulated daylight on models. Our team was supported by the brilliant team at the UW Integrated Design Lab (IDL), who built and tested digital models. The IDL ran calculations, and we continued to build physical models, experimenting again and again with the light on our wooden box, twisting and turning the models for all angles, morning and evening, summer and winter, solstice and equinox light.

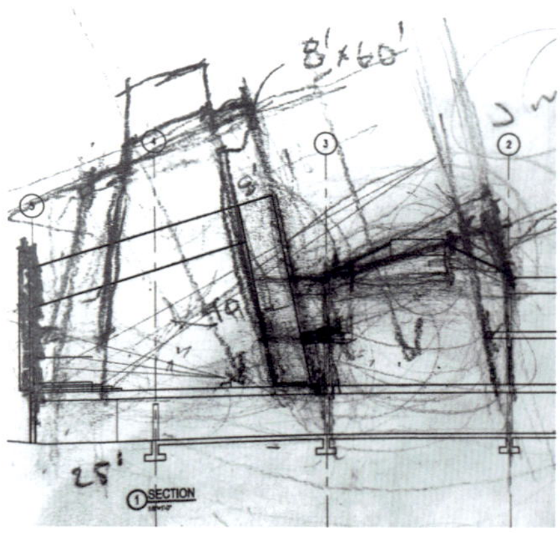

In the end, we brought the light down through five skylights and in through two 30-foot-high narrow side windows, extending outwards from the box of light to conceal the source of the daylight. Only the movement of light across the giant wall of wood reflects against their awkward folded planes. Witnessing them, we leap upwards with their height and follow their light bending down towards us.

Light on Wood. Light Leaps.

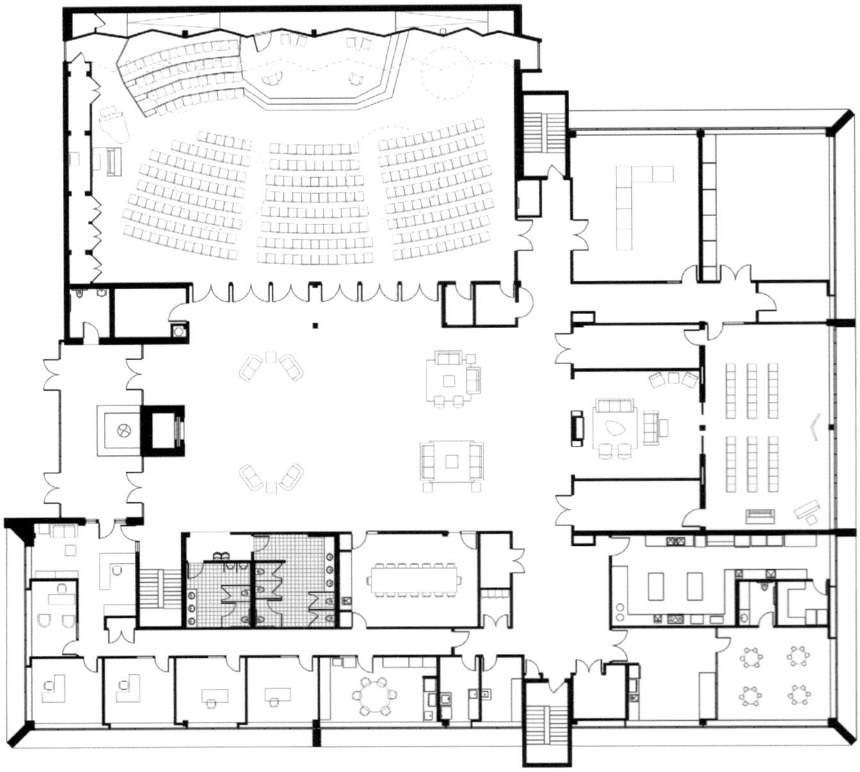

Level 1 Plan

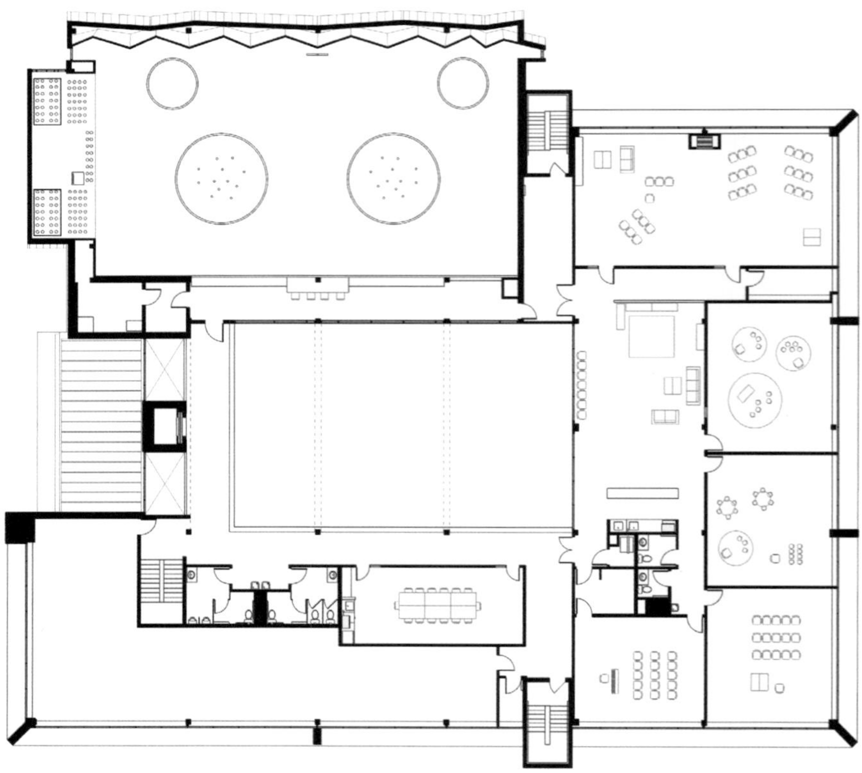

Level 2 Plan

EXIT

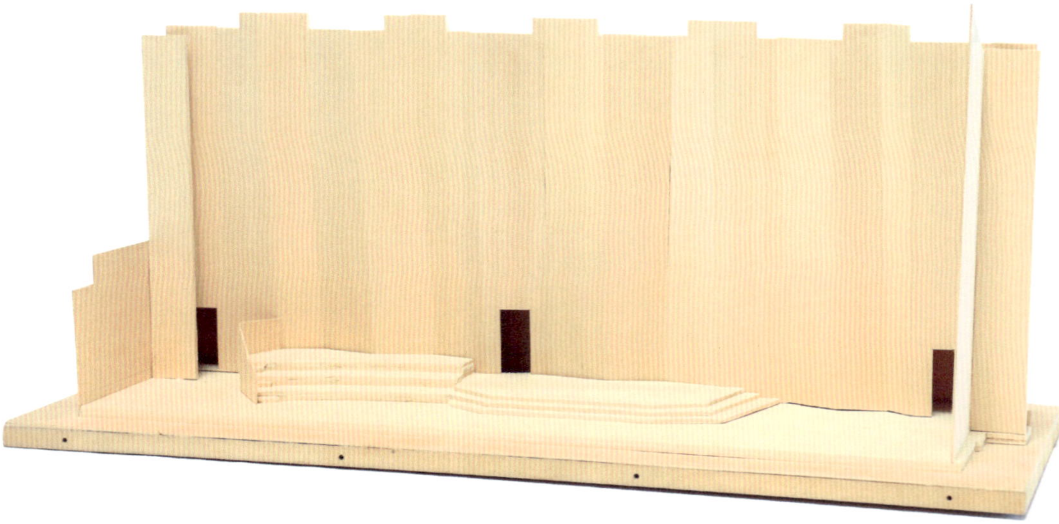

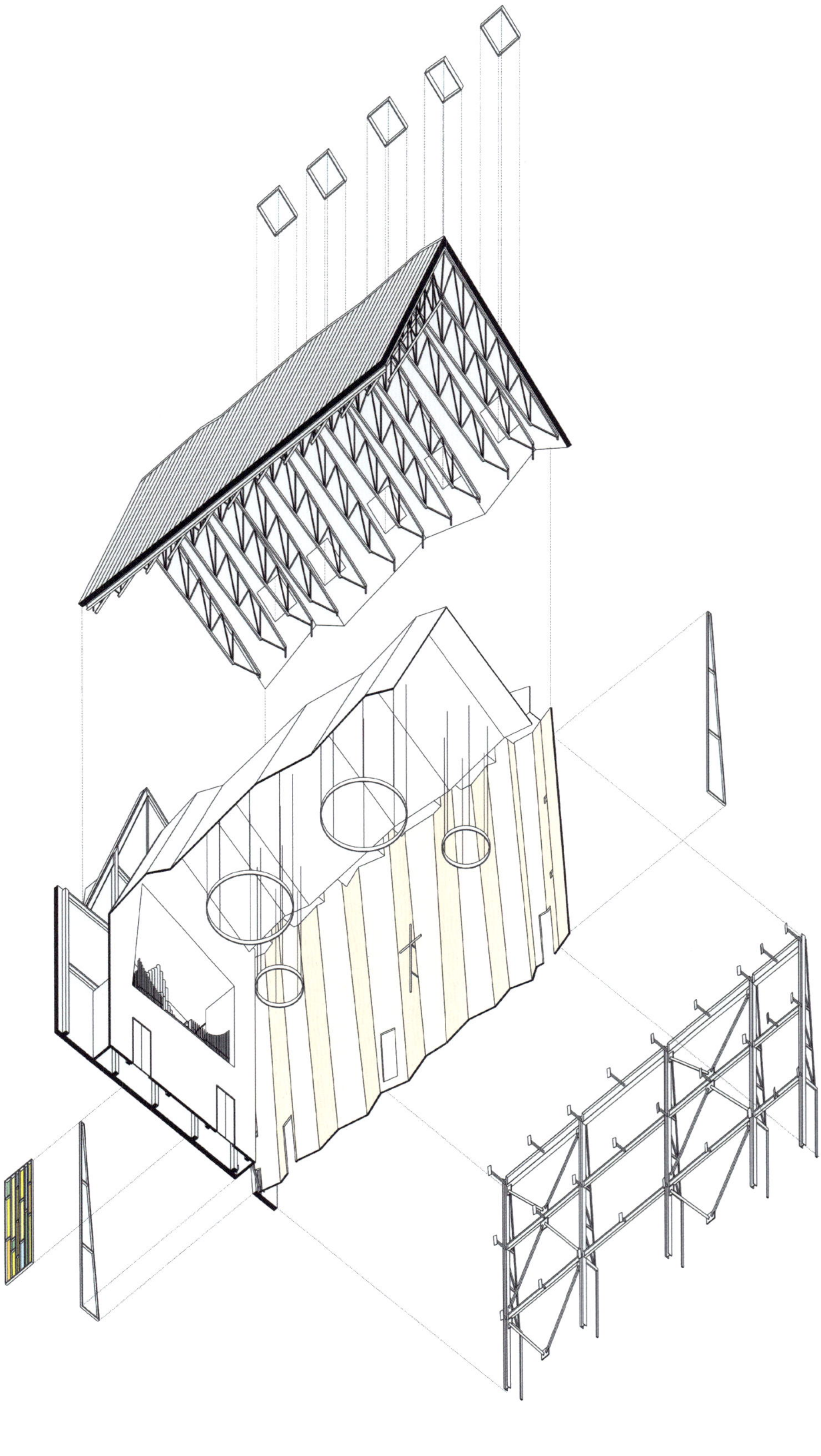

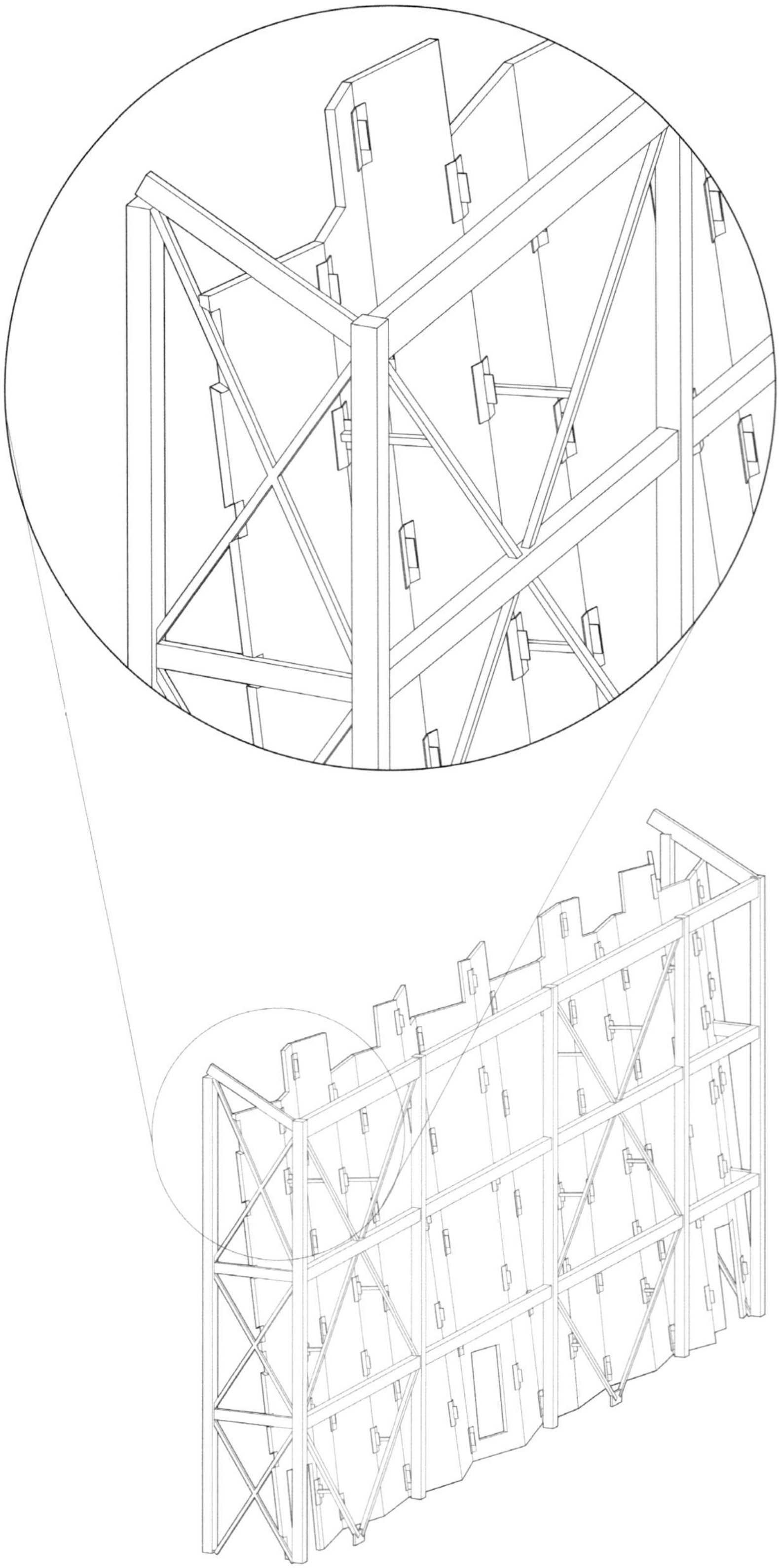

III.

Unconsciously, we experience the tree as our friend and relative. Like us, the tree has its origin in nature and even when crafted into an object or a house, it reminds us of its organic origins.

Juhani Pallasmaa

h o m e

Eco / Oiko

It was around 2010, against the backdrop of an economic recession, that I had to take stock. None of our inspired, potentially catalytic projects had been built[3], much had they disrupted our wasteful 20th-century ways of building. I had stayed focused, as an architect does, working with time honored tools of design—drawings, models, and renderings—to attempt to make ideas of change, provocations of disruption. We had won awards for our work. But then we raised our hands, gave the work to our clients, and said *okay, now you build them*. Which also meant *you pay for them*. But they declined. The disrupters stayed quiet and inert.

3: See "Disruption," p. 264

I was living my life in multiple silos, not letting them intersect. My family—my husband, Marco and my children, Rogan and Domenica—lived in a small, 1,000-square-foot condominium on the Seattle Waterfront. The condominium stood in the shadow of a 1950s concrete double-decker viaduct, with thousands of cars roaring by per day. Domenica and Rogan were 10 and 11 by this time and growing quickly. Our home was growing smaller as they grew into themselves. We needed to find a new home.

At the same time, my family was growing in other ways. The policies of regulating our family's forest had evolved. The Washington State Department of Natural Resources (WADNR) introduced new regulations, asking my then 76-year-old mother and 80-year-old aunt to become ecologists, foresters, and loggers in exchange for the time-honored property tax reduction. This new stance on privately owned forest lands asked for a Forest Management Plan (FMP) to be carried out by the owners, in exchange for the Forest Designation and its tax status.

We learned that our forest was badly overstocked, and we would need to thin and harvest parts of it. This meant hiring ecologists, loggers and truckers. All with the threat of losing the property tax benefits that we had accrued over the years. Concerns around the family dinner table grew, as my anxious mother explained what the State and the County were asking her to do. The option of selling my grandfather's forest outright was always on that table.

Those dark discussions also coincided with the deepest days of the economic recession as we felt it in the Pacific Northwest. I became aware that I had a mere sliver of an economic window to find what felt like the last piece of somewhat-affordable land in Seattle. After months of scanning real estate offerings, I took a deep breath and made an offer. In February 2011, we closed on the lot: a tiny, triangular divot of 2,500 square feet, facing a bank parking lot and a busy alley with dumpsters. At least it faced south.

Experiencing the brunt fact of ownership, having taken the first, hardest risk, the design models flowed immediately. The triangularity of the lot, its tiny size, the front-and-back play between the conventional neighborhood west elevation and the

raw triangle of the alley elevation, needing both visual privacy and light, made for a severe economy of means to pack every ounce of life into the spatial geometries of the house. The 12 models that survived the three-year design process stand today as talismans of a dark recession. All I could do at the end of some long, not-so-busy weeks in the office, was to stay late on a Friday night and craft yet another small wooden model of a house that could one day hold our bursting family.

I began to see the house as a respite of space and light that could provide us with a sense of peace, shaped by wood. I was inspired by my grandparents' tiny 1950s cabin on Orcas Island. Crossing the threshold of that wooden cabin, after a five-hour journey out of the city by car and boat, we were always met by a sense of beauty and calm. Why not replicate that homecoming in the city? An urban beach cabin.

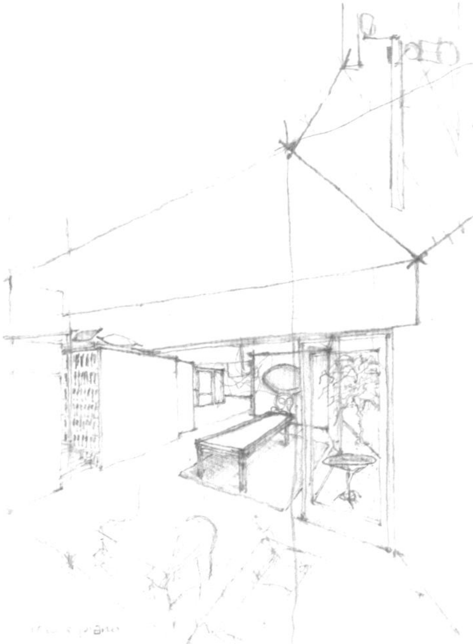

A vague image rose up, of beautiful, softly sanded white wood. It was one I recalled from a catalog of small Austrian homes that a friend had sent me the year before. What was that material on their ceilings? A large, solid plane of wood, without the familiar veneer or 4-by-8-foot divisions of plywood sheets. It must have been substantial, as it spanned the entire living and dining rooms. How did I not know this material?

While it would make a nice, neat story to say that my decision to buy a tiny, underutilized lot to build the CLTHouse, as well as my decision to step up and help my family manage this badly overstocked forest and meet current, evolving regulatory positions on private forest ownership and their management, influenced my decision to focus on mass timber design at atelierjones, it was not what happened. At least not at first.

Design, Research, Risk

The opportunity to design my own house, one worthy of the love and lives of my family, pushed me towards a cautiously entrepreneurial stance. The fact that I was considering spending 20 years' worth of my own carefully saved funds further sharpened this instinct.

A single-family house is the smallest of development projects, but for me it represented a risky leap into entrepreneurship, and an opportunity to demonstrate the innovation that I had long been seeking in our firm's work. Embracing the earlier ideals of our practice and projects, I realized I had the perfect opportunity to make this small house impactful on a broader level, expanding the architect's often solipsistic process of designing one's own perfect house. The silos of my personal and professional lives were beginning to collapse.

But my choice of material was a huge risk. At the time, cross-laminated timber was a material barely known in North America, especially in the United States. There was a paucity of information about its fabrication and use, and no experienced engineering or contracting partners to turn to. As one of the first cross-laminated timber structures in the United States, the *risk* I was taking keenly focused my research instinct to hunt for questions and answers about this new material, this new construction system.

As an architect, I have long been inspired by Alvar Aalto. Not only for his exquisite entwining of space, structure and the muted light of Finland, but also by his fluid and outward-focused practice model of designer-led research. From the relative isolation of Finland, he writes passionately about the value of reaching out to other countries, cultures, and industries. Of communication, languages, and collaboration. Of talking to others. Of asking questions of them and learning what they know. Of taking risks by asking questions.[4]

4: Mateo Kries and Jochen Eisenbrand, 2014. *Alvar Aalto: Second Nature*

Alvar Aalto Museum, Jyväskylä, Finland

Aalto's biography presents a lifelong journey of design, research, and good-natured engagement with the people in his and Aino's and later Elissa's lives together, be they patrons, university or religious leaders, or owners of sawmills. His long-standing design experimentation, research, and advocacy of plywood, the then-newly emerging building material, and its entwined importance for the timber industry of Finland is well known. Experimentation with plywood connected Aalto with industry, furniture, and arts communities that enlarged the platform for his prodigious talent.

My miles-long walk on a cold Finnish summer afternoon in 1990 to experience both the humility and grandeur of Aalto's Sunila Factory was electrifying for a young architect. Reflecting on the fact that it was designed in the economic bleakness of the 1930s, I began to understand of the range of his engagement with the diverse communities of urban and rural Finland.

Against this backdrop of personal and professional inspiration, a framework for the value of linking design with research started to come into focus through two opportunities. First, I was asked by the American Institute of Architects (AIA) to write about how to incorporate research within the context of a small firm. Writing in 2013, I started to articulate the power of entwining design with research, and how designer-led research is uniquely suited to a small firm, in turn generating design:

Susan Jones, 2014. "Research and Small Firm Practice: Integration and Implementation". Published in *AIA 2015 Handbook for Architectural Practice.*

> Research that applies design intelligence to existing knowledge to develop new design knowledge can be strategically scalable to the small firm. Where traditional research generates new, deeper specialized knowledge within one field, design research generates new, broader knowledge out of existing, specialized knowledge. The opportunity for design firms–large and small–is to leverage existing knowledge and generate new, innovative design.
>
> […]
>
> by creating and cultivating a permeable knowledge boundary around the firm, a small firm can embrace broader circles of knowledge by intersecting with recognized national and international primary sources of knowledge. Mining these external fields for productive methodologies and design opportunities allows the small firm to leverage this knowledge in ways unique to its practice, usually through the curiosity and passion of its founder.
>
> Leveraging mutual areas of passion is the backbone of fruitful collaborative partnerships between external non-profits and architecture firms. Driven by issues born out of an ethical or personal imperative, the small firm that identifies similarly driven non-profits or related corporate entities can collaborate and leverage each other's complementary strengths, and work together to create stronger, more authentic, and more valuable design research.

As I was writing this text on the relationship between design and research, making early models of the CLTHouse, and helping my mother implement our forest plan, another opportunity presented itself, to teach a graduate architecture studio at the University of Washington (UW) in the fall of 2013.

The idea crystalized to bring the design problem presented by my CLTHouse to my UW studio. More silos in my personal and professional lives collapsed. I proposed a design and research studio that would investigate the emergence of this new (to the US) building material, *cross-laminated timber*. Designer-led research. We would all try to learn together. Gratefully, it was accepted.

Cross-laminated timber is not a new invention. It was first patented over 100 years ago by timber industrialists in Tacoma, Washington.[5] But the modern CLT panel wasn't created until the 1990s, by brilliant Austrian and German architects and engineers. In Europe, this material system evolved rapidly, adding an important new material system for 21st-century design. But in 2012, there were still only two plants in North America producing the material, both of them in Canada. Even that information took me months to discover; finally, after a prescient cold call in 2012 to an ever friendly and garrulous Pete Kobelt, then working to set up a mass timber fabrication plant in Montana, which would become Smartlam.

5: Frank J. Walsh & Robert L. Watts, "Composite lumber," US Patent 1465383A, issued August 21, 1923

Fig.1

A year later, in the UW Studio, as background research to design a large, institutional center made from CLT, the students and I were scouring the multitude of European fabricators of cross-laminated timber. We studied the differences between 3-ply, 5-ply, and 7-ply CLT, and how its commercial lamstock was milled from a tree. We looked at forest health. We looked at architectural precedents from Austria, Germany, Great Britain, Finland, and Sweden. We connected with UW Professor Kate Simonen and her classes on Life-Cycle Assessment (LCA), and ran our students' designs through early LCA tools that quantified the CO_2 expenditure of different wall assemblies, comparing mass timber to concrete and light wood frame with gypsum wall board. The research from the 2013 and the later 2016 studio, focusing on a University of Washington Wood Innovation Center is well detailed and credited in my 2017 book, *Mass Timber | Design and Research*.

2016 studio trip to D.R. Johnson Wood Innovations, Riddle, Oregon

The teaching and research of these two UW studios while designing, permitting, developing and building the prototype CLTHouse, would become the model for how atelierjones practices architecture. With the studios, I created a platform to better understand the deeper entwined systemic relationships between architecture and our material sources. Together, we started to quantify questions of embodied carbon, and their material origins at the scale of landscape, engendering basic questions of forest health. Most importantly, designing the house and designing in studio explored how to take the constraints of this nascent material and make architecture. The experiences in these two UW studios remain some of the most important design and research collaborations of my professional life. The experimental CLTHouse had become not just a home for my family, but a vehicle for learning, awareness, research, and a way to tell the story of mass timber in the United States. It also became a way to connect back to the forest landscape that was a deep part of our family history. The house helped us see the forest.

Log Deck Operator at North Fork Lumber Mill, Korbel, California

Measurement

We did not originally set out to study the scale of landscape. We were trying to understand this new actor, cross-laminated timber within the existing 20th-century compendium of materials, based primarily on concrete and steel. But as the Studio progressed, it occurred to me that we could measure wood in very different ways to how we measure concrete and steel. Wood invites the measurement of its origins—the trees and the forests in which it grows.

One day, late that spring quarter of 2013, I asked the students to quantify the amount of lumber required to build their projects. They responded with typical enthusiasm, and provided robust digital models of their projects, calculating the volume of wood based on our understanding of the thickness of the CLT panels. Emboldened, we went a step further, and used our earlier research on softwood lumber production to give us the approximate number of trees harvested to build each of their projects.

Then, we advanced, calculating the equivalent number of acres required to grow the trees, based on typical planting ratios. Comparing this area to our family's forested land on Mt. Constitution gave me a clear and humbling view of just how much of our natural landscape had been used to grow the lumber for their projects. Clear, succinct diagrams emerged to explain these concepts, connecting buildings to trees to landscapes.

Later, in our 2016 studio, we deepened this research, focusing on how trees are used to make merchantable lumber. When trees are cut, their roots typically remain in the ground, their carbon decomposing into the soil. But much of the slash—branches and debris left after the logs are harvested—is burnt or decomposes above ground, releasing the carbon previously sequestered in the living tree. Only the carbon sequestered in the tree trunk remains stored in the milled lumber.

Based on industry data, we calculated that an average commercially logged Douglas fir yields 58% of its total biomass as merchantable stem. Of that trunk/stem, 52% is usable as planed, dried lumber, while the rest is left over as sawdust, bark, and wood waste.[6] Thus, when a mature Douglas fir tree is harvested, approximately 31% of its biomass becomes actual lumber, on average about 260 board feet for a single mature tree.[7] In other words, to replace a single tree's worth of stored carbon in the built environment, one needed to plant approximately three trees. The landscape-scale implications of these simple calculations came into focus.

6: Francis G. Wagner, Maureen E. Puettmann, & Leonard R. Johnson, 2009. "Life Cycle Inventory of Inland Northwest Softwood Lumber Manufacturing." CORRIM Phase II Final Report.
7: Ibid.

As the spring 2013 studio developed these methodologies, the CLTHouse was progressing from models to permit plan sets. I drew the CLTHouse final permit set for weeks on end in the fall, and we received the permit relatively easily by April of 2014. In June, I signed a contract to procure the CLT panels, glulams, one steel beam and two columns from Structurlam. That November, I made an excited visit up to Penticton, BC to tour their plant and witness the creation of my home's walls and ceilings, just weeks before they would arrive on site.

Using mass timber revealed the power of the prefabrication process. Over the last decades of the 20th century, we architects have often ceded responsibility to the contracting community, and along with it cost control, design control, and the ability to directly influence how buildings are made. But the CLTHouse showed me the power of being not only the owner—holding the contract with the mass timber fabricator—but also the lead entity coordinating the mass timber shop drawings, along with our structural engineers. Because we were working directly with the fabricator, small design changes during the shop drawing process would not become change orders and potential cost increases. After the bid was accepted, we had more control to adapt the construction to fit the design intent, not the other way around. We had been willing to absorb the *risk*.

The process of CLT production is tightly controlled. Each panel is cut using large, Computer Numerically Controlled (CNC) machines according to the architect's and engineers' specifications and drawings. Leading the prefabrication process allowed us as architects to become intimately familiar with each of the house's 67 panels. The shop drawings were explicit about the dimensions of each panel. We knew the different thickness of the 3-ply and 5-ply CLT panels. It was basic arithmetic to calculate the volume of lumber used in the panels for the CLTHouse: 47,796 board feet in total.

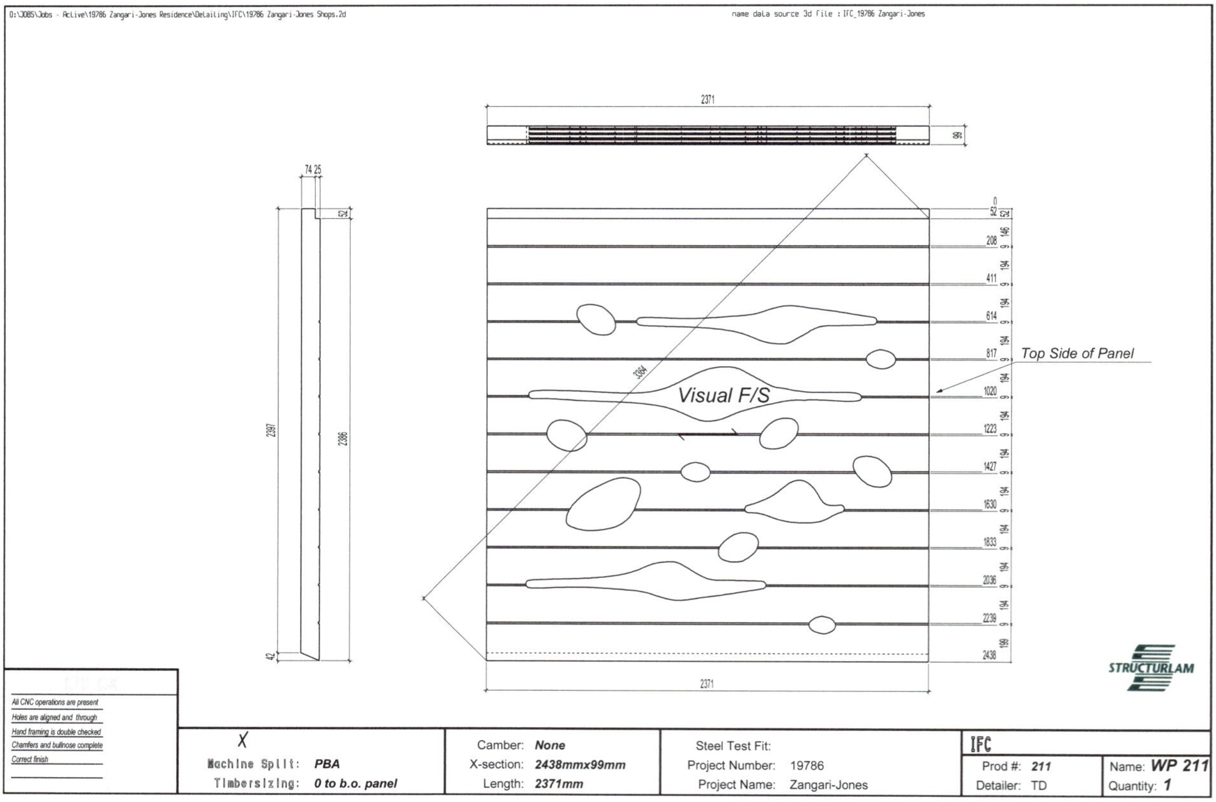

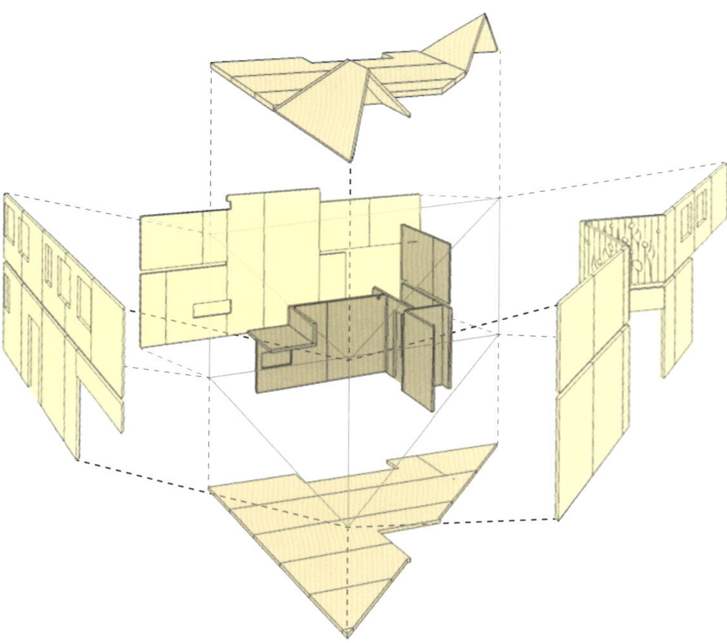

3-ply 27,411 board feet

5-ply 20,385 board feet

total 47,796 board feet

We could also calculate that those 47,796 board feet represented approximately 184 mature softwood trees that had been harvested to build my 1,500-square-foot mass timber house. In a healthy Pacific Northwest forest, that would represent just under one acre of harvest.[8]

8: The Washington State Department of Natural Resources recommends between 250–680 Douglas fir trees per acre as a healthy density. WA DNR, 2019. "Planting Forest Seedlings"

Connecting these analytics back to experiences in our family forest, where we had replanted trees the year before, on three acres, was a thrilling moment. The 700 trees that had survived from our planting represented almost four times the number of trees utilized for the CLTHouse. Along with the Sustainable Forestry Initiative (SFI) practice of replanting trees upon harvest, some five trees had been planted for every tree harvested for the CLTHouse, in addition to the 31% of harvested wood storing its carbon within the structure.

Sourcing

As these landscape visualizations emerged, showing mass timber in terms of trees and forests, even as it became the walls and ceilings of my home, the almost childlike moment of re-seeing the forests for the trees also emerged, encouraging a new way of thinking about our work as architects. It created an urgency within our practice to better understand where our materials come from, to better understand our forests, with their complex connections to industry and ecology, and our own responsibility as individuals and professionals in keeping those forests healthy.

While many early mass timber projects in the United States relied on more widely available European timber sources, I made the decision to procure the mass timber for the CLTHouse regionally. I felt that working within our Cascadia biome was critical for understanding this material and its sourcing, from the fabricators and the lumber mills, to the forests themselves. It placed our mass timber firmly within the cultural context of rural communities where the forests grew and were managed.

By limiting our sourcing to the Cascadia biome, representing an approximately 500-mile radius from Seattle, our firm has been able to visit and personally get to know almost all the mass timber fabricators in the region and many of the lamstock mills and glulam timber fabricators. Getting to know them, their sources of milled lumber, and the forests they harvest within, ensures a greater success of understanding of the supply chain of softwood logs, and their legal, certification and forest management practices.

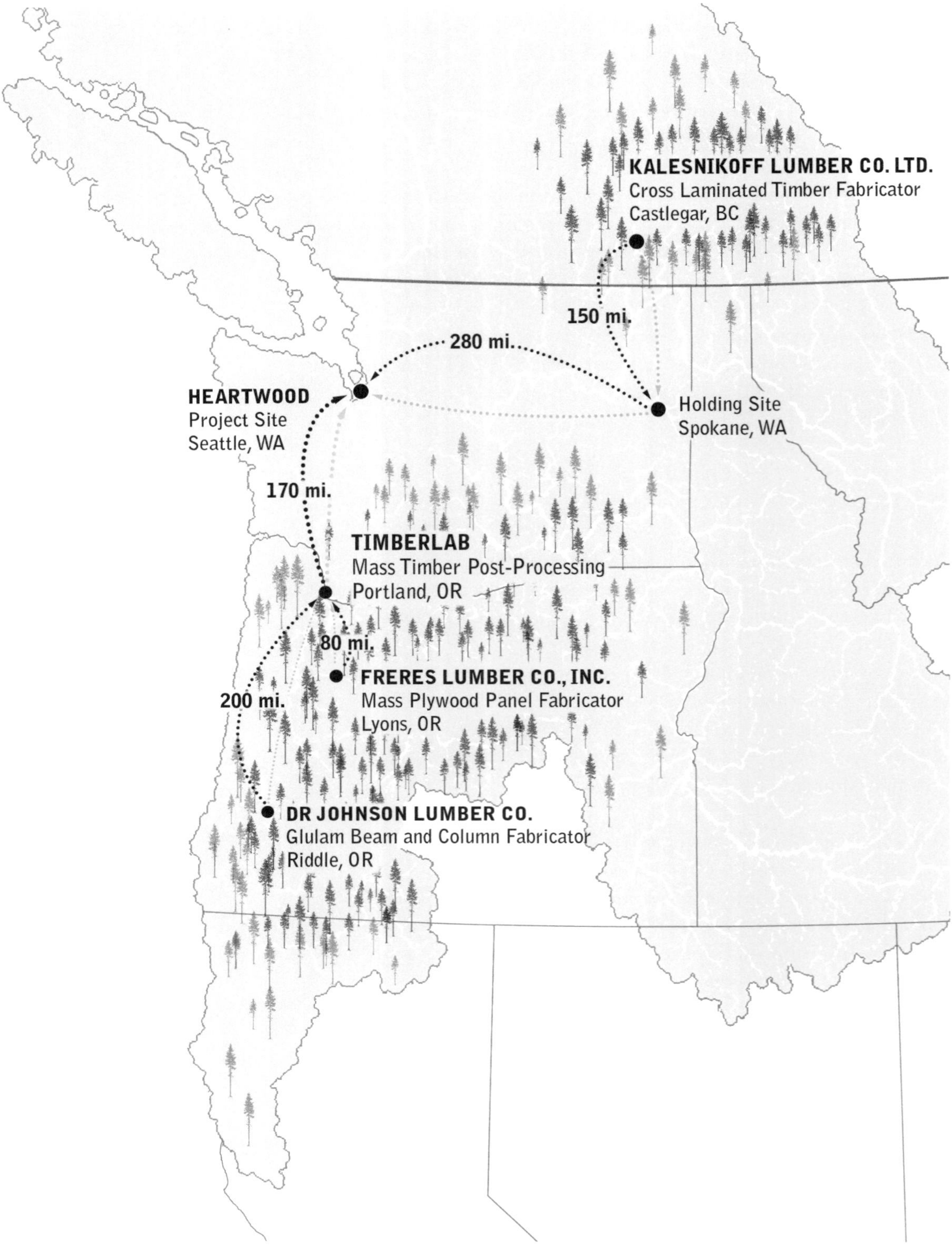

Timber sourcing "woodbasket" for Heartwood (p. 166) within the Cascadia biome

Even within the Cascadia biome, understanding the different legal regulations for logging is complex, as both the US and Canada regulate their Best Management Practices (BMPs) by U.S. state or Canadian province. The US Forest Practices Act and related state laws are adopted on a state-by-state basis. Those states and provinces also include different sovereign entities like the Colville, Yakama, Makah and many other First Nation communities in British Columbia who source and mill their own timber from tribally managed forests. Additional complexities arise from the spectrum of forest certification programs, from the US and Canadian Sustainable Forestry Initiative (SFI), to the global Forest Stewardship Council (FSC) and Programme for the Endorsement of Forest Certification (PEFC).

I realized early on that understanding, documenting and clarifying the complexities of all of these differing regulations and certification systems was critical to backing up the sustainable sourcing profile of the mass timber we were using to design and construct our buildings. With others, atelierjones advanced this thinking rapidly, and is now considered as a model for certain key regional projects, notably the Portland International Airport, completed in 2024.[9]

9: Jacob Dunn and Paul Vanderford, 2024. “Sustainable Northwest, Breaking Down the Wood Supply Chain for PDX Airport.”

Geographic proximity makes it easier to ask questions and get to know the various layers of agencies and individuals involved in these complex regulatory processes. The landscape of laws and certifications crossing state, tribal and national borders is hard enough to track regionally. It is far more difficult to do that on different continents, under different political systems and different countries, even those under the tight regulations of the EU.

Working regionally, I have met with multiple coalitions that are working together for the good of a healthy working forest. These are perhaps the most inspiring examples of all, watching and learning how highly diverse communities of interests—environmental groups, tribal leaders, publicly traded logging companies, and small private ones—can come together and create practices that ensure thriving, healthy forests.[10]

10: See also USDA US Forest Service, 2024. “Colville National Forest advances innovative partnerships through A to Z Projects.”

Since 2014, all of the mass timber projects executed by atelierjones contain wood milled only from trees in Washington, Oregon, Idaho, Montana, or British Columbia. We intensely value and nurture our relationships with local mass timber fabricators, mills, forest managers, and owners. Working regionally helps us understand our forests and the rural communities that support them. Promoting continued transparency of the mill sourcing of the lumber, as well as sustainable forest management practices, remains critical for the future viability of mass timber as a renewable, sustainable building material.

Oikos

The home and forest stories of my personal and professional lives had long run parallel to one another. They finally converged as I sought to put language and images together, when I was asked to tell a story one October evening in 2015 for the Northwest Eco-Building Guild. The constraint of condensing this journey to merely ten images and five minutes finally crystallized the intimate circular story of forest to home to forest. The power of that moment of systemic understanding, even as I had been acting in a systemic manner, was thrilling. Understanding is not a linear process, nor an additive one.

What my story gave me was a broader understanding of ecology. The word itself was first coined by Ernst Haeckel in 1866, combining the ancient Greek words *oikos*, meaning 'house', and the suffix *-logy*, meaning 'study of.'[11] For Haeckel this "study of the house" meant the study of our collective home on Mother Earth.

11: Ernst Haeckel, 1866. *Generelle Morphologie der Organismen.*

The process of designing, researching and building the CLTHouse, the study of a home–my home–had become the process of studying our *home on earth*.

From *Oikos* to *ecology*. From house to earth.

The design and research methodologies we developed to help understand the CLTHouse became the foundation of our architectural practice at atelierjones. Given the harm that 20th-century building practices continue to inflict upon the earth, *the study of our house and its systems* presents an ethical necessity. We must attempt to understand these practices, and imagine how we might disrupt them, even in the face of resistance to change. And through this lens of understanding, over the last decade we have helped lead this discussion, helping to define the role that architects can play in sourcing sustainable building materials, including timber from well-managed forests.

Designing the CLTHouse sharpened our understanding of the landscapes, processes and communities from which lumber comes. We began to understand how mass timber could both encourage healthier forests and healthier communities, both urban and rural.

Our work with mass timber encouraged a deeper awareness of how, when managed, restored and harvested wisely, our forests are truly renewable resources. Ironically, today in the Pacific Northwest, with second- or third-generation forests of even-aged, overstocked stands at high risk of fire and disease, it is often under-harvesting, rather than over-harvesting that poses the greater risk to our landscapes. Strategic logging and replanting can reduce these risks and create more resilient, ecologically-rich, uneven-aged forests, a lesson long understood in Austria and Germany, where forests have been continually harvested for centuries.

The forest landscapes of the Pacific Northwest lie deep within rural communities and are often managed with local labor to thin, log, and replant the forests, relying on vastly different systems and time scales to nurture healthy forests. Mass timber is a constructed material, industrially fabricated with digital computer tools, and requires skilled, better-paid labor to mill the timber, fabricate, program and cut the prefabricated panels near the forests themselves. During both its sourcing and production, mass timber can help provide jobs for these often-vulnerable communities, all while producing the material to build lower-carbon, more resilient, and more beautiful cities.

We learned how wood stores sequestered carbon from the forests as harvested lumber, and how mass timber could address the need to lower our construction industry's carbon footprint by building lower-carbon and more durable buildings. Storing high levels of carbon in our cities, in timber harvested in tightly regulated, regional sustainable forest ecosystems also helps raise awareness of forest management issues to denizens of our cities.

The concept of *ecology* suggests the importance of studying entire systems, themselves by nature circular. We learned to collaborate and understand how design can see issues not in separate silos but in networks, in how they affect each other. It was a lesson in how we can design a livable future for our *home on earth*.

2010–2015
Seattle, Washington

atelierjones:
Susan Jones, Brian Gerich, Joe Swain,
Maria Ibarlucia, Brooks Brainerd,
Mesa Sherriff, Marisol Foreman,
Megumi Migita

Owner:
Susan Jones and Marco Zangari

Structural Engineering:
Harriott Valentine Engineers

Contractor:
Cascade Built LLC

Mass Timber Supplier/Fabricator:
Structurlam

CLT Support:
Pete Kobelt, Hans-Erik Blomgren,
Ethan Martin

Photography:
Lara Swimmer

CLTHouse

Living with Wood

The CLTHouse is an experimental house testing a new *21st-century wood.* It is an experiment in how to build with lower-carbon materials, how to understand where our materials come from, and in how to create new spaces and volumes with that new wood. Its rich phenomenological living experience has been written about, spawned multiple videos, and inspired architects and students internationally. For the last ten years, it has been a relatively maintenance-free, warm and loving home for our family of four.

Inside and outside, light dances across its wood structure, in small fleeting moments of life and in dramatic seasonal transitions. We have had it photographed twice professionally: once fresh, naked, and newly-built in the heat of summer, and again a decade later, now subtly silvered and robed in its small but richly verdant garden, encompassed by a weathered cedar fence.

The impact of these fruit-bearing orchards, with apples, plums, raspberries, figs, and pomegranates are a study unto themselves in how 2,500 square feet of land can produce its own biohabitat. The shade and shelter under these trees in the heat of summer creates a softened buffer of green that shimmers against the Douglas fir cladding, blackened by fire treatment and softly graying with age under the brushed black burn of ashes.

The house recalls the ubiquitous Pacific Northwest beach cabin, a space of respite and relaxation. A closeness to nature is evoked, from the smell of the wood panels—a mix of spruce, pine, and fir (SPF)—to the feel of them underfoot, and the soft reflections of light on their whitewashed surfaces. An airy, open feel, with light in three directions—east, west, and south—persists throughout the year.

Its small footprint, on two vaulted stories, comprises just 1,500 square feet of living space. Crossing the wooden threshold at a compressed entry, the interior opens into the high volume of the ground floor, with living and dining rooms delineated above by a Miesian steel beam in gloss white. The complexity of the small triangular site is visible from the first moment of entry. The rear wall slices forward diagonally from the back entry, into the wooden dining room, outside to a small green court, back in across the wood of the living room, and out again through large windows to the green orchard and the neighborhood beyond.

Simultaneously, a slow-to-rise wooden staircase ascends to the left. Light descends from an unseen source to fall on a wooden sleeping loft, bookcase, window seat, and built-in storage walls that step down to mediate the sectional transition.

For both better and worse, our world today is indelibly shaped by the impact of humans. So much of our landscape is the result of the intense relationship between nature and humanity, stretching back to pre-industrial times. Because of this, what we think of as *natural* is often a *constructed nature*. As a material, CLT is one such expression of this condition—at once natural and fabricated, where both these qualities are perceived and amplified. The essential, emotive quality of natural wood is abundantly present, even if this is a hybrid, constructed solution for an era where the purely natural is under increasing threat.

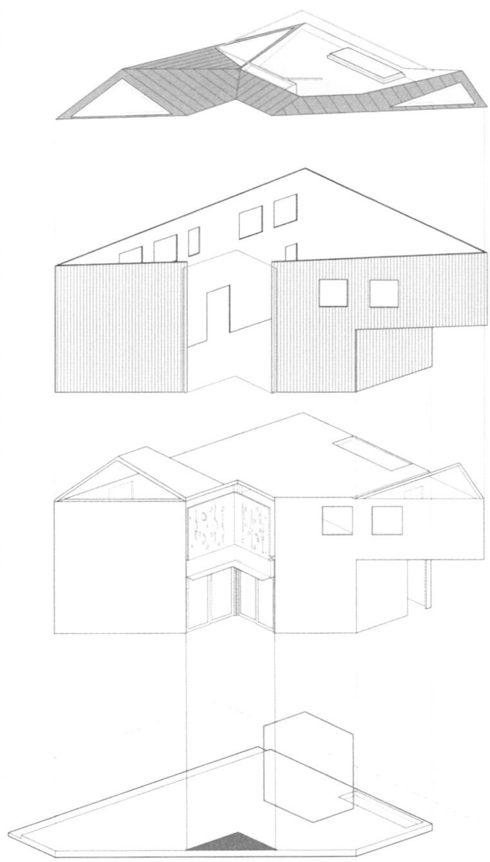

Its additional levels of constructed meaning are revealed upon closer inspection. First, a familiar one: the ubiquitous 2-by-6-inch lumber that comprises the submatrix of the CLT panels is evident everywhere—it is the base material of the house. But as familiar as the 2x6 is to Americans, it is uncanny to see it exposed and turned horizontal to the viewer, as both a structural and finish material, rather than in its conventional position as a perpendicular framing member. The presence of the workhorse 2x6 lamstock within the sanded and whitewashed field of the large CLT panels provides handmade, yet highly crafted sensation to the viewer. The subtle wash of white-diluted paint and a matte UV clearcoat, further provides a layer of reflections that alternatively subdues and intensifies the natural properties of the wood.

The uncanny continues, for upon closer inspection, the homey and familiar 2x6s are not divided in conventional lengths but spliced—almost randomly—with finger-joints to form continuous members. These create large, uniform surfaces of walls, ceilings and floors. Like paper, they are pressed together with no visible connections, simply wrapping volumes. This volumetric reading is enhanced by the careful orientation of grain direction, creating the impression of stereotomic mass in a tectonic system.

Although the panels have an obvious weight and muscular presence, their thickness and connectors are largely concealed, obscuring their structural function, and it is not until one moves up through the house that this logic is slowly revealed.

From the stairs, section cuts of the CLT panels become visible, showing their structural heft, their *constructive matrix*. The structural stacking of these walls becomes apparent on the second level, where wooden vaults crown two ends of the triangular plan in office and bedroom. Finally, one passes up through an oversized skylight to perch on a roof deck atop the wooden structure, nestled in the tree canopy.

The CLTHouse provides sensations at multiple levels. With its triple-glazed windows and doors and 13-inch-thick walls, the house is strangely quiet inside. The solid wood walls create soft but acoustically very live aural experiences unusual in a residential setting. Because of the high mass of the walls, with 4 inches of wood and an additional 6.5 inches of rock-mineral wool on the outside, they hold the sound, especially the bass tones, making it a classically live space with longer reverberation times. While subtle, these additional verbal and musical sound patterns engender an almost spiritual and emotive release.

With the sweet smell of the wood surrounding, its hypernatural visual surface and its smooth, soft feeling underfoot, four out of five senses are engaged. Without resorting to sentimental treatment of wood, its enhanced natural and experiential qualities are deepened by its constructed materiality and high-performance construction system. Phenomenologically rich, the materiality of the house rises beyond a sentimental experience of wood and becomes a technological clue that points to a new relationship between wood, our forests, and our built environment.

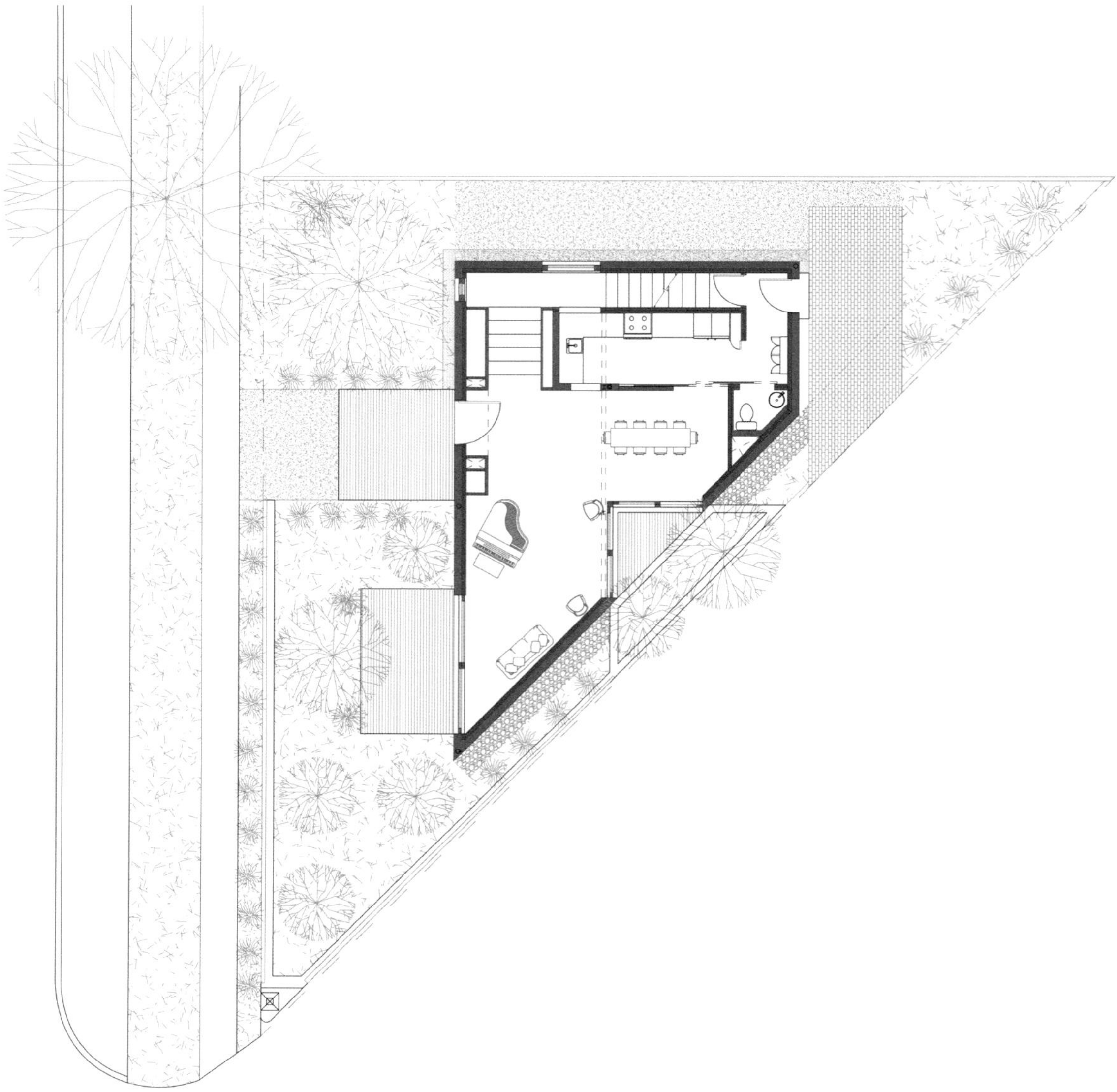

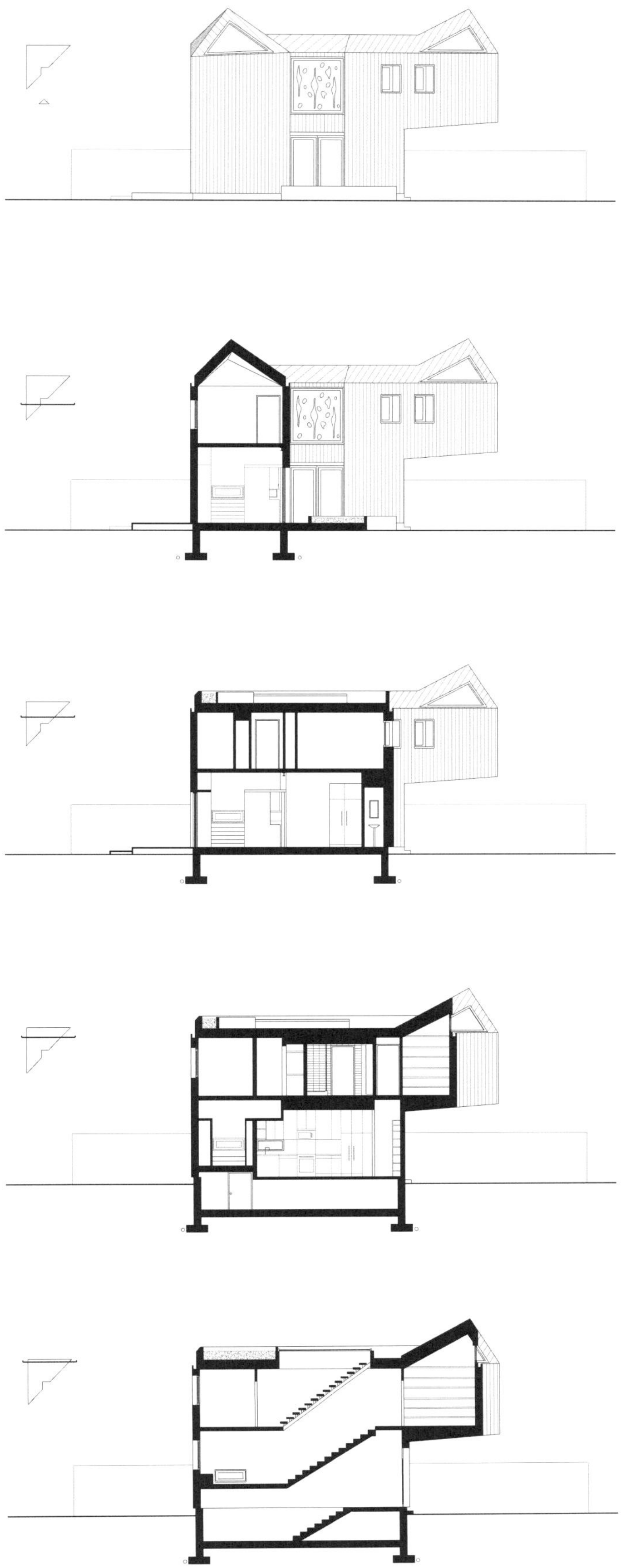

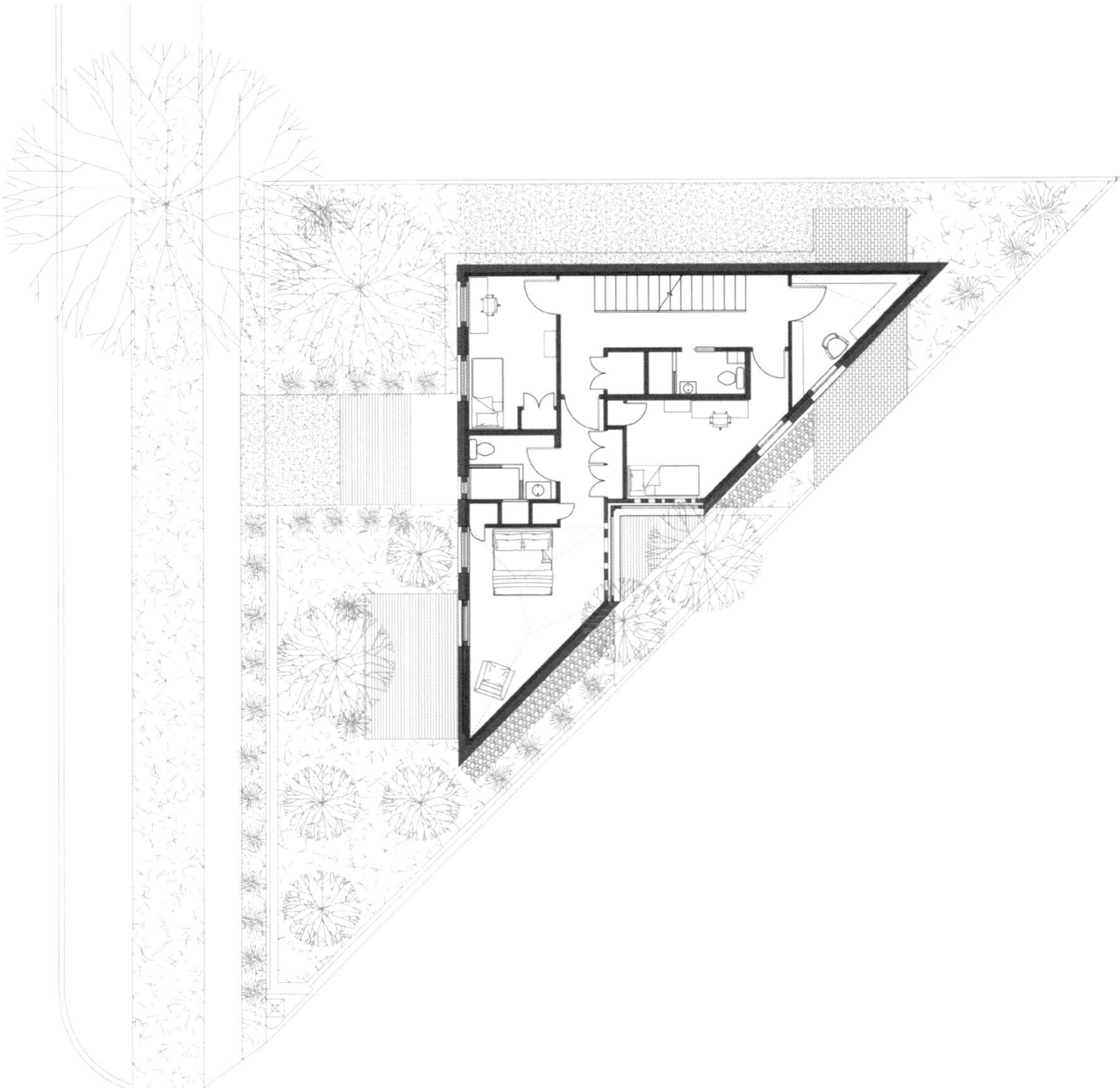

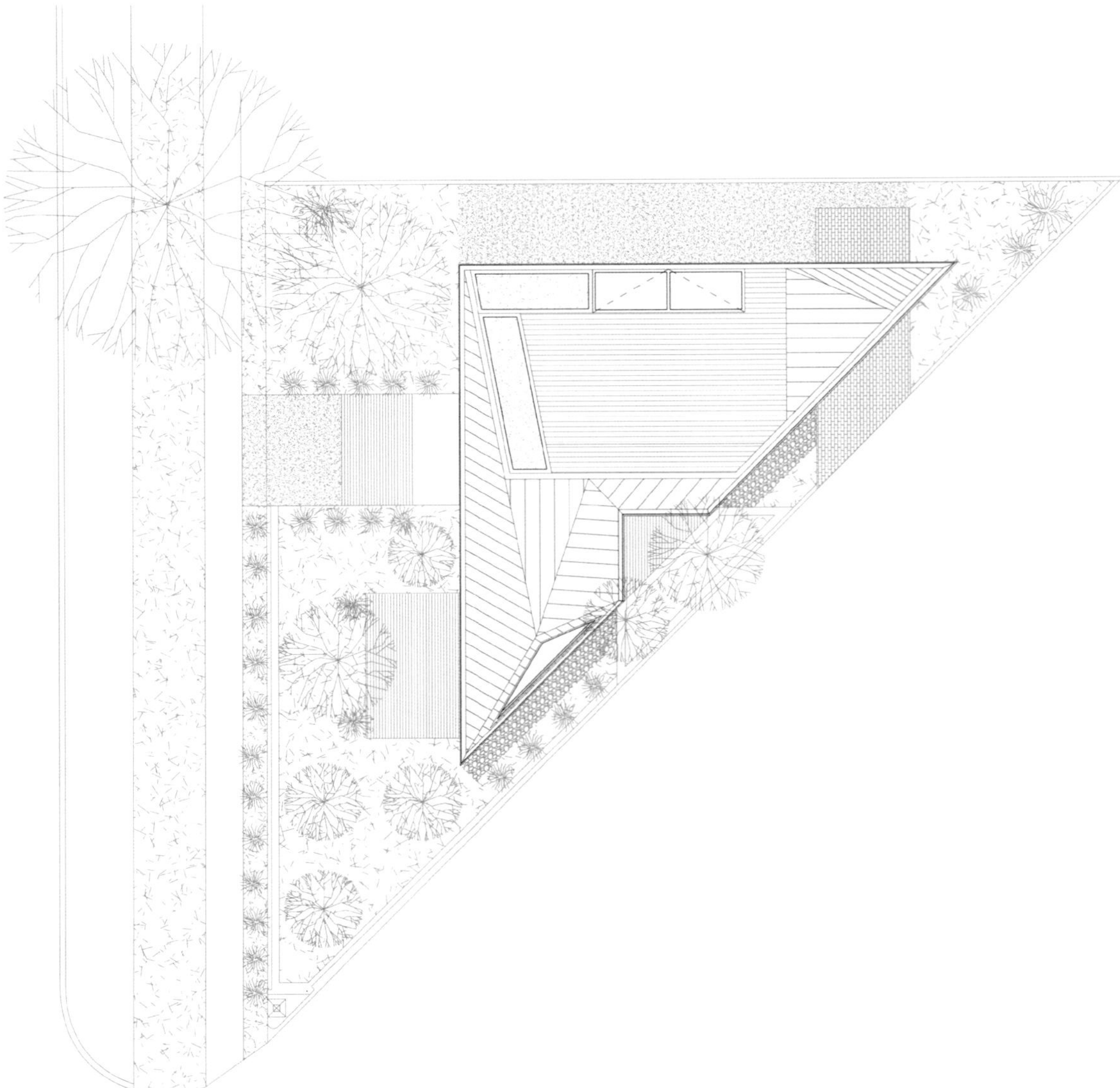

They paved paradise and put up a parking lot

Joni Mitchell

IV.

s c a l e

Going Up?

From the inception of atelierjones in 2003, I focused on designing for a more sustainable built environment. I had spent my time as a young architect in the 1990s focusing on lowering the operational energy of buildings and their environments. Inspired by my colleagues, early *Greenbuild* conventions in Portland, and partnerships with UC Berkeley's Center for the Built Environment, I learned about transit-rich neighborhoods, low-flow toilets, heat-recovery systems, solar shade systems, and building-integrated solar panels. I studied Norman Foster's seminal Commerzbank high-rise in Frankfurt and its innovative twin-wall facades. Later, airtight *Passivhaus* wall assemblies developed in Europe were crossing the Atlantic to impact residential construction.

12: Lloyd Alter, 2024. *The Story of Upfront Carbon.*

But throughout this process, a growing unease was developing that we were, in the words of Lloyd Alter,[12] expending an enormous amount of *upfront carbon* in exchange for small gains in the future. Materials used to create wall, floor, and roof assemblies with better energy performance were often carbon-intensive, such as thick, petroleum-based polystyrene insulation, aluminum triple-glazed windows, or mineral-intensive solar panels As a profession, we had effectively ignored the importance of finding lower-carbon materials and creating regional supply chains to source them locally.

We needed to go deeper. By 2011, when I had the opportunity to design and build my own house, it was clear that I needed to confront this uncomfortable reality. We needed to distinguish the upfront carbon—the carbon it actually took to build a building—from the energy it took to operate it during its lifetime.

Through my Austrian architect friends, I kept hearing about new approaches to wood construction, distinct from the typical residential stick-frame construction in North America. There were new emerging *mass timber* materials that could supposedly harness wood in new ways for greater strength and environmental

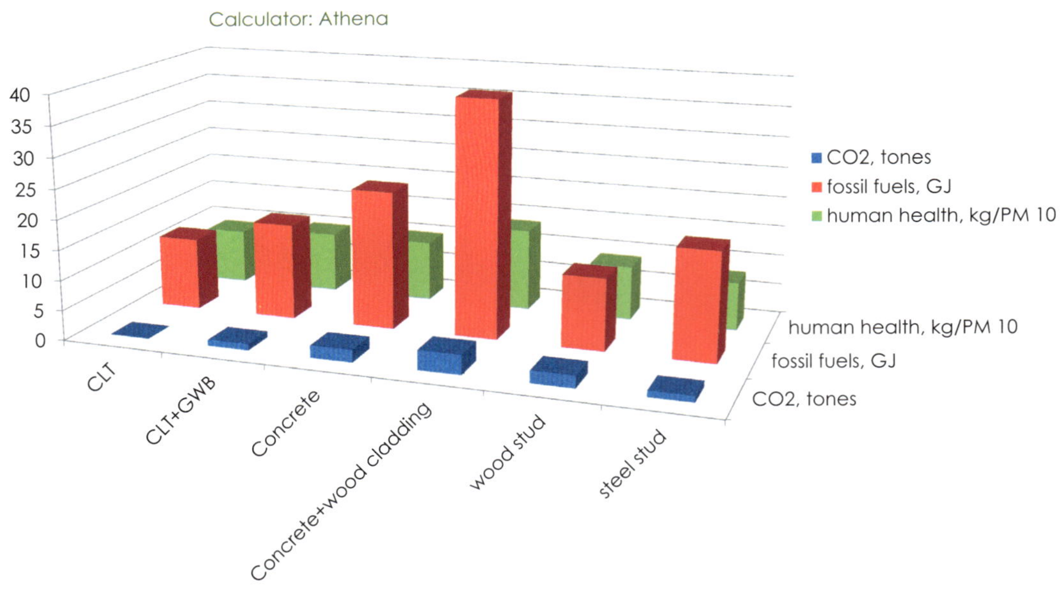

Comparative material carbon analysis Olga Amigud, Dhara Goradia, Justin Schwartzhof University of Washington, 2013

resilience. The differences were fundamental. In Europe, centuries-old deforestation had led to hundreds of years of regrown, replanted and renewed forests. In the 1990's those forests provided the basis to engineer large pieces of lumber from small, regrown, carefully tended trees.

Wood-rich America was still accustomed to using large, raw heavy timber beams cut from older trees, even until the 1970s and 80s. The 20th-century use of old-growth timber had serious impacts on forests everywhere, and the 'Timber Wars' of the 1990s had settled the issue. Larger, older trees needed to stay as forests.

While reusing reclaimed heavy timber, as practiced by many high-design architects in the Pacific Northwest, was one way to preserve the strength, longevity and biophilic beauty of these large timbers, this was only a boutique application. Reusing this limited quantity of reclaimed early 20th-century wood inspired an outsized desire for large pieces of heavy timber in rarified and mostly private environments. Trying to recreate and keep these primordial experiences of wood for all people and all scales of work, was a driving factor of our practice. With *21st-century wood*, we could recreate all qualities of large timber from smaller pieces of lumber, allowing us to harvest from sustainably managed regenerated forests, and do so at scale.

For me, mass timber was compelling for its beauty, the opportunities for prefabrication, and for its carbon impact. It became the basis of our design and research work at atelierjones, starting with design of our CLTHouse from 2012—2015, the CLTChurch, from 2013—2016 and the CLTSchools from 2016—2017. Astonishingly, having completed these four projects by 2017, atelierjones had likely completed more mass timber buildings than any other architectural firm in the United States at the time.

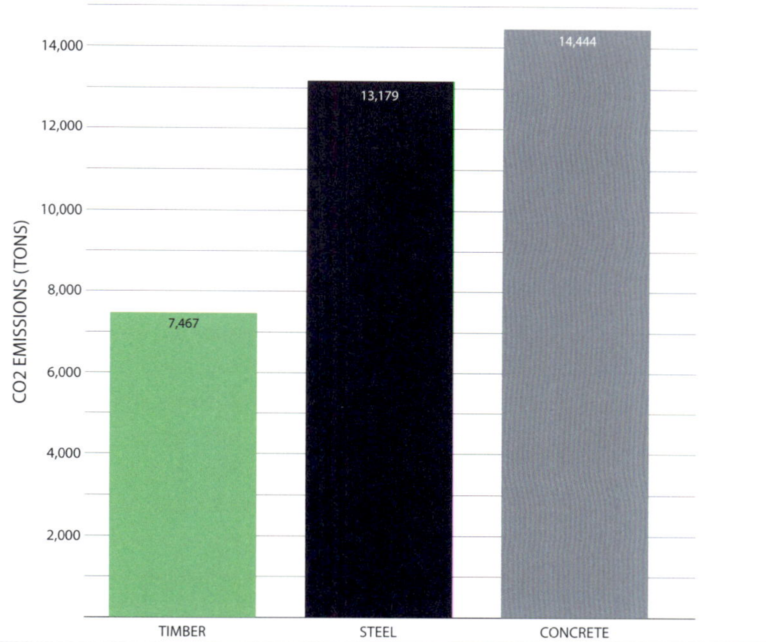

Whole-building carbon comparisons
Tyler Moench, Vy Nguyen, Shazia Ahmad
University of Washington, 2016

TIMBER COMPOSITE CONSTRUCTION

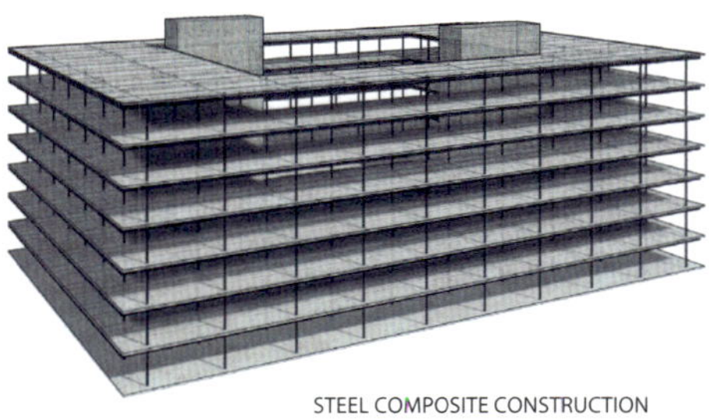

STEEL COMPOSITE CONSTRUCTION

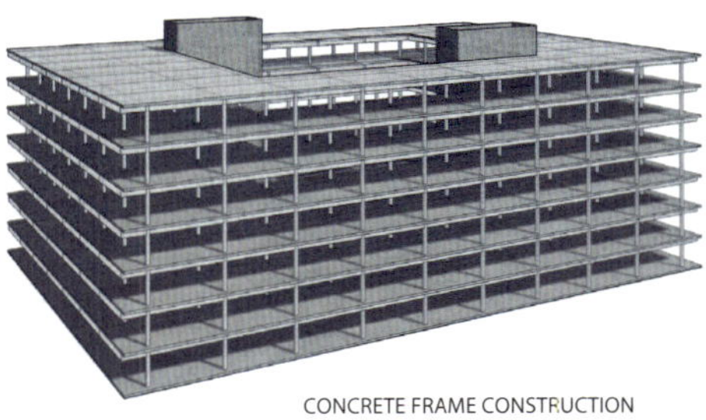

CONCRETE FRAME CONSTRUCTION

As satisfying as these small projects were, I that mass timber could have a bigger impact. Were we really harnessing this material's potential ability to lower our building industry's carbon footprint? While it was exhilarating to design and build some of the first buildings of this kind in the United States, our early student research from my University of Washington studios suggested that we needed a much more nuanced understanding of carbon.

In 2013, my UW architecture graduate students partnered with Professor Kate Simonen, today well known as the founder of the Carbon Leadership Forum, to perform lifecycle assessment (LCA) studies using Athena software. In those early days tools were scarce, and carbon LCAs for buildings were in their infancy.

In those early student analyses, cross-laminated timber performed very well as a stand-alone material in comparison to concrete or structural steel. But as a full-wall assembly, compared to a typical American light-frame wood construction, it yielded surprisingly little difference in carbon footprint, even when the stored carbon in the wood was included.

While we did not perform a comparative LCA of the CLTHouse and a similar light-wood-frame structure, it is likely that the mass timber house would actually have a higher carbon footprint than its light-wood-frame counterpart. While that intuition did not shake my will to build our experimental house out of cross-laminated timber, nor did it factor in the longer durability of a mass timber house, it left me pondering the issue of scale. I was starting to sense that if mass timber was going to disrupt business-as-usual concrete and steel development, we needed to go bigger.

In the fall of 2016, I had the opportunity to test the hypothesis differently, again with my UW students. Building on the 2013 design and research studio, I decided to give the students a larger program. To take a jump in scale.

I assigned the studio to design a 12-story mass timber institutional building, the Wood Innovation Center. At this height, a comparative, conventional building could only have used concrete or steel construction. We again took on LCA work.

We had data, published by Alan Organschi at Yale, to measure the relative carbon intensities of 20-foot-long structural members of wood, steel, and concrete.[13] But floor assemblies for large buildings are not just made from wood, steel or concrete. Steel pan decks support concrete and rebar, for instance, and mass timber floors require layers of acoustic material and gypsum. So, we developed full assemblies, and tracked carbon data for each of the composite materials.

13: Alan Organschi, 2015. *Timber in the City*.

From there, we calculated the carbon footprint of a typical structural bay, and finally extrapolated the results to the scale of a generic high-rise building in mass timber, steel and concrete. Each time we jumped in scale the carbon analysis became truer to life. Eventually, we came up with whole-building results that showed a 30-50% lower Global Warming Potential (GWP) for larger-scale mass timber superstructure when compared to conventional construction.

These studies were carried out by graduate students of architecture, not professionals, and were some of the earliest we had seen attempting to understand these carbon issues at a mid-rise scale. But even before they were later refined (and largely confirmed) by Kate Simonen and her University of Washington colleague Indroneil Ganguly, the lesson was clear: substituting mass timber for steel and concrete at scale was where the real carbon benefits would be found.

In over five years of research and design, from 2011—2016, we had helped introduce mass timber, particularly cross-laminated timber, into the US building supply chain. But this early work with mass timber had focused on smaller-scale prototype buildings. While beautiful and compelling, they did not represent a significant step forward in our need to lower our building and design industry's carbon footprint.

But substituting wood for concrete or steel made a measurable difference. Scale mattered.

The only direction was to go up.

Codes

As architects, we are trained to use and respect building codes. Depending on jurisdiction and building type, these codes can be thousands of pages long, and with their corollaries—structural, energy and fire codes—cover topics from stairways to slot machines,[14] concrete to Christmas trees.[15] A building design must adhere to them all.

14: *2021 International Building Code*, section 1110.16: Gaming Machines and Gaming Tables
15: *2021 International Fire Code*, section 806: Natural Decorative Vegetation in New and Existing Buildings

Currently in the US, the International Building Code (IBC) developed by the International Code Council (ICC) predominates as the architectural code applied in most major US jurisdictions, and the ICC leads a rigorous, consensus-based process to continually update it. As architects, we design and submit building permit drawings to an *Authority Having Jurisdiction* (AHJ), a cumbersome term describing the wide variety of city, state, and county institutions authorized to approve building permits in the US. Buildings undergo extensive reviews by multiple code officials, each focusing on their area of expertise. Architects are responsible for ensuring that our drawings meet the letter of the code, as interpreted by these myriad authorities.

As Principal Architect of atelierjones, I have signed and stamped every single page of drawings submitted over the life of the firm. Nevertheless, this does not make me a code expert. Architecture is a complex discipline, and requires an incredible variety of different skills, at different scales, from the highly creative to the highly technical. Young architects learn—often in painstaking and painful ways—in which areas of the complex building process their particular creative talent will best manifest itself. It takes tremendous discipline, patience and perseverance to master the incredible variety of skills and talents required to bring a building into existence.

I knew early on that, while I could navigate the incredible tapestry of building codes, mastering both their requirements and their full design potentials would not be my strength as an architect. I was happy to rely upon those who had greater patience to search, absorb, and understand the codes. At least that was what I thought.

So, when the International Code Council issued a call for members for a new, mass timber-focused committee in December 2015, I demurred. With my Seattle mass timber colleagues, we discussed the opportunity over beer. We all agreed that the effort was critical for mass timber to succeed. They were eager and extraordinarily adroit with code language. They talked about strategies to rewrite the codes, how would it be done, and whether tall mass timber would fall under a new or existing code building type. They had been collaborating for months with the City of Seattle to consider options. They applied. I was sure one of them would be appointed and felt the new TWB committee would be in great hands. *Thank goodness.*

It was much to my surprise, then, in February 2016, when I took a call on my mobile phone from a Washington, D.C. area code. I was standing in an alley in downtown Seattle, outside the large brick theater building that housed my second-floor office. It was from the National Codes Director of the American Institute of Architects. He explained that the AIA wanted me to apply to the code committee. I explained that there was no need: they already had some great applications from highly capable and qualified folks. Who also had designed with mass timber. Who were passionate and highly knowledgeable about building codes. That they didn't need me. He again asked me to apply.

At that time, the Bellevue First Congregational church was nearing completion, and the CLTSchools were on track to be completed in the summer. We were in the thick of realizing three proof-of-concept mass timber buildings, advancing the field. I had already agreed to teach another UW Wood Innovation Design and Research Studio in the Fall. So, I said, no, thank you, that running my own firm, teaching and building mass timber prototypes was already a tremendous load, not to mention raising two teenagers at the time. He said to think about it, and that he would call back later. And that he would send me an application form. I said, "thank you very much, but no thank you." This ballet of *"please think about it"* and *"no thank you"* went on for about a week.

On the evening before the application deadline, I was sitting at my dinner table in the CLTHouse, spring light falling across the cross-laminated timber walls. I tentatively raised the subject with my kids. They were 15 and 16 at the time, one in a large, diverse public high school, the other in one of the most venerated private schools in the US. Dinner table debates were often vigorous and strenuous. I tentatively raised the issue. Administrative code. Writing, potentially changing policy, bureaucratic meetings, travel, etc. I tried to make it as dry sounding as possible. But I did say "I mean, to design and build this house is one level of innovation, changing codes to allow everyone in the country to build with this material at scale, is another."

My 15-year-old daughter was particularly articulate. She said it sounded interesting, and that it would have more impact than just a house made of CLT. She waved her hand towards the wall of our dining room. I was not expecting that reaction. I sent in the application the next day.

One month later, I received an email welcoming me to the committee and asking me to attend in person an initial three-day meeting in July at a hotel outside Chicago O'Hare Airport.

ICC Code Committee Members view the solar eclipse of August 21, 2017

Changing Codes, Part I

2016–2019

Starting in 2016, I represented the American Institute of Architects in the International Code Council's (ICC) tall timber code development process, having no idea it would take over three years. The work would grow to involve 18 months of collective discernment, research, debating, and writing, followed by 18 months of the ICC's ratification process. Collective wordsmithing, amongst an 18-member committee—several of whom were strongly opposed to the use of mass timber in taller buildings—to write 200 pages of new, data-driven building codes would be an enormous undertaking. It completely changed my small architectural practice.

The process would require new, original research and testing that would ultimately create consensus to write and defend the new codes. Much of work of the ICC's Tall Wood Building Ad-Hoc Committee (TWB) work revolved around understanding the safety limitations of mass timber and its performance under fire conditions. We would need to collectively define a set of data-driven performance criteria and perform multiple rounds of fire testing. To agree on the codes, the committee would need to rise above industry interests and agree to use data as the decision-making criteria. Challenging as that would prove, the passing of these prescriptive codes would mark a huge success for the large-scale adoption of mass timber and the pathway toward a lower-carbon built environment.

The State of the Codes

The International Building Code has long recognized "heavy timber" under the Type IV construction category. In 2015, the IBC added a definition of cross-laminated timber within the Type IV heavy timber definition. These updates also increased the height allowance of Type IV construction from three stories to six. But, since light-wood frame or hybrid ("5 over 2") buildings can also be built at this

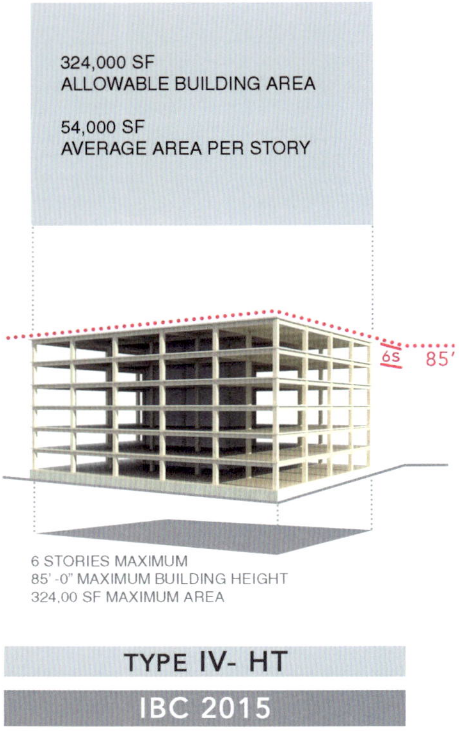

Maximum mass timber building height and area allowance per the 2015 IBC code

scale in the United States, this increase was still not enough to affect the heavy carbon footprint of concrete and steel. We needed to go to 8 stories and above to substitute for concrete and steel.

For those looking to go taller, alternative pathways did exist. Individual jurisdictions could approve mass timber buildings on a case-by-case basis through Alternate Materials and Methods Requests (AMMRs). These performance-based approvals were difficult however, requiring extensive and expensive upfront project-based testing to convince local officials that the proposed design could meet the intent of the building codes.

Key early projects, such as Carbon 12 in Portland by Kaiser/Path Architects, completed in 2018, or Ascent in Milwaukee by Korb + Associates Architects, completed in 2022, used these pathways, but they required the developer/owner to assume a great deal of risk. Project teams and jurisdictions alike needed the will and the resources to invest in these pilot performance-based projects. In 2016, there was no prescriptive path for tall timber buildings *as-of-right*.

The Tall Wood Building Committee

Demand for such a prescriptive tall timber code was increasing. The early tall timber projects on both coasts had exposed the challenges of the AMMR approach. It was clear that AHJ's all over the country could soon be faced with many one-off, performance-based code approval processes. This put both jurisdictions and project teams at risk of delays and additional expenses to secure approval. Even if approvals were successful, diverse state and city-based approvals could create a chaotic patchwork of methodologies across different jurisdictions. Deeper questions, like structural and fire/life safety testing, might not be approved uniformly, leading to confusion, and possible failure to launch mass timber successfully. A coordinated approach was required.

With leadership by the US Forest Service and the American Wood Council, the ICC agreed to convene the TWB committee to take on this challenge. The 18 voting members included a cross-section of the US building industry: architects, structural and fire engineers, code officials, and representatives from the wood, concrete, steel, and gypsum-wall board industries.

The first three-day session of the committee in July 2016 was exhausting and disorienting. The 18 of us sat in a circle of plastic banquet tables strewn with computer cables, under the weak borrowed light of a skylight. The windowless, beige room behind us was packed with an audience of over 100 highly motivated stakeholders, sitting in rows of folding chairs.

Key individuals who acted as leaders, buffers, and bluffers on the committee began to emerge. Statements of disregard, inaccuracies, and casual slights were volleyed back and forth across the table, all burnished under the guise of "protecting the code." *Well remember what happened last time, they can't even define mass timber. Why are we wasting our time?* Whether or not this was a hazing experience intended for the likes of me or not, my shock and concern for what I was witnessing grew hourly.

By 2016, I had been in this profession for over 30 years. I had walked, invited or uninvited, into new situations, always filled with fear, again and again. In concrete studio trays at the Harvard Graduate School of Design, in large stone Ringstrasse offices of Vienna, walking through concrete and stone rubble of the newly opened East Berlin, or sitting at sleek formed plastic tables of new business partners in Seattle, I had had over 30 years of experiences encountering groups of professionals (mostly men) recounting their culture, their ways of designing, building, making a living, of *how we do it here.*

I had learned that my presence as a female often elicited additional, extraneous energy, sometimes highly destructive to getting work done. Listening as the outsider, again and again, I had heard the voices of groups reinforcing their perspectives, transmitting their values, telling me their ways. From loquacious Harvard reviewers to Handwerkers in Venice thinking through welded steel connections, to corporate business partners discussing bonus tier structures, to contractors value-engineering my buildings over and over, these conversations taught me again and again how to design, how to build, how to be in this world I loved so much. That we all loved so much.

As I ventured outwards, I had first learned to be quiet. To listen. Being naturally quiet that was easy. And my fear and always my pounding heart made it easy to step back and listen and watch. To understand the groups' ways of being. To understand their language, whether GSD, Viennese or German, but also, the way these groups interacted, created social capital, creating tacit agreements with one another on what was acceptable and what was not. Raised in an early 1960s highly educated female culture that praised, supported, upheld and benefited from patriarchal systems of power and social capital, that came naturally. The difficulty, always, was finding my own voice within those different realms.

Several hours into the session, I began to focus on one person. Large and relaxed, with a large grin and a twinkle in his eye. It was Sam Francis, the AWC National Programs Director. I checked quickly around the table. Besides him, only one other 'wood' person was there, a gentle Canadian. Through the emotion of the hours, I began to focus on Sam's reactions to the most absurd statements. He would often fire back a cocky but good-natured retort, or sometimes, just a quiet smile. At worst a sigh. Without his genial warmth and disarming charm, I likely would not have lasted through the first session. I so often credit his dogged and brilliant leadership skills as the most essential factor in the passage of the Tall Wood Building Codes. His presence convinced me to make it through the first three days.

But on that first day, one presence emerged above all others: Sean DeCrane, the former Fire Chief of Cleveland, an enormously tall, well-built man. He had brought us to tears earlier in the day, with his talk about what it meant for him to *have a bad day*. Commanding your boys, your *boys*, to climb a burning tower and watching only some of them come back down. Sifting through ashes to find their bodies later. Telling children that their parent would not be coming back. *Having a bad day*.

We understood the emotion. We shared it. At the end of the day, I approached him cautiously and thanked him for putting our work in perspective. He peered down at me skeptically. His gruff Irish countenance forced up a thanks to my shy gratitude. I left, with my head down.

We heard ten presentations those first three days, most from people who had never touched a cross-laminated timber panel. They spoke eloquently of their structural capacities, their ability to be assembled into 40-story towers. They spoke eloquently of wonderous European wood buildings, Australian wood buildings, Canadian wood buildings. They spoke knowledgably about French fire tests, Canadian fire tests, British fire tests.

But somehow, none of it touched the bullish heart of the large former Fire Chief of Cleveland. We asked him why. Astonishingly, he spoke plainly: "a European Fire is not an American Fire, a Canadian Fire is not an American Fire. We need real-life fire tests." Relishing his role as game master, he declined to explain further.

By the end of three days, we had agreed to divide up into subcommittees: Definitions, Code, Structural, and Fire. The TWB Committee met regularly, including two or three times yearly for tightly prescribed, multi-day in-person meetings in Chicago. Meetings lasted two to four days, depending on content, and agendas were tightly prescribed. Outside stakeholders were invited to attend in person, and committee members were required. On its own, TWB represented a large commitment, but I had also agreed to join the Code Subcommittee, with its own set of additional meetings and efforts.

But it was also clear that the real group to convince was the Fire Subcommittee. The Fire contingent on the TWB seemed ill-informed, perhaps willfully so, of mass timber. They would regularly conflate the fire dangers of light wood frame construction with mass timber construction. They had not felt the enormous heft of these panels swinging on a steel cable, floating down into place on massive, paneled walls settling into place with barely a shiver, creating a solid 6-5/8 inch floor plate that would become the floor of your bedroom. Their children's bare feet didn't graze over the soft surface of the huge wood panels every morning.

Now, joining the Fire Subcommittee would mean yet another huge commitment, one for which I knew I had little training. What did the Fire Chief mean by *"real-life fire tests"?* The enormity of the task was beginning to dawn on me.

I did have choices. This was a completely pro-bono effort. There were no contracts, other than the handshake that AIA National would pay for my plane tickets and hotel rooms. I could resign in the face of an impossible task to which I felt I was completely unsuited. I could show up late, sit on the sidelines, and use excuses like *"sorry, gotta save the life-blood of my small, female-run practice!"* and no one would know the difference. I was no one to them.

The code effort might have still squeaked through, or perhaps floundered, who knows. It had floundered before. During the previous code cycle this same effort had failed, opposed by concrete and steel lobbies and voices like the Fire Chief. Whether they overtly or innocently mixed the massive mass timber panels with light wood frame structures when discussing fire was nobody's concern. No one had stopped them. The committee failed, folded and went away, pushing us back, deeper into the 20th-century carbon frenzy of concrete and steel buildings that dominated some 40% of the global carbon footprint.

I could stay on the sidelines or double down and learn more about Fire.

What to do?

Fire and wood are conjoined in our collective, human consciousness. Fire burns wood. Rock, Paper, Scissors. Fire always wins. Fire only loses when Wood is depleted or absent in the first place. City regulations have been designed, often directly, in response to catastrophic fires. The role of the International Code Council is to protect lives. To regulate the Life Safety of buildings for their inhabitants. The logic of the argument against wood was impenetrable.

At the end of those excruciating three days, I rose. The voice that I finally found at this raucous, conflicted and interest-strewn table called for collaboration, for working together. *"This is an extraordinarily intelligent and informed group of people sitting at this table. If this group cannot come together to change the ICC codes to allow for lower-carbon Tall Wood Buildings, then I do not know if we will ever be able to do so."*

My words were also a stake in the ground, to the table, to myself, that I had committed, unknowingly or willingly, to this pathway toward a vision of a new way of building tall, with lower-carbon materials.

I agreed to join the Fire Subcommittee.

Fire Test 3 in progress at the ATF Fire Research Laboratory, June 20, 2017

Fire Protocol Design

We had one piece of ammunition: the TWB committee had agreed to use data-based outcomes as the basis to move forward. After much discussion, the committee agreed to charge the Fire Subcommittee with developing real-life mass timber fire tests to augment the large body of international fire tests, both real and simulated.

To move the code language further, past the conservative fire community, it became vitally important to develop a US body of fire tests that skeptics like the Fire Chief would accept. I found myself suppressing fury and swallowing hard instead, learning the hard way to accept that, sometimes, we learn the most from those who disagree with us. It was a very humbling process.

We asked him: "Sean, what is it going to take to get you to agree these buildings are safe?" His answer was "real-life American fire tests."

I soon found myself learning about American fires over my mobile phone.

Before the pandemic forced the practice on all of us, the ICC had perfected the art of convening virtual meetings. The Fire Subcommittee met weekly, all remotely. Some of these calls involved hundreds of people. Subcommittee members spoke first, then questions and comments were requested from the stakeholders present. A neophyte member of the subcommittee, I began to realize how much I just needed to listen to understand fire, so I could parse those words of the Cleveland Fire Chief: American Fires vs. European Fires. Listen first, learn why they said what they did, find the tools to help design a Fire Test Structure that would address concerns. Listen, Learn, Design.

There was a technical language which I had to learn. ASTM E119 tests. Flashover. Fuel Loads. Thermocouples. Fire modeling. Compartments. People went to school for this. I learned it over hours of video calls, on speaker phone, muted, often taken while I was in the shower or lying in bed, in the early hours of Pacific Standard Time.

Over these calls, I began to know my allies and my foes, the mild detractors, the dangerous ones, and the disruptive ones. I learned how and when to insert just the right amount of doubt into my voice, to assemble and alert the other voices to stand strong, to rally to the danger approaching. The most casual of comments could disguise a Trojan Horse, casually sowing discord or creating massive detours that could take weeks or months for the subcommittees to dig out of.

After much deliberation we agreed on a structure. Each design decision endured tremendous scrutiny and skepticism.

The test structure was designed to represent a typical US apartment. As is common with new, US multi-family structures, it was designed with long, wide corridors, leading to a vertical exit stair enclosure. This corridor layout, as opposed to a typical European configuration with a single point or scissors stair, would feed the fire with greater airflow, an understanding that was critical in designing the tests.

The tests were conservative by design. They were also conservative because of the limitations of the facility in which they would be tested. Given the urgency of the tests relative to the code cycle, we had to work with the limitations of available facilities. Only the Bureau of Alcohol, Tobacco and Firearms (ATF) could accommodate us in the spring and summer of 2017, giving us just barely enough time to build, conduct and process the results and then finish writing code language for submission by the end of the year. The urgency was real. But the limitations of their indoor facility would limit the amount of fuel load, hence the amount of exposed wood, that we would be able to test.

Fire Testing

In the summer of 2017, the two-story, load-bearing test structure was complete and ready for the fires inside the ATF's huge steel warehouse outside of Washington D.C.

Despite their conservative design, these would still be the largest mass timber fire tests yet performed, with the largest fuel loads ever tested. Because of the prevalent fear that the mass timber structure itself would unduly contribute to the fuel load of an ongoing fire, for the first test, the CLT panels were protected with multiple layers of gypsum wallboard, limiting the exposure of the wood. Progressively, each of the five tests would remove sections of this drywall covering to test greater exposures.

The apartments were outfitted with kitchen cabinets, Ikea furniture, books, and papers, carefully calculated to add fuel load to the fire. They would be replaced for each test to ensure consistency. The tests would be conducted one at a time, each started with a ziplock bag of gasoline-soaked gauze, placed in a kitchen cabinet on one of the two levels. An array of smoke detectors, gas analyzers, thermal imaging cameras, and hundreds of heat-sensing thermocouples were placed throughout the compartments and bored deep inside the wood panels.

The first fire test was hardly a mass timber test at all. Completely encased in two layers of fire-resistant gypsum wallboard, the structure predictably held up well during the fire. The second test would be the real challenge. With two sections of the ceiling exposed, would the panel be quickly consumed and magnify the fire exponentially? Or would the timber form a protective char layer and smolder slowly? The experts in the fire community needed to see the results with their own eyes.

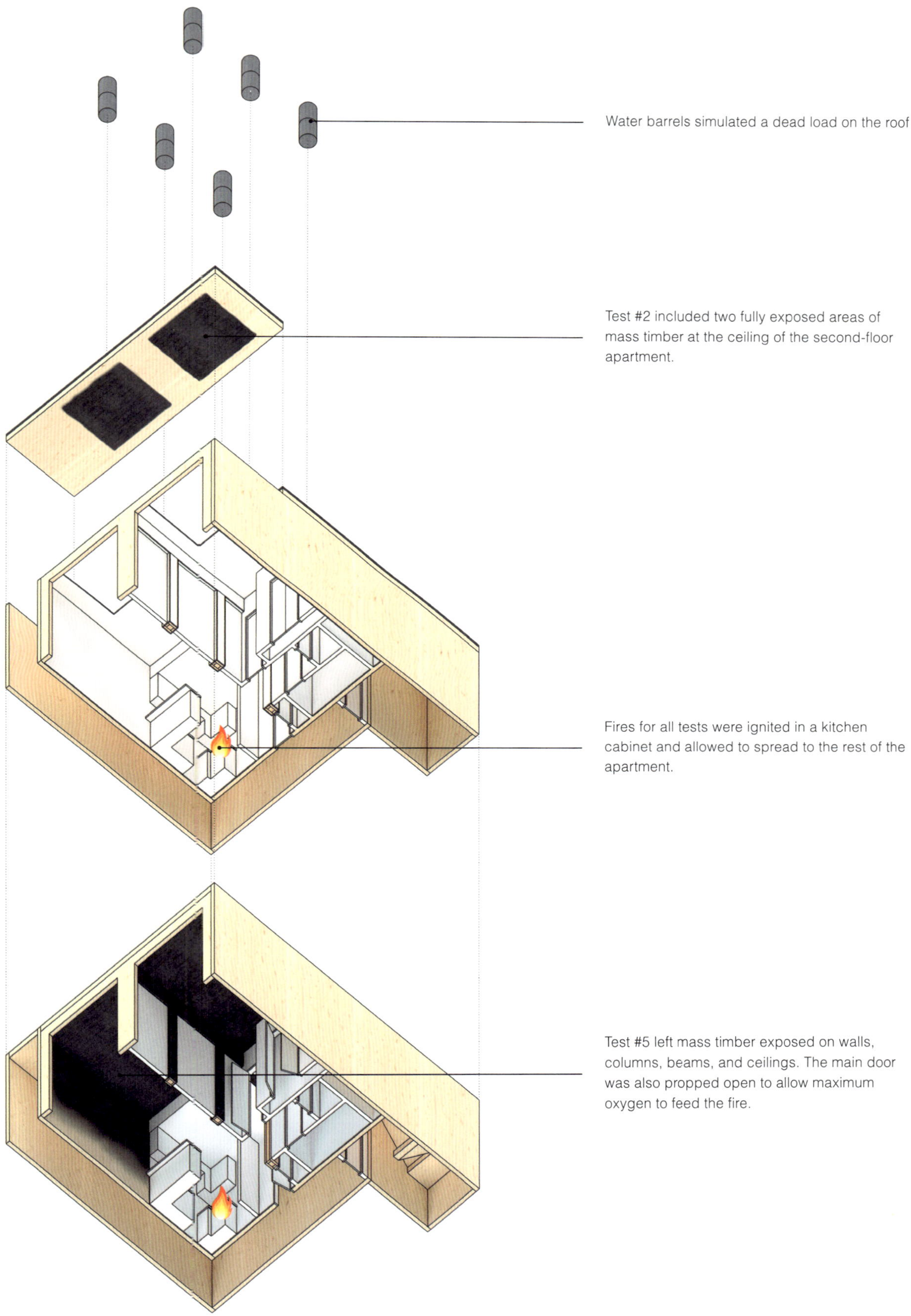
Water barrels simulated a dead load on the roof
Test #2 included two fully exposed areas of mass timber at the ceiling of the second-floor apartment.
Fires for all tests were ignited in a kitchen cabinet and allowed to spread to the rest of the apartment.
Test #5 left mass timber exposed on walls, columns, beams, and ceilings. The main door was also propped open to allow maximum oxygen to feed the fire.

After four hours of intense fire, the last of the embers were drenched and the smoke exhausted through the gargantuan collection hood above. In the end, with no sprinklers or firefighter response, the CLT ceiling panels were still intact. The first of the five layers of laminated 2x6s had burned away, but the char layer that formed had protected the remaining inner four layers, enough to keep the structure sound.

Fire did not conquer wood.

The 40-foot-long 5-ply CLT ceiling panel was lifted away. It revealed black squares of char against the untouched wood that had been protected by drywall. Underneath the charred wood squares was light, strong wood, still intact structurally.

Wood had stopped fire from conquering wood.

For the final three tests, fresh panels were installed, and the rest of the structure restored. These would expose the CLT walls of the bedroom and living room and ultimately the ceilings as well, testing as much exposure as the team was comfortable with in the indoor facility.

The tests all went well. The char layer hypothesis appeared to be confirmed, as the wood burned but was not reduced enough to compromise its structural integrity. Rather than burning quickly like kindling, the mass timber panels were like large logs on a fire: slow to burn and more difficult to ignite. This would allow residents more time to evacuate and give the Chief's boys a chance to more safely enter the building and put out the fire.

In the fourth and fifth tests, the fire sprinklers were activated. The Fire Chief was interested to see how quickly these mass timber fires would be put out.

The fires were put out within conventional time limits.

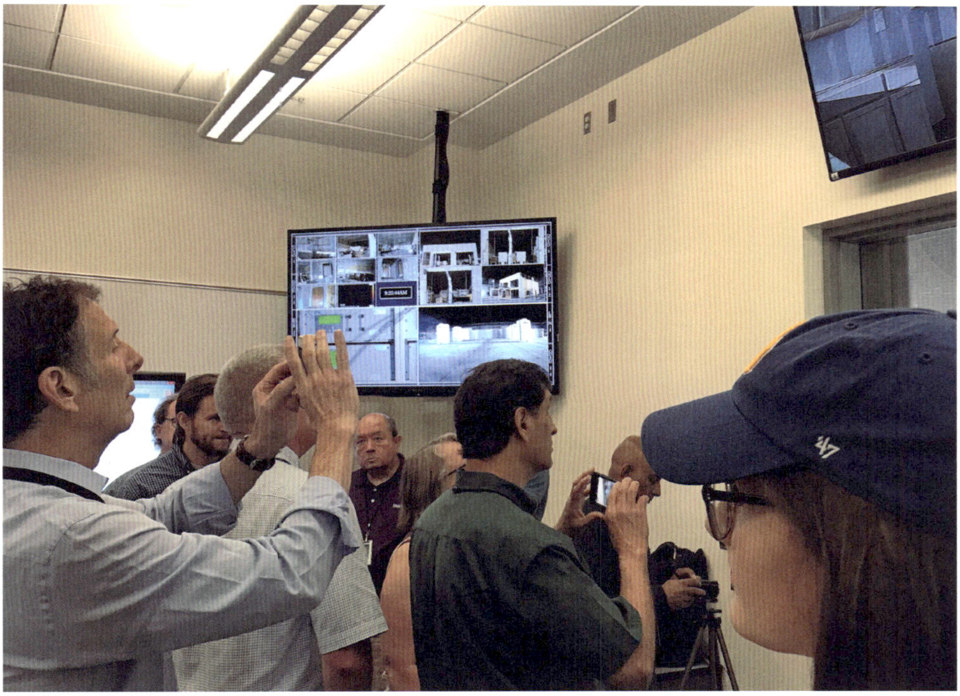

Table 1: Test matrix

Test number	Experiment ID	Amount and location of exposed cross-laminated timber (CLT)	Windows in Wall A	Fire sprinklers	Story
1	193825	None; all CLT surfaces encapsulated	No	No	1st
2	193871	Partially exposed CLT on ceiling in bedroom and living room	No	No	2nd
3	203923	Exposed CLT on walls in bedroom and living room	No	No	2nd
4	203924	Exposed CLT on ceiling and walls in bedroom and living room	Yes	Yes	1st
5	223940	Exposed CLT on ceiling and walls in bedroom and living room	Yes	Yes, but delayed	1st

Table 2: Major events during the cross-laminated timber test series

	Time to event after ignition (mm:ss)				
Event	**Test #1**	**Test #2**	**Test #3**	**Test #4**	**Test #5**
Flashover in living room	13:27	11:42	12:37	N/A	N/A
Flashover in bedroom	17:20	17:20	17:00	N/A	N/A
Flames in corridor outside of apartment door	26:51	30:38	13:06	N/A	~9:00[a]
Failure of entire apartment door	57:46	63:59	29:42	N/A	N/A
Sprinkler activation	N/A	N/A	N/A	2:37	23:00[b]

[a] Apartment door was open at the start of the test.

[b] Sprinklers were manually activated.

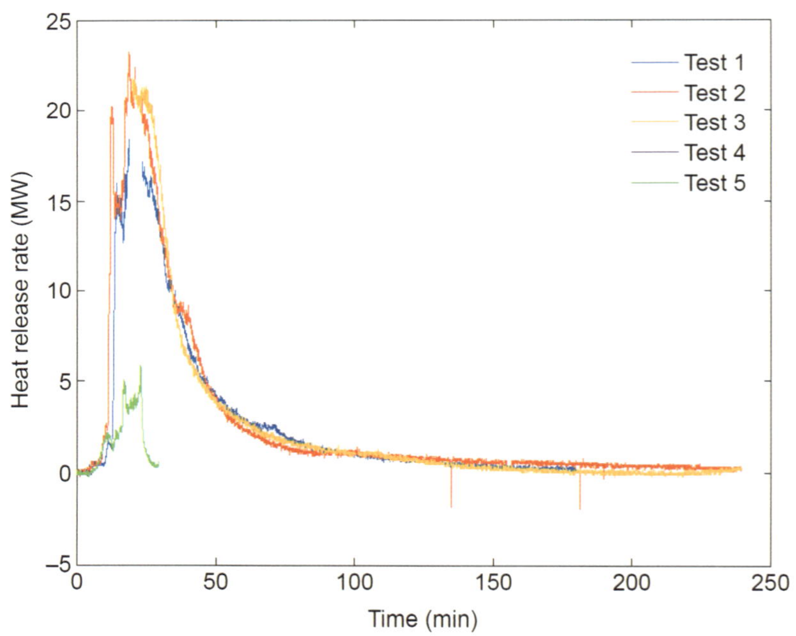

Heat release rate for each test.

ATF Test parameters and results

Zelinka, Hasburgh, Bourne, et al."Compartment fire testing of a two-story mass timber building" *US Forest Service Treesearch,* 2018

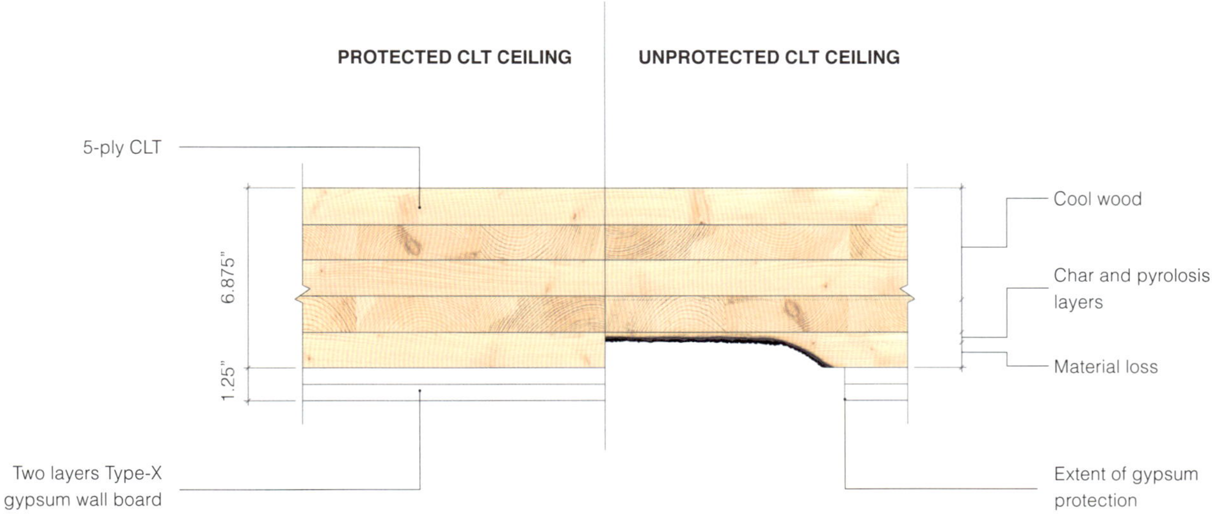

Charred section of ceiling panel from Test #2

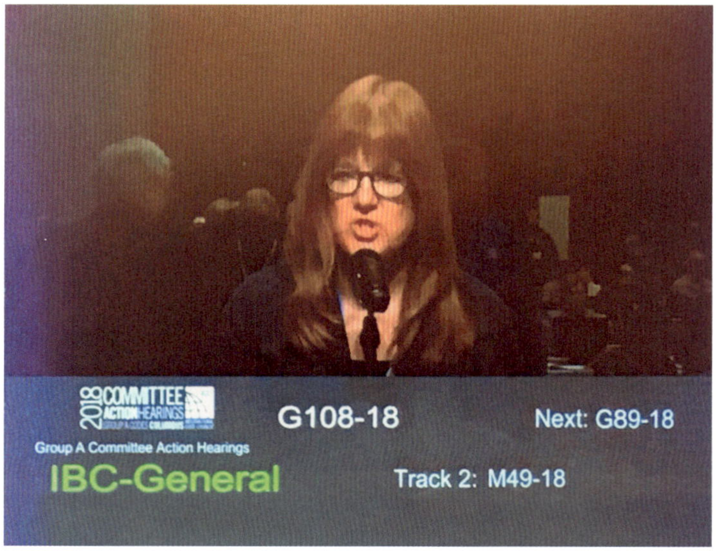

Ratification

The fire community professed to be shocked at the decisive performance of the mass timber under the intense fires. When the results of the tests were officially unveiled to the entire TWB committee, the tenor of the Committee's discussions grew noticeably lighter, and much more productive. Code passages that had earlier been held up by skeptical voices were now inserted into final code language with ease. The next few months were a flurry of action to finalize the written codes for submittal to the Committee Action Hearings by December of 2017.

When our proposals were completed, the last formal meeting of the TWB committee was held to conduct a final vote before submitting them to the next stage. It passed 15-3. Two negative votes were cast by individuals representing concrete and steel industry organizations. The other negative vote was cast by the Fire Chief, unwilling to break ranks with his professional community that still regarded wood as a danger.

Despite their official no-votes, these individuals had still helped by articulating their industry hurdles in the clearest of terms, allowing us to overcome them. The Fire Chief would go on to become a friend and ally. In some ways, his stubborn, emotional 'no' helped to build the trust of the fire community as he later opened doors for us to the New York City and Tokyo Fire Departments.

We submitted the model code language just in time for the ICC Committee Action Hearings. The hearings in Columbus were a tightly choreographed line of speakers, each given two-minute statements and a two-minute rebuttal. If a speaker exceeded their two minutes they were cut off mid-sentence, under the gaze of a huge digital clock. The process took place in a huge convention center, with hundreds of onlookers, before a large committee seated on a dais. Even the code veterans were nervous. I rehearsed my statement shown opposite, word by word, to keep it under the two minutes. I can still feel the cadence and rhythm of the words.

My name is Susan Jones, founding architect of atelierjones, a nationally recognized firm leading the transformation to mass timber in the US. A member of the 18-person ICC Tall Timber Committee, I represent the American Institute of Architects which advocates on behalf of over 90,000 architects in over 260 locations worldwide.

As professional architects we lead and collaborate with hundreds of thousands of building professionals including engineers, contractors, AHJs, and owners making millions of choices every day to design, specify materials to create our nation's built environments.

As professionals, we know that our sector is responsible for nearly half of our nation's nations' carbon emissions, including the construction and operations of buildings.

Climate change is the issue of our generation. When our children and grandchildren ask us later, what did you try to do, we want to answer with focus and action. As professionals, we have an ethical responsibility to lead.

We seek more choices.

Wood, when sustainably harvested, is renewable. A handful of seeds can create enough timber to design a lower-carbon building, as high as 15 to 20% lower greenhouse gas emissions.

Today, current codes restrict our choices to build with wood.

I have volunteered hundreds of hours for this ICC Committee effort. The Tall Wood AdHoc is a balanced Committee. We worked extremely hard and with the utmost professionalism to craft a balanced and conservative system of new regulatory codes for our nation.

Our work was based on testing real-life fire conditions, designed by fire professionals on our committee who live to protect our buildings and their inhabitants. These codes were developed directly out of these fire tests.

And these codes are conservative. They are an initial step forward for our design and industry professionals, and all who seek a lower-carbon alternative to design our built environments.

Thank you for your consideration.

Two-minute statement to the ICC Committee Action Hearings Code Committee, Columbus, Ohio. April 16, 2018

Over the next year, the ICC continued to hold forums for public comments on our proposals. The process culminated in a vote at the end of 2018 that included online voting by all the code and fire officials in the United States. This large, diverse body voted 68% in favor of the new codes, and tall wood was adopted into the IBC 2021.

The months-long deliberations were intense and difficult, as different communities sought to represent their values and interests. Those who supported mass timber fought hard to move ahead with productive language, while those that resisted tested us constantly, to find yet another hole in our arguments, our logic, that had to be carefully parsed out, yet again. Ultimately, however frustrating this tried-and-true negotiation tactic of wear-out-the-other side was, it also created a rigorous, hardened code language that would be a shield against future detractors. We worked intensely within the limits of the existing system to make changes to the ways we had been allowed to build in the 20th century.

What held us together, no matter how much we argued, was that we respected the code: its structure, its precision, its interrelationships, and its logic. Not to mention its paramount duty to safeguard the life of building inhabitants. We knew that it took all of us—fire experts, engineers, industry experts, architects, and materials experts—to write the 70 new code passages that we submitted to the ICC for approval. The leadership and commitment of key individuals, Sam Francis, the chair of the TWB individuals, such as Steve DiGiovanni, the ICC secretary, Mike Pfeiffer, as well as key leaders Carl Baldassarra and Jon Sui, had been essential.

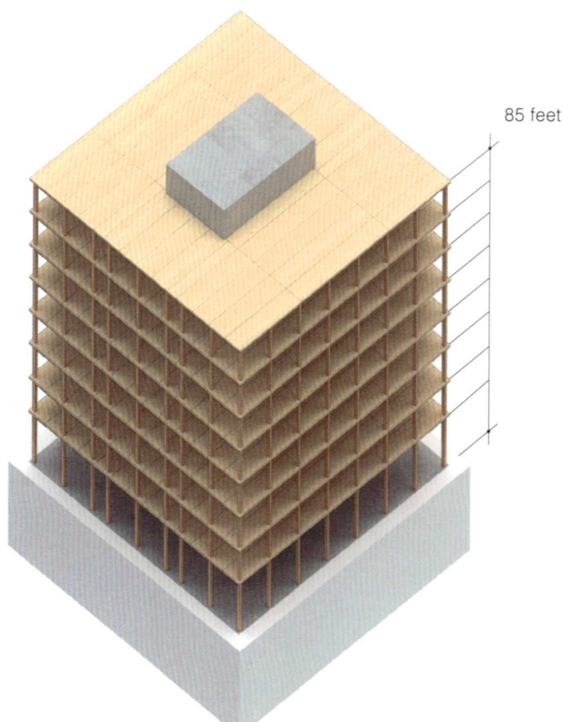

Type IV-C
Residential Allowable stories / height: 8 stories / 85 feet
R-2 Total Allowable Building Area
(varies with frontage): 230,625–307,500 gross square feet (GSF)

As an outsider to the formal process of developing building codes, the civility of that group, divergent as the industries represented were, was remarkable. It was also in sharp contrast to the larger political environment we were situated in. While we had been engaged in this process, starting in 2016, the United States was undergoing a harsh shift on the larger political level. As political divisions deepened, creating silos between communities, families, and individuals, the TWB Committee, with its collective allegiances to the rigor of the Code, became in my mind a model of how messy, divergent interests could still hold together in a democracy. Galvanized by this bleak political situation at large, in the late fall of 2016, I leaned into my earlier decision to focus on the ICC TWB work.

Collaboration had been necessary to reinforce institutions created for the collective good.

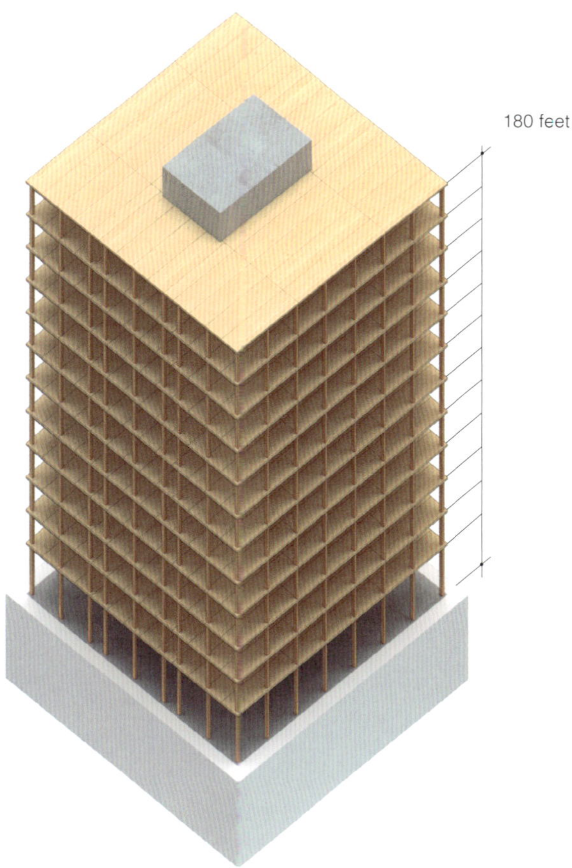

Type IV-B
Residential Allowable stories / height: 12 stories / 180 feet
R-2 Total Allowable Building Area
(varies with frontage): 369,000–492,000 gross square feet (GSF)

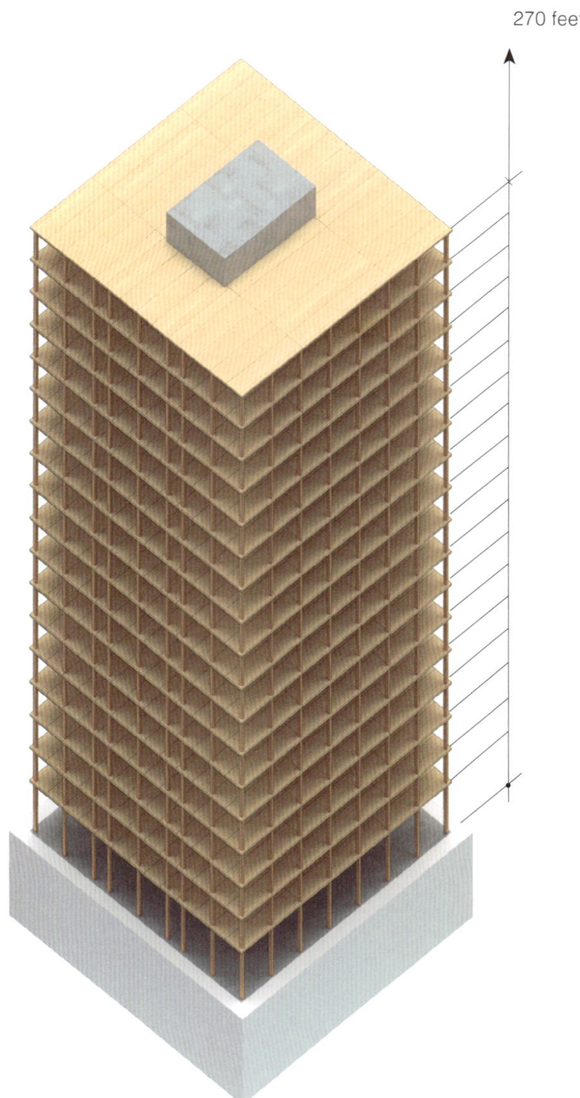

Type IV-A
Residential Allowable stories / height: 18 stories / 270 feet
R-2 Total Allowable Building Area (varies with frontage):
553,500–738,000 gross square feet (GSF)

The ICC Tall Timber Building Codes

The new codes set a resounding precedent for building at-scale with mass timber, and a pathway to reducing the carbon footprint of our built environment. The final, ratified changes to the codes were extensive: some 200 pages of new code language, including three new code building types—an action only taken every generation or so of code revisions.

In the 2021 IBC, tall timber is categorized in three new building type classifications: IV-C, IV-B, and IV-A. These types have different height, story, and area allowances, based in part on the intended use of the building, with IV-C up to 9 stories, IV-B up to 12, and IV-A up to 18 stories tall.

As the types increase in height, they are required to include progressively more fire protection elements. Type IV-C buildings can have the majority of their mass timber elements exposed on the interior, with only shafts, concealed spaces, and outside exterior walls requiring a noncombustible covering (usually a layer of gypsum wallboard). Type IV-B buildings can only have 40% of their mass timber structure exposed on the interior,[16] and Type IV-A buildings must have their structure completely enclosed and protected to a three-hour fire rating.

16: Further efforts would go on to lower this percentage. See part II, p. 194

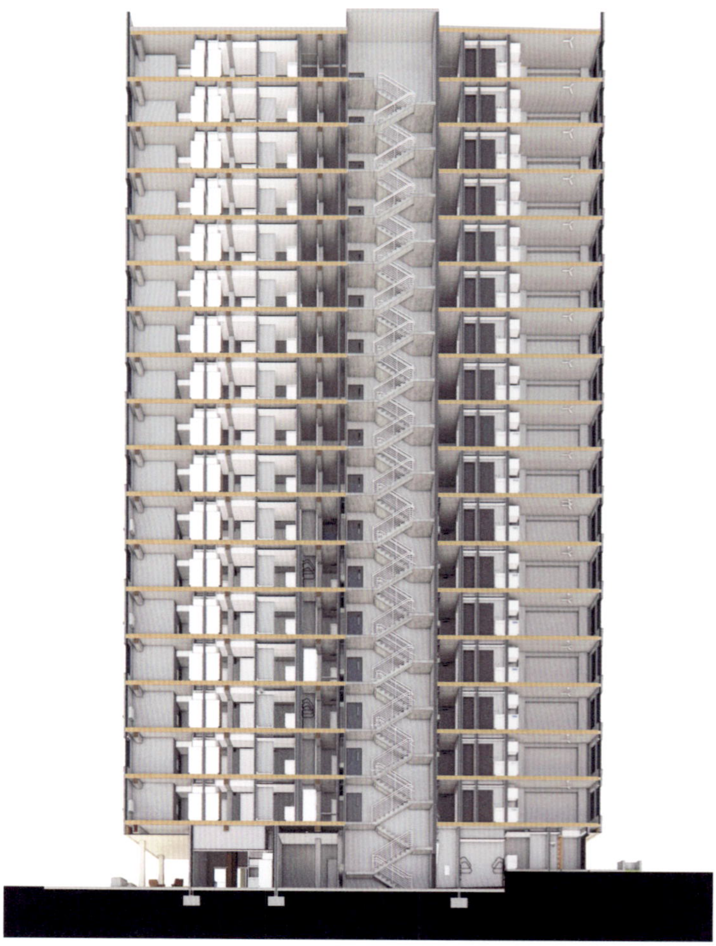

Type IV-A with full encapsulation

Check Your Work

With the ICC Tall Wood Building code changes finally ratified in January of 2019, mass timber had the green light to flourish in the United States. The US had finally agreed on a building code framework. As my European friends, ensconced in the complex bureaucracy of the European Union would say, "Susan, thanks to the fire tests, and the PRG320 glue standards, the US agrees on fire. The US agrees on glue." [17] While it sounds almost comical, it was now a fact that any authority having jurisdiction (AHJ) had a nationally agreed series of standards to use to grant a building permit. The regulatory barriers to mass timber were gone.

17: Daniel Brandon, RISE, conversation with author, Bordeaux, France, October 18, 2023

But what about that carbon? My investment of time and effort into the codes process was driven by my motivation to lower carbon emissions from the built environment. And while the early studies suggested that would be the case, a true, deep understanding of carbon accounting was still lacking.

We were still learning about carbon: *embodied* vs. *upfront* carbon and *sequestered* vs. *stored* carbon. How could we be sure about the carbon performance when we were still clarifying terms? Tall mass timber buildings would still be complex, hybrid structures—with concrete foundations, woven together with tight knots of carbon-intensive steel reinforcing bars, needing tall lateral structural systems, typically out of steel or concrete. There were code-mandated layers of acoustic protection on the floors and walls, and fire protections around the exterior. The emissions of each system would vary with their regional context.

My middle and high school math teachers had always taught me to check my work. As one of the strongest proponents of Tall Wood Buildings, I knew it was my responsibility to try to fully understand the carbon proposition. How could I begin to bring clarity and transparency to that question? The path forward was not obvious.

Our earlier studies had scratched the surface of the complexity of the work, but it was clear that, once again, had with our forests, the building codes, and the fire tests, we needed to reach out to collaborate with others.

The University of Washington studios had given us a good start on understanding the lifecycle performance of mass timber buildings. In the 2013 studio we compared mass timber assemblies to conventional alternatives, and in 2016 we had extrapolated this work to the scale of a larger building. The results were promising—showing significant carbon emission benefits for large mass timber structures—and provided some of the only data available at the time. However, these were still just rough student studies using early software tools, a far cry from true, peer-reviewed and publishable research. It was clear that more needed to be done, at a larger scale.

Sitting at my desk one day at my busy office, in early 2017, I received a call from a trusted colleague from the University of Washington. She said she had access to a considerable gift of money from a donor that wanted to put it toward mass timber. She asked me what I thought would help move mass timber the furthest the fastest. I remember holding my head in my hands, bending over the phone. With all of the pressures of finding work for my small firm while balancing pro-bono ICC Code meetings and practically pro-bono UW studios, I was desperate to tell her: "Hire atelierjones to design a tall mass timber building with these building codes I am helping to write!" But instead, I heard the words softly emerge from my mouth: "Elaine, it's about the carbon. We've got to prove out the carbon to everyone, including ourselves."

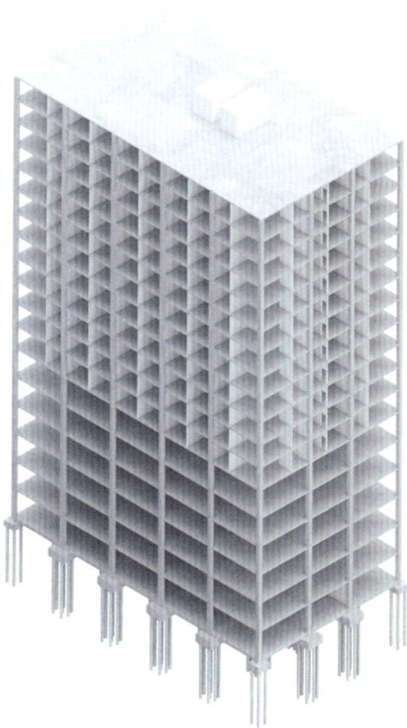

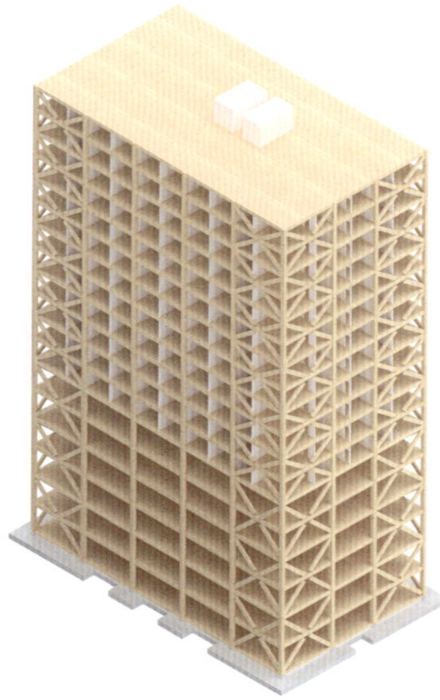

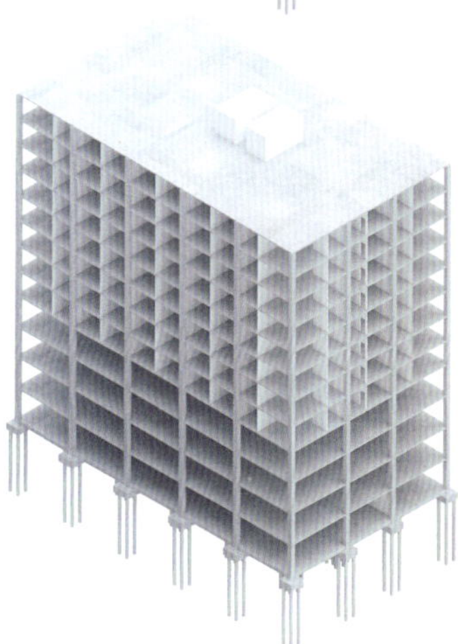

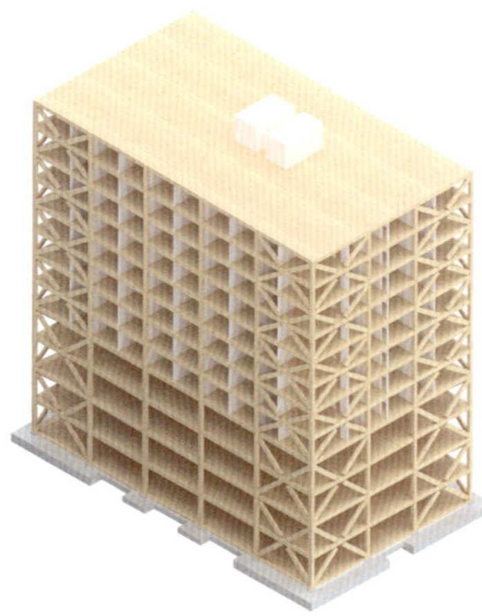

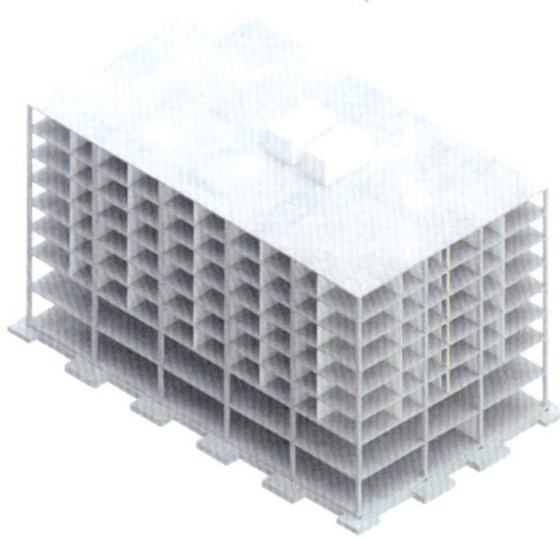

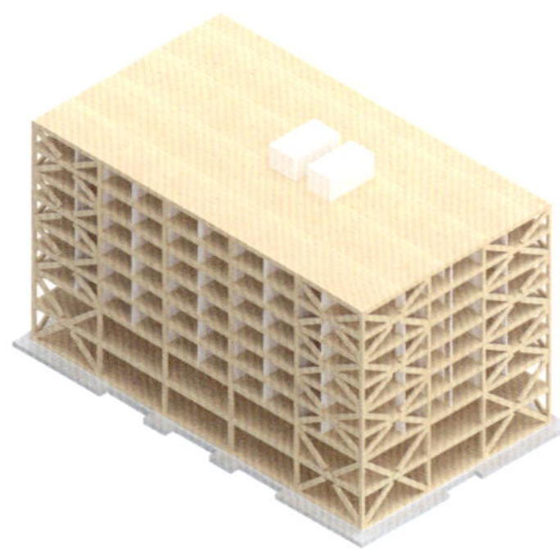

The Nature Conservancy Life-Cycle Assessment

The following year, The Nature Conservancy, funded by The Doris Duke Foundation and the US Forest Service (USFS), asked atelierjones to help them understand the carbon benefits of large mass timber buildings. Led by Mark Wishnie, then Director of Global Forestry and Wood Products with The Nature Conservancy, we would develop building designs that would become the basis for lifecycle assessments in regions across the United States. LCA scientists from The Consortium for Research on Renewable Industrial Materials (CORRIM), the University of Washington School of Environmental and Forest Sciences, and the USFS Forest Products Laboratory would lead LCA analyses based on these designs. We would design 18 Building Information Models: nine with mass timber and nine as concrete equivalents. Each would represent one of the new 8-, 12-, and 18-story ICC code building types we were still in the process of ratifying, within three different United States geographic regions: the Pacific Northwest, the Northeast, and the Southeast.

Foundations were included, and the entire superstructure would be analyzed by the LCA team. Fire-protection considerations, such as required gypsum wallboard protection, were also included. In a later phase, the work would be expanded to include regionally-based studies in China, Chile, and Austria.

The results of these LCAs were released as three papers in a special Mass Timber issue of the peer-reviewed journal *Sustainability* in December 2021. The study found that, across all regions and building heights, the mass timber projects had reductions of 22% to 48% in embodied carbon compared to their concrete counterparts.[18]

18: Puettemann, Pierobon, Ganguly, et al., 2021. "Comparative LCAs of Conventional and Mass Timber Buildings in Regions with Potential for Mass Timber Penetration." Published in *Sustainability*.

The LCAs showed regional variations due to the differences in timber stock, distances from production to building sites, energy grids, soil variations, and, in the case of the Pacific Northwest, necessary seismic considerations. In all locations, the 8- and 12-story mass timber buildings outperformed their 18-story counterparts, due to their reduced cores, foundations, and fire-protection requirements.

This was significant. With this study, we now had a solid body of modeled data that gave greater weight to the argument that substitution mattered. That our building materials mattered. That how we sourced materials mattered.

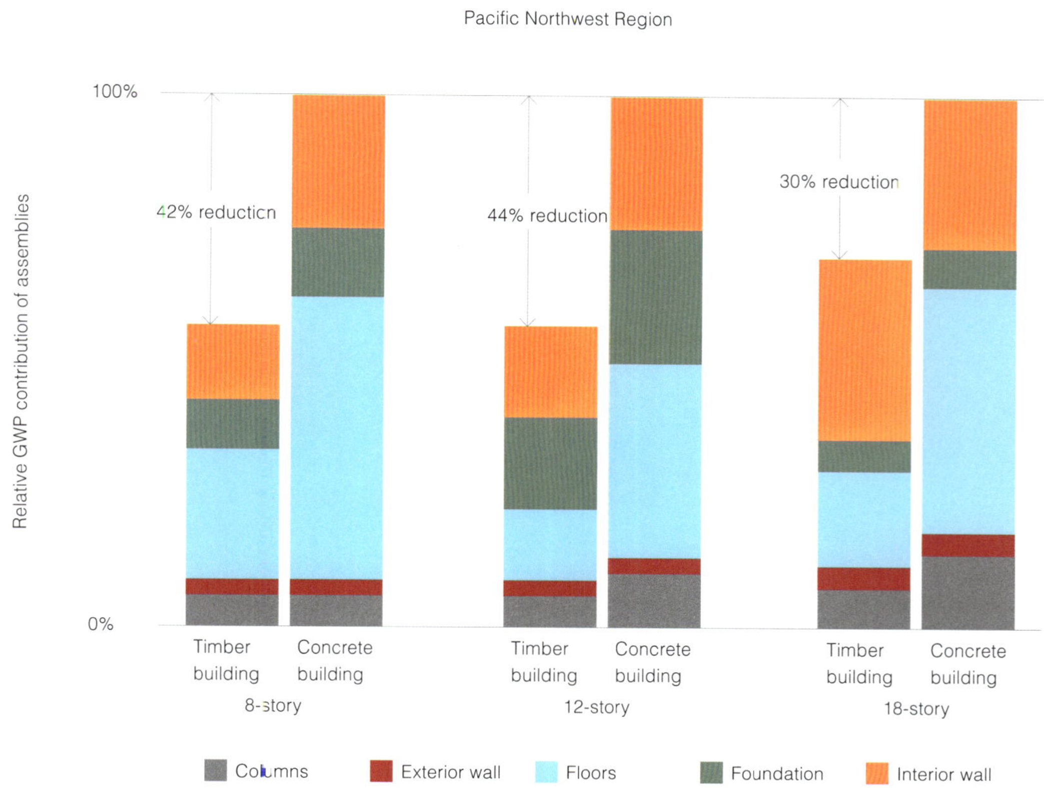

Comparative Global Warming Potential results for the Pacific Northwest region. Each of the mass timber building types outperformed their concrete counterparts by a significant margin.

These results also validated the premise for our onerous work in changing the building codes. I felt even more confident that the new tall timber codes had the potential to disrupt conventional 20th-century *building as usual*. We had the tools now to create a new type of building at scale, one built from healthier and renewable forests, stored carbon. It would represent a small but tangible measure against the devastating effects of climate change.

Now, with testing, legislation, and carbon accounting, the foundation for tall timber was in place. But the only way to truly understand the opportunities and constraints of the codes we had spent three and a half years working, was to build the first Type IV prototype. The opportunity was there. Someone would need to take it and move forward.

2019–2022
Seattle, Washington

atelierjones:
Susan Jones, Ian Maples, Olga Amigud, Lenore Wan, Bron Heinz, Alex Zink, Eleanor Lewis, Meghan Doring

Owner:
Community Roots Housing

Developer:
Skipstone

Structural Engineering:
DCI Engineers

Contractor:
Swinerton

Mass Timber Suppliers:
DR Johnson, Kalesnikoff, Freres

Mass Timber Fabrication & Install:
Timberlab

Photography:
Lara Swimmer, Timberlab

Heartwood

Building Tall Timber

In January 2019, as the reality of the passage the Tall Timber Codes had begun to sink in, our Heartwood building did not exist, even as a vision. As I sat down to complete atelierjones' application for a USFS 2019 Wood Innovation Grant, the idea of building a strategic tall timber prototype with the new codes began to take shape.

Build the building I had helped design the code for.

In mid-August 2019, I called my friend, A-P Hurd. A highly successful developer during Seattle's tech-driven, post-recession buildup in the 2010s, she had recently stepped aside to start her own company, SkipStone Consulting. I could hear the gravel crunch under her feet as she said hello. I asked where she was. "Up in Quebec, visiting my home with my family." Canadian-American, she wore her name, Anne-Pierre proudly, and made sure her daughter was fluent in French. She told me she almost didn't answer the call because she was out, picking blackberries with her daughter under the warm sun.

"I have a grant for a mass timber project" I said, "Do you know of anyone who could use it?" Typically quick, she cut to straight to the point: "Yes, I do. Would housing work?" *Yes.* "Eight stories?" Yes. "10,000 SF lot?" *Yes.* "Ok, I am on vacation and won't be back to my emails for a week. But I will reach out to Chris, the CEO of Community Roots Housing. I will call you in a week. I have to get back to my walk. I'll let you know."

Two weeks later we were standing in a parking lot in the Capitol Hill neighborhood of Seattle, planning the eight-story middle-

income apartment building that would become Heartwood. Two months later we had a concept design and a cost estimate. I had hand-picked our experienced, vertically integrated grant and design team.

The estimated costs for the mass timber structure were comparable to a conventionally built building and the visionary owner, Community Roots Housing, gave us the approval to move forward with a mass timber building. The opportunity to test a tall timber building and the Type IV-C codes was in our hands, with a highly capable and collaborative team.

Designing a building with a dedicated team and a motivated client is one of the joys of my professional life. It is thrilling to bring a vision to life at every scale. But the opportunity to build a prototype of the codes I had just written, that had the potential to reshape building culture, gave me an entirely different level of drive and focus. My motivation and energy spilled over to the entire team, and we were keenly focused on the outcome.

March 13, 2020—the day the US declared a National Emergency for the Coronavirus Pandemic—barely touched our team's focus. We moved to our homes, onto our VPNs, and launched into ten hours of Zoom calls a day. By mid-April, I started to schedule walks and a lunch for myself on my calendar, so I wouldn't schedule a meeting with some cohort of the team for each and every hour of the days between March 13 and June 13, 2020, the day we submitted for the building permit.

As a team we were designinga wooden building at a scale that was entirely new to the United States. We were all learning and had to develop new sets of details that would satisfy the Type IV-C codes and its required 2-hour fire-rated connections. While mass timber would be the primary vertical gravity structure, tall wood lateral resistance systems are not approved for high seismic areas yet,[19] and the building would still have to be a hybrid—using each material where it could have the most impact. An efficient steel Buckling Restrained Braced Frame (BRBF) was used to resist horizontal forces. For the foundation, concrete was unavoidable, although mass timber's relatively light weight meant that the foundation volume could be reduced by approximately 30% compared to a comparable all-concrete structure, further decarbonizing the superstructure.

19: Emily Williamson et al., 2023. Design and Cyclic Experiments of a Mass Timber Frame with a Timber Buckling Restrained Brace." Published in *Journal of Structural Engineering.*

Since this was the first of its kind, we would need to figure out for ourselves how the required complexity of mechanical, electrical and plumbing (MEP) systems would come together in a new, Type IV-C building.

From the beginning of the codes process, exposing the maximum amount of mass timber had been the goal. In a Type IV-C building (85 feet and below) the entire mass timber superstructure could be exposed, from the glulam columns and beams to the cross-laminated timber ceilings. Nevertheless, multi-family units each require services, from ventilation of bathrooms, stoves and air movement, to heating and cooling, plumbing and electrical runs.

A standard design strategy is to make the entire ceiling a large, dropped gypsum wall board or acoustic ceiling soffit, and run required services inside. However, not only did we want to expose the maximum amount of the wood ceilings, but the Type IV-C codes require an additional layer of fire-protection in concealed spaces, adding cost. Unlike with standard multi-family projects, we started our design of the ceiling soffits, floor assemblies, and beam depths extremely early in the project, knowing it was critical to resolve both code and acoustic issues as early as possible. Not only did we need to know the costs early on, and avoid surprise impacts, it was critical that we exposed as much wood as possible on the unit interiors.

The All-Wood Joint

It seemed so straightforward during the fire tests. Two large pieces of laminated wood come together to create a joint between a column and a beam. Then, together, they hold up a laminated wood panel ceiling. Three different pieces, so three different tiny gaps between them. Horizontal, vertical, horizontal again.

This is the most ancient of structures. The Parthenon exhibits this post-and-beam logic in its columns, architrave, and triglyphs, albeit with the original wood replaced by a marble facsimile. It is Marc-Antoine Laugier's *Primitive Hut*, with a light, vernacular version using tree limbs as columns, beams, and roof pediment.

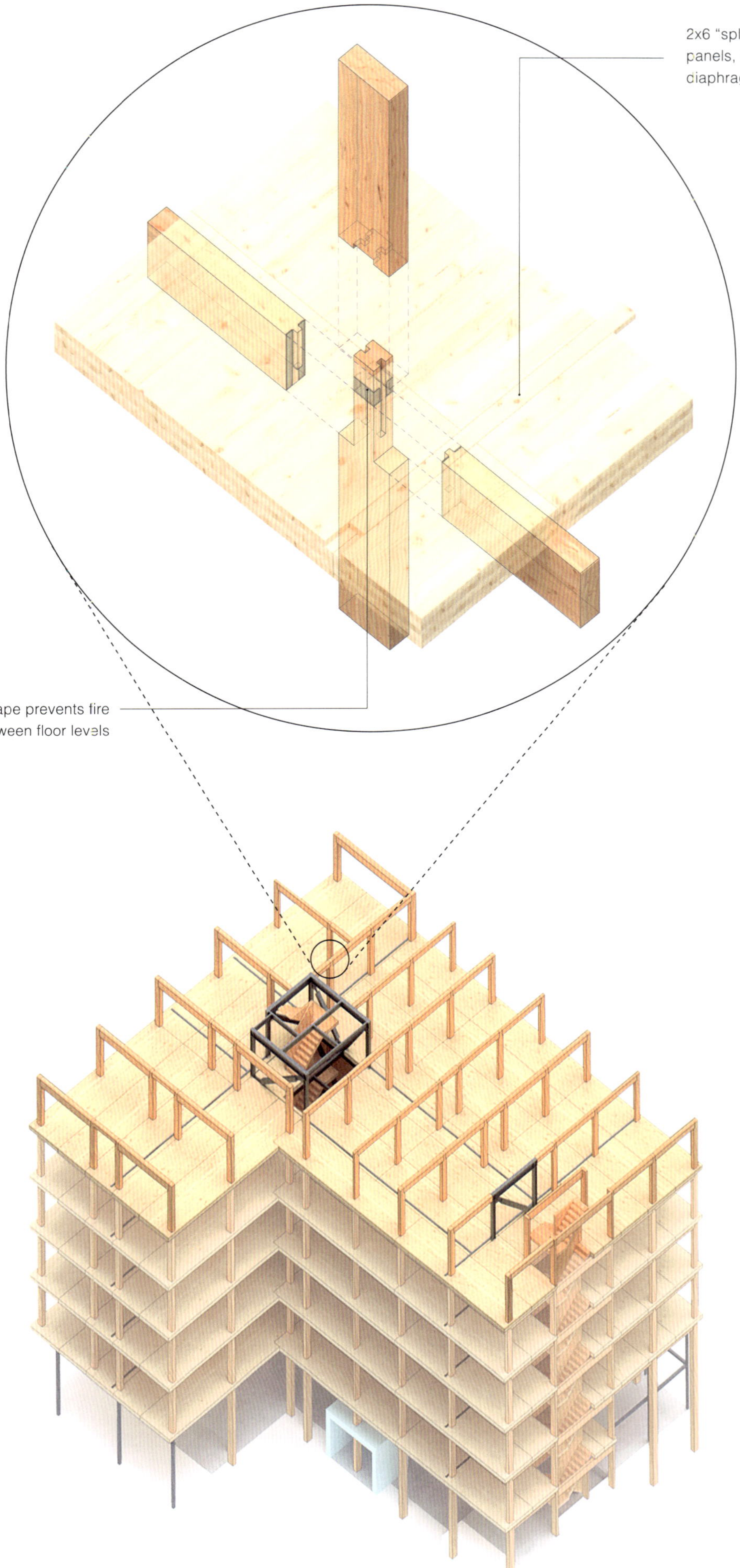
2x6 "splines" connect mass timber panels, adding rigidity to the floor diaphragm
Intumescent tape prevents fire spread between floor levels

Later, settlers of the Pacific Northwest found massive Douglas firs and cedars—unlikely to again be grown on this earth—that they ravenously harvested to make huge, squared off columns and beams for construction up and down the west coast. Sometimes we call the simple wooden post-and-beam structural system *back to the future*. It is a humbling thought.

Ancient as this system is, our buildings today have more acute requirements. We would have to meet the standards of the 21st-century codes, mandating structural, fire, energy, and acoustic performance. Together, all these systems had to work. In wood.

Though prefabrication would enable us to design to tight tolerances in wood, we still would never be able to create perfect, airless joints between mass timber column, beam, and floor. This meant that although each unit was sprinklered and separated with layers of insulation, the tiny gaps between each member remained a concern for the transfer of air, noise, and flames.

While our TWB committee had established a largely prescriptive building code for tall timber, there were still aspects that had to be left up to interpretation. The design of 2-hour fire-rated joints and assemblies was one. Even after spending hours and hours wordsmithing with some of the finest code minds in the United States, we chose not to dictate a specific prescriptive answer for every foreseeable condition. Instead, we determined performance standards for each joint and assembly, that each collaborative design and engineering team would have to meet for the specific conditions of their project.

As such, leading the Heartwood design team meant an intense series of design iterations, meetings, and revisions during two months in the spring of 2020, and then further during the corrections process later that year. Our rich, multi-talented team, including atelierjones, Timberlab, DCI, Wiss, Janny, Elstner, Greenbusch, and Swinerton, with the close collaboration of the Seattle Department of Construction and Inspection, constantly tested ideas back and forth. It was only through this collaboration of architects, fabricators, structural, fire protection, and acoustic engineers, contractors, and city building officials that a solution was possible, working together to unearth the practical implications of this new code.

Ultimately, we arrived at an elegant solution. The primary joint for the structure, between column, floor, and beam, would be all wood. A simple, massive, mortise and tenon joint. The team's solution to the remaining small air gaps between members was to use an intumescent tape routed into pockets within the wood joint, which, if exposed to fire, would expand and harden to seal the gap. This novel solution meant the structural connection could meet the 2-hour fire rating that the tall wood codes required. In mass timber buildings before Heartwood, joints were usually designed with heavy steel plates and connectors. In Heartwood, only two steel screws were needed to secure each joint. The rest was all wood.

This joint is used extensively in Heartwood, some 875 times. The team estimated that this reduction in steel saved some $5/ft on the project budget[20] and lowered the building's carbon footprint. We saved valuable time and labor by routing the connections at Timberlab's Portland, Oregon fabrication facility, and adding the fire tape inside the joints before the prefabricated wooden elements were delivered to the construction site.

20: Timberlab presentation, January 19, 2023, Portland, Oregon

The large columns, beams, and floor plates were delivered to the site sequentially, floor by floor, to Heartwood's tight urban lot. Heartwood shares a site with the Helen V, a deeply-affordable three-story apartment building also owned by Community Roots Housing. In order for the Helen V to remain open for residents, site disturbance during Heartwood's construction had to be kept to an absolute minimum. The site had no laydown area and a time-restricted unloading lane large enough for only one truck at a time.

Mass plywood panel stairs in Frerez factory (above) and assembled in the core with steel BRBF lateral system

The talented Timberlab installation team choreographed the process as, one by one, columns were erected, beams placed gently on columns, and huge floor plates slipped over the top of the columns. The installation process was quick and elegant, with the mass timber installed at the rate of one floor every ten days, including the erection of the steel BRBF core and the prefabricated Mass Plywood Panel (MPP) exit stairs, taking only four months as planned. With prefabrication and just-in-time delivery, mass timber allowed the team to construct a project that would have been almost impossible with conventional methods, and the construction site stayed relatively quiet and clean.

With the Tall Wood Building Committee, we had written new codes and new policies, in order to bring lower-carbon mass timber to scale. Our team then proved them out by designing, permitting and building Heartwood during a global pandemic. We demonstrated that a tall mass timber building could be realized under typical multi-family budgets—indeed, the per/unit construction cost of some $225,000 per unit is competitive in the Washington State multi-family affordable housing market.

That budget also explains the deep simplicity of the building, the straightforward massing, the cost-effective materiality of the facade, and the simple repetitive windows, each placed within the units to maximize the impact of natural light into their spaces and highlight the interior wood superstructure. We had used mass timber as efficiently as possible, as both superstructure and finish material for maximum impact, exposing it in the areas where it could be most fully experienced by the residents of the workforce apartment building.

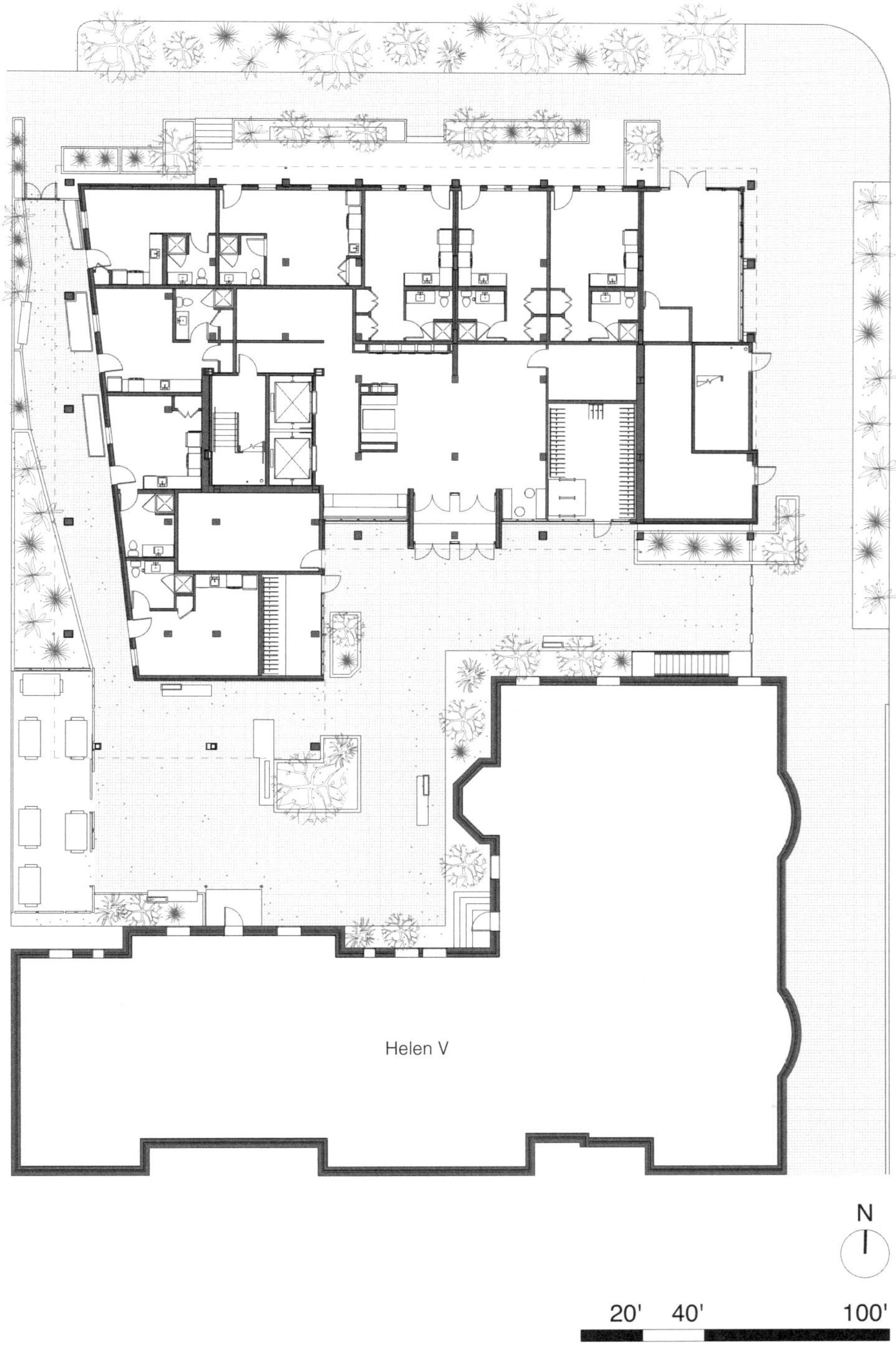

Heartwood ground floor plan

Unit Exploded Axon

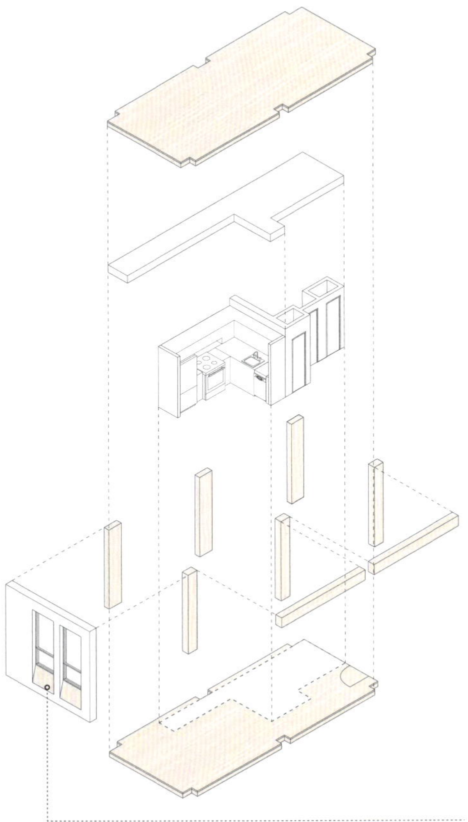

Typical Studio

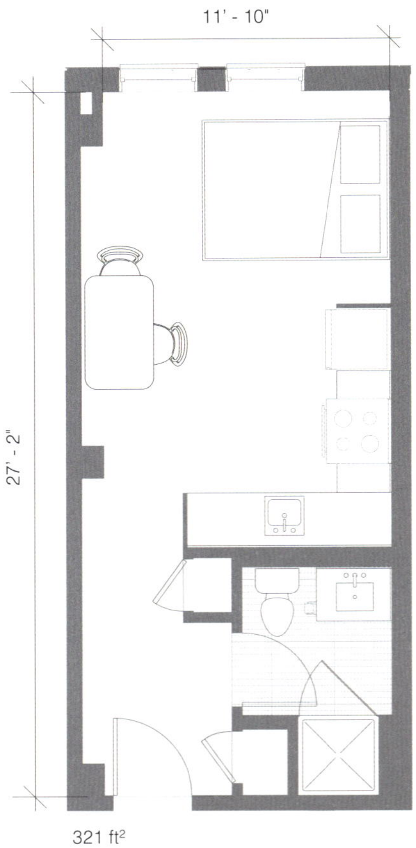

1323
HEARTW

Wood in the City

Today, in the completed Heartwood, the large, ruddy columns and beams support the lighter, whiter CLT floor/ceiling panels, their slightly different grains and tones acting as reminders of the regional origins and species of the timber. The wooden superstructure is a natural part of every living space, its warm solidity inviting a touch of the fingers, a lean back up against it with shoulders. Its solid proportions reminding everyone—including the bank appraisers and the excited Seattle Fire Department when they toured the construction—of just how durable the building is.

Living in the CLTHouse, surrounded by wood, has been a deep source of calm and peace for me. While a house cannot control the rhythms and emotional bonds between a family, I know as the mother of our energetic and often hyperactive household, that our wooden house has been a softly soothing influence. As I began the design of Heartwood in August of 2019, I knew the last four years of living in the CLTHouse had been a tremendous source of delight, beauty, and, yes, privilege.

Designing this experience for a missing-middle workforce housing community was a huge honor. The idea that living with this natural material could be shared with so many others, of all backgrounds was deeply moving and motivating. After months of intense technical collaboration during the pandemic, isolated as we were from one another, the impact was tremendous when we had finally progressed far enough to create renderings of the interiors. Seeing those space come to life, with broad spruce/pine/fir (SPF) ceilings from forests in southern British Columbia, and darker Douglas fir columns and beams sourced from forests in southern Oregon was thrilling. We were bringing nature into the city.

By late 2023, the small, simple units were realized, and in 2024, became homes for some 150 people. In each, two wooden beams and three wooden columns - large enough to barely wrap your arms around them, thanks to their safe char depth - support a broad wood ceiling. Two vertically proportioned windows look out to the city, casting light gently across the wooden ceilings.

At night from the exterior, windows glow within the quiet dark facade. They send the warmth of wood, of being surrounded by nature, to all who look up at the building, and especially to those who walk in from the busy, noisy city, up the wooden stairs and open the door into the warm, natural space they call home.

Check Your Work, Again

Heartwood Lifecycle Assessment

In November 2021, with client approval, permit in hand, and loans secured, Heartwood was quickly becoming a very real building. With construction on the horizon, we had an excellent opportunity to perform a lifecycle assessment based on a real-life building.

As excellent as The Nature Conservancy LCAs were, they still only analyzed generic designs, not real-life conditions. As I had learned from my colleagues on the ICC Code Committee, research based on modeling, as good as it is, is not as good as real-life test cases.

And we had a real-life building. With the help of another USFS grant, we were able to work again with Indroneil Ganguly and his team at the University of Washington School of the Environment and Forest Sciences (SEFS) for a comparative LCA of Heartwood's superstructure and a concrete equivalent. Along with our structural engineers at DCI, we already had a highly detailed, mass timber 3D Building Information Model. The next task was to model a functionally-equivalent concrete version of the same size, same unit layout, same eight-story height, and in the same seismic zone as Heartwood, producing material takeoffs for the UW team.

Our teams compared details, assemblies, and shear wall locations, with the fireproofing, acoustic and structural elements required for each system. We made sure to add the appropriate additional concrete foundation volume for the heavier concrete building. We worked through the definition of a "functionally-equivalent" building again and again. What was distinct, and what was the same for both buildings? We analyzed the recycled steel content of Heartwood's BRBF core and checked with the construction team to see what deviations in materials and assembly installation were necessary from the original design.

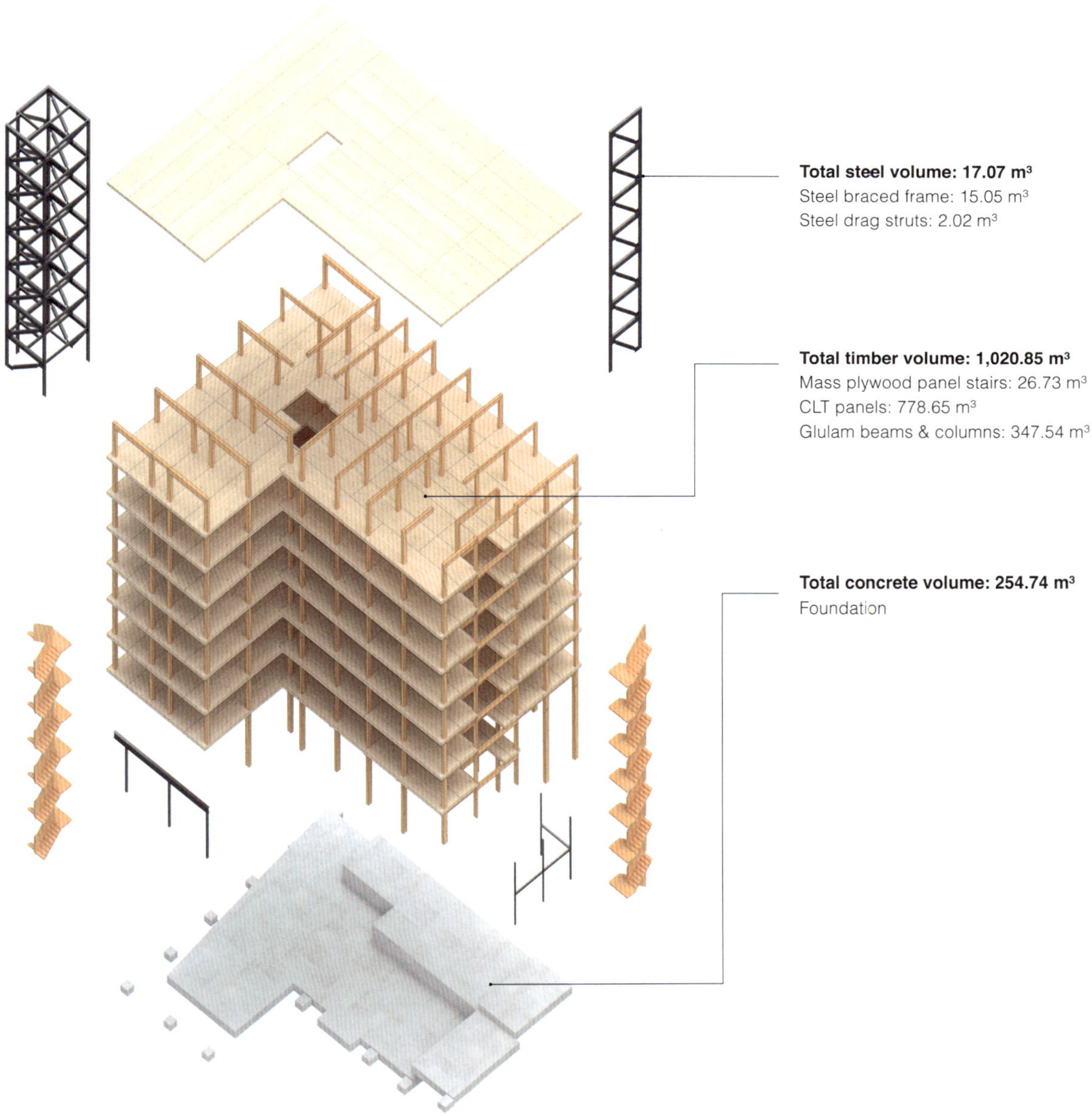
Total steel volume: 17.07 m³
Steel braced frame: 15.05 m³
Steel drag struts: 2.02 m³
Total timber volume: 1,020.85 m³
Mass plywood panel stairs: 26.73 m³
CLT panels: 778.65 m³
Glulam beams & columns: 347.54 m³
Total concrete volume: 254.74 m³
Foundation

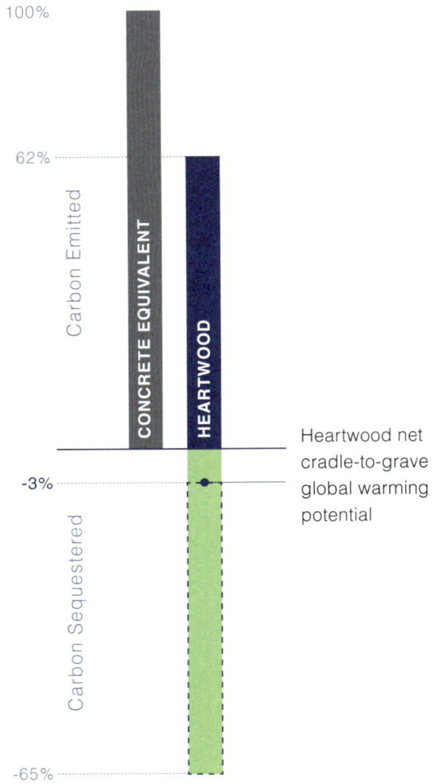

21: "The Heartwood Project: North America's First Type IV-C Mass Timber Building," publication forthcoming in 2026

This stretched across months of calls with seven careful, detail-oriented architects, scientists, structural engineers and contractors. The process was vigorous, interactive, often confusing, and always relentless. And, with the Seattle Teamsters' concrete strike dragging out the Heartwood construction schedule, it was usually the most fun call of the month.

Eventually, just as the strike ended, and the concrete foundation could finally get moving, we received the results. The final number was 38%. That is, the material production, transportation, and construction required to build the superstructure of the mass timber building expended 38% less CO_2 than the concrete equivalent. This was highly gratifying and validating to the earlier Nature Conservancy studies that had arrived at a 40% number.

But the most thrilling moment was seeing the results after factoring in the carbon stored in the wood. The 38% number represented the upfront carbon, the amount of carbon it took to produce the building in the first place. But as trees grow in the forest, they absorb carbon from the atmosphere, which remains in the wood even when it is harvested. The trees can then be replanted and go on to absorb more CO_2 in a positive cycle. When this stored carbon, the carbon footprint of Heartwood's superstructure became net negative—a 108% reduction compared to the carbon used in the concrete building.[21]

End-of-Life

When I present our work along with these LCA conclusions, there often emerges a thoughtful question: "What happens to all that stored carbon when the building is taken down?"

The Nature Conservancy and Heartwood LCA studies had only focused on the A1-A5 scope, which includes the comparative emissions of material production, transportation and construction. The results of the LCA were only valid as long as the building was standing. We know that, if properly detailed and maintained, concrete buildings can last many years—maybe centuries — and we believe that mass timber can have the same kind of lifespan. But, whether in 50 years or 500, all buildings' lives will come to an end. What happens to the carbon then?

We've all seen demolition sites. The implosion of Seattle's Kingdome was a stupendous event. As the concrete behemoth, only 21 years old, was demolished on a Sunday afternoon in the summer of 2000, the entire city was on hand to watch. Clouds of concrete dust went up into the air for hours, blanketing downtown.

We didn't yet know what would happen to a tall mass timber building at the end of its life. While we knew it wasn't a pretty end for concrete, we could only speculate about that of mass timber. This is rich work for research, and in 2023, few, if any, studies of a mass timber building had been conducted to this extent.

Fortunately, a PhD student at the University of Washington decided to take this question on. Christina Bjarvin, who had been working with the UW team on the Heartwood LCA, decided to extend the study to focus on Heartwood's end of life conditions.

We finally had the chance to think through how long Heartwood's life would be.

It was clear that Heartwood was not just another light wood-frame building with a 50- to 75-year lifespan. The fire, appraisal and real estate communities in Seattle had seen Heartwood in person and sensed its solidity. The mass timber elements themselves were not likely to deflect with gravity over time like their light wood-frame counterparts. Nor were they likely to burn.

Moreover, we had future-proofed the building. Heartwood was designed so that any failure points of the interior wet walls for kitchens and baths would occur against non-load-bearing, light-gauge metal walls. And the demising walls were also non-load-bearing. As such, they could be removed or adjusted if the unit layout or equipment of the building became outdated. We had set the columns 18 inches back from the facade, so that any exterior moisture intrusion over time would only damage the exterior cladding, and the building could relatively easily be re-clad in the future.

For me, seeing the wonderful condition of 140-year-old heavy timber buildings on the Seattle waterfront told me that Heartwood could easily last 200 years, but, to be conservative, we compromised at a 100-year lifespan, recognizing that even if the structure did not lose its soundness, demands for land use could change.

But what would happen to the mass timber elements upon Heartwood's eventual demolition?

Typically, demolished wood elements are chipped, ground into OSB or particle board, or sent to landfill. But, from my daily experience living surrounded by CLT panels, I couldn't imagine that these immense, 40-foot-long, 8-foot-wide panels of solid wood would be simply ground up into woodchips.

Instead, we assumed that they could be dismantled. Their all-wood joints would come apart as simply as they were attached, and they could be reused in a second building,[22] allowing for 10% material loss during this transition. Then, after another 100-year lifespan for the second building, the remaining elements—minus another 10% for waste—would be recycled into particle board and OSB. These recycled products would have their own 40-year lifespans, and then be recycled again into new particle board for another 40 years. Finally, 280 years from the completion of Heartwood, the original wood fiber would end up in landfill.

22: A design problem of recycling that we would go on to explore in our 2025 "CLT Cannibalism" studio at the University of Washington

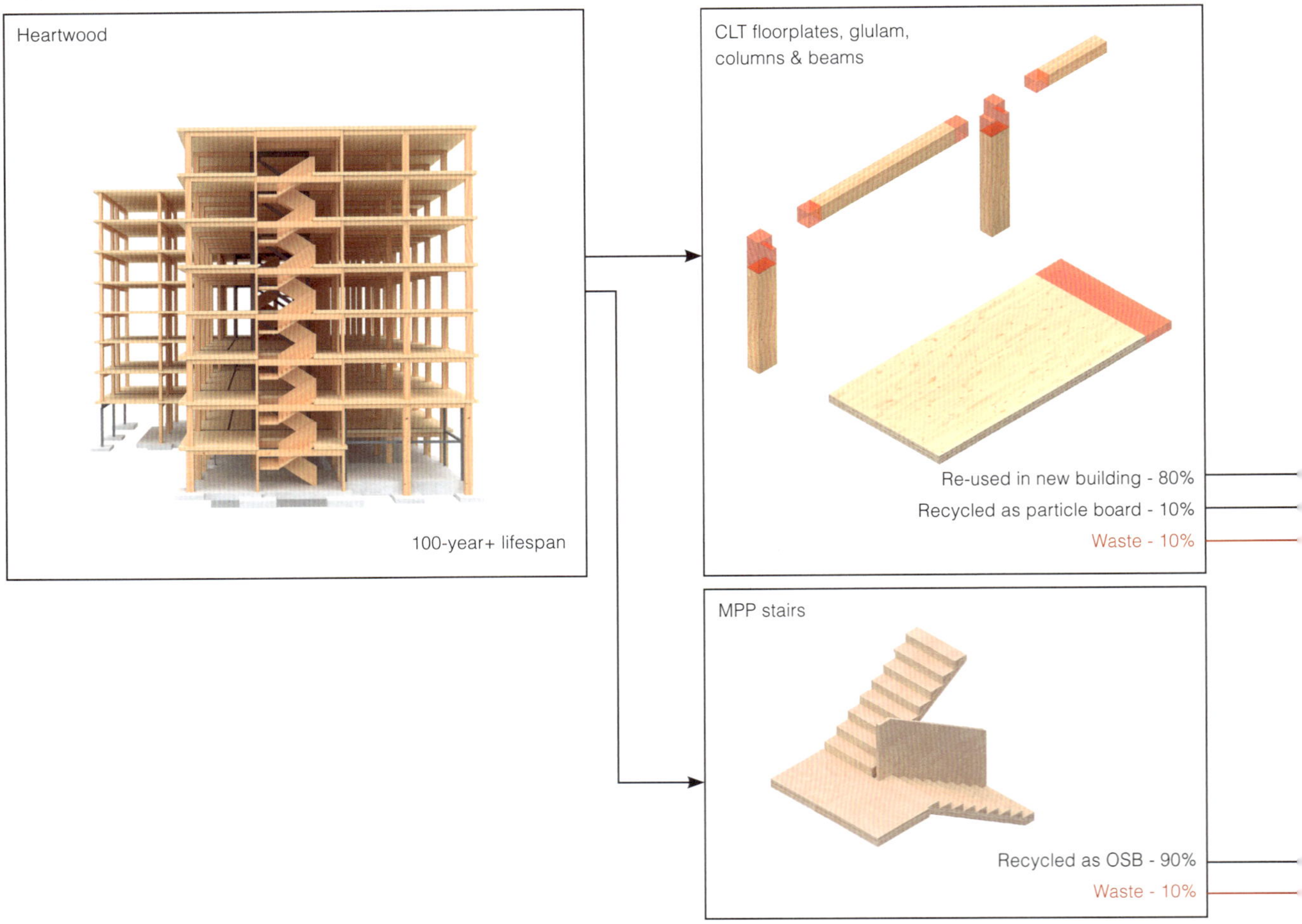

Heartwood End-of-Life scenarios

Oftentimes, this transition to landfill is imagined as a complete loss for carbon storage—a 100% offgassing of stored carbon as the wood decays over decades. However, a 2020 EPA study showed that this is hardly the case. Indeed, because landfills are capped with earth, approximately 88% of the decaying carbon is absorbed by the soil rather than released to the atmosphere.[23] So, even after the wood served several long, productive lives, the vast majority of its precious carbon would remain stored indefinitely.

23: EPA Waste Reduction Model (WARM), 2020

Altogether, this study adjusted our final result to be a 103% reduction in Global Warming Potential for Heartwood's superstructure against a concrete one. The concrete building represented 1,713,681 kg of CO_2 equivalent GWP added to the atmosphere, while, after factoring in the carbon stored in the wood, Heartwood represented negative 59,549 kg.

While this showed that a small percentage of the carbon performance would be reversed at the end of the building's life, it was a much better result than many of us had expected. And it meant that I could now confidently answer the skeptics asking if all the stored carbon benefits of mass timber were lost at the end of a building's life. We had indeed built a net-negative building superstructure.

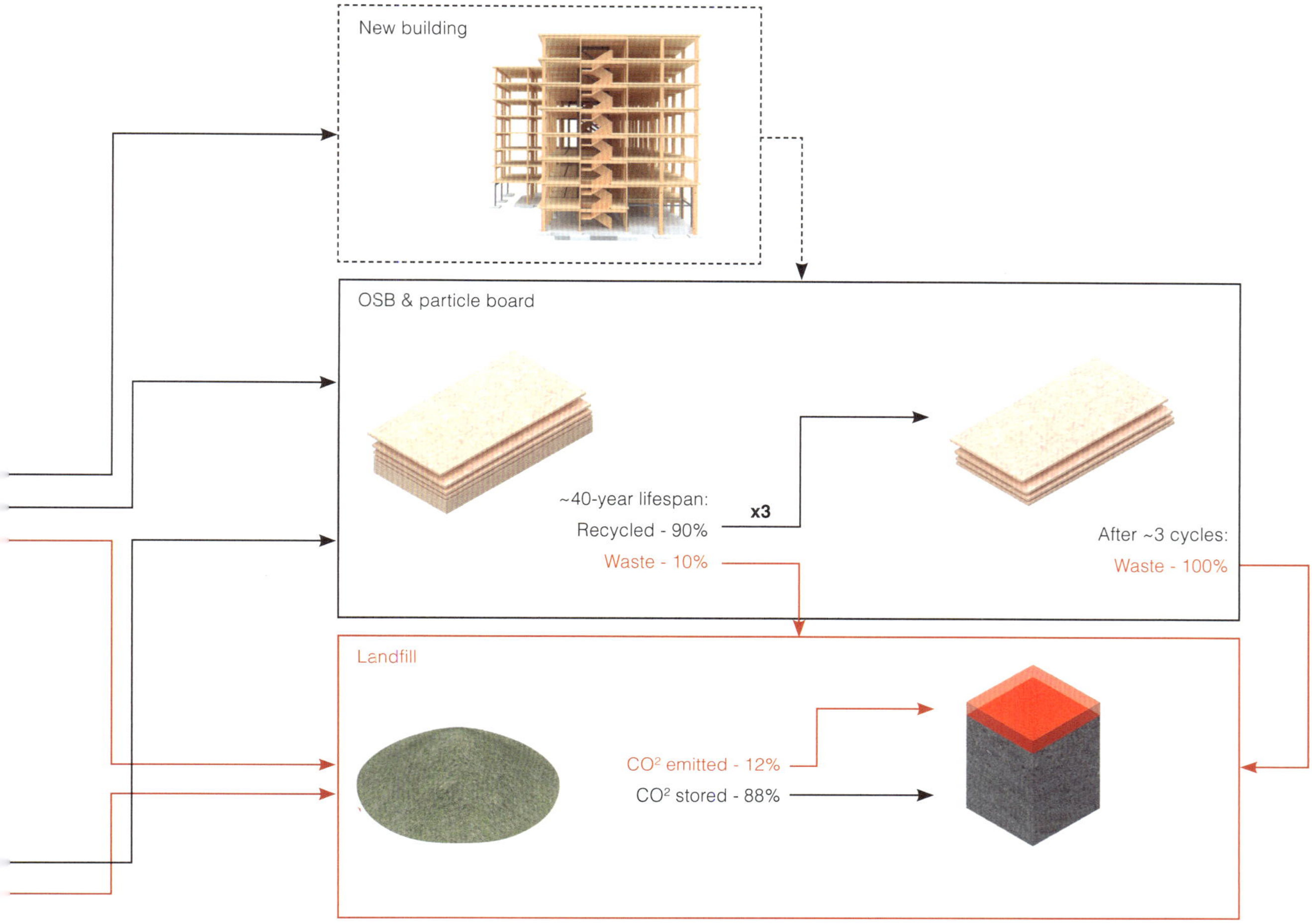

Thoughtful critics sometimes ask why it's fair for mass timber projects to factor in the carbon sequestered in their wood, while concrete or steel construction does not get the benefit of *not* cutting down those same trees. Exploring visually, we sought to explore the long-term landscape-scale implications of Heartwood and its concrete equivalent.

The diagram that resulted illustrates the difference in Global Warming Potential (GWP) balance between one scenario where a forest is repeatedly harvested and replanted over 240 years, with the lumber used to build mass timber buildings, and another where the forest is left untouched, with a series of concrete buildings erected at the same interval.

For the mass timber scenario, this land is harvested every 60 years to build another Heartwood-type building, and then replanted. The carbon sequestered by trees in the forest is stored in the superstructure of each building, with some loss from harvesting. The emissions required to fabricate and construct each building are then added to the negative sequestered carbon to find the net GWP balance. At the end of the lives of each of these buildings, they are dismantled, recycled, and reused per the end-of-life scenarios in the UW study.

The concrete equivalent structures are (generously) given the GWP benefit of the carbon sequestered if the forest had remained untouched. However, this unmanaged forest slows down its carbon sequestration and becomes roughly neutral on carbon balance after 100 years.[24] As such, the GWP balance of concrete buildings with untouched forest climbs massively with the construction of each new concrete building.

24: Consortium for Research on Renewable Industrial Materials, 2013. "The Role of Forests, Management, and Forest Products on Carbon Mitigation."

After 240 years, the series of mass timber buildings remain net-negative, even after the oldest ones are fully given to landfill. In reality, the longer potential lifespan of timber buildings and the vulnerability of unmanaged forests to fire and disease would likely make this difference in performance even greater.

Every lifecycle assessment study we've collaborated on has furthered our understanding of carbon in the built environment, and we are committed to continuing and expanding this research for as long we

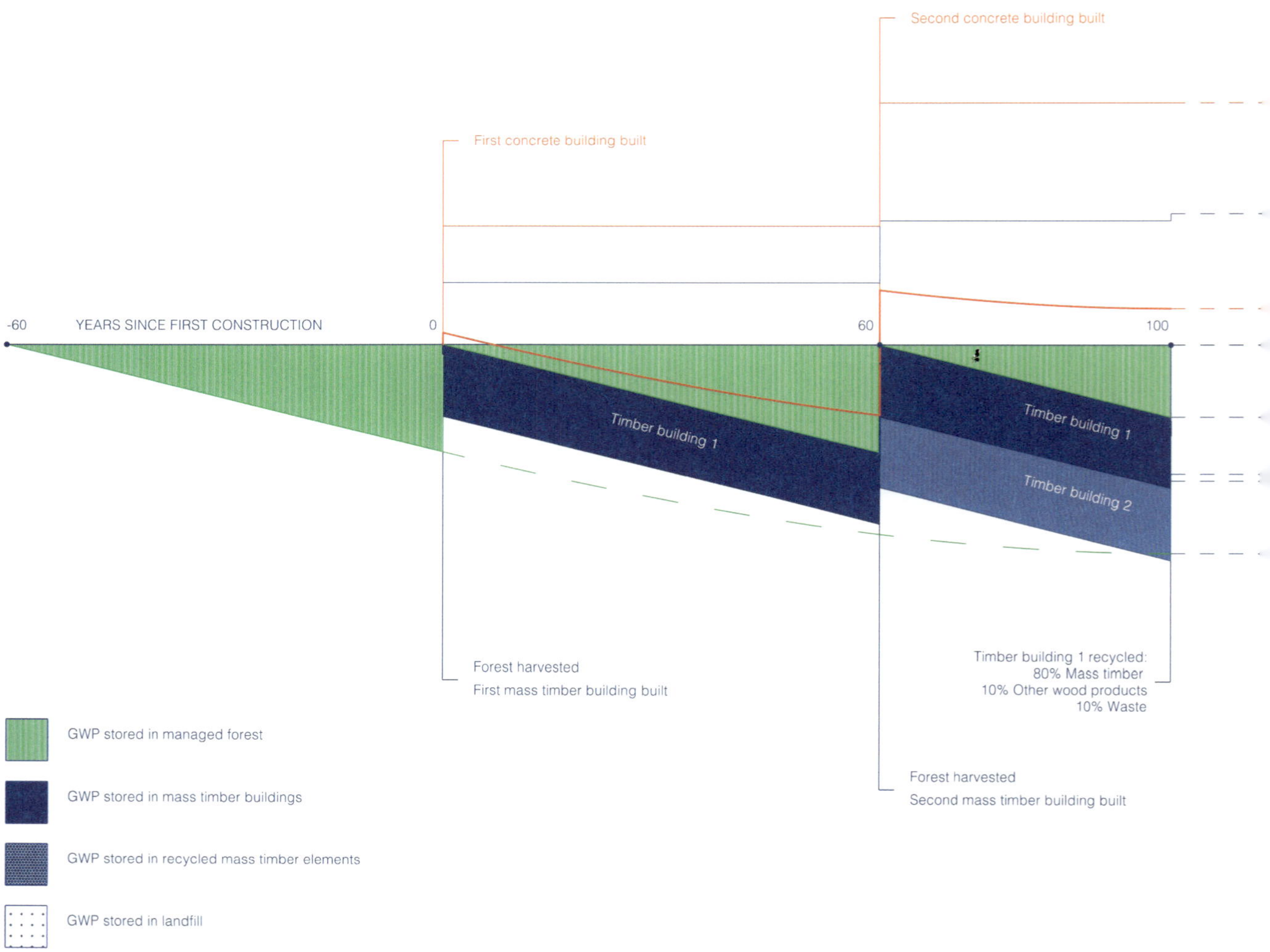

can. As I write, we are working on another end-of-life study with Christina, this one examining the *actual* disassembly of a large-scale mass timber prototype building.

Like the questions of disassembly, lifecycle assessment is still an evolving science, and these wonderful, in-depth studies do not claim to be the final answers for all mass timber buildings. We are keenly aware that each LCA is only as good as the information and assumptions it relies on, and that there are many different methodologies used within the LCA community. But in the pursuit of transparency, we are curious about asking these questions, as fast as we can, and to share results as they become available. We are proud to be part of a broad *collective intelligence* that is exploring how mass timber buildings can help lower our building industry's carbon footprint.

There is more work to be done.

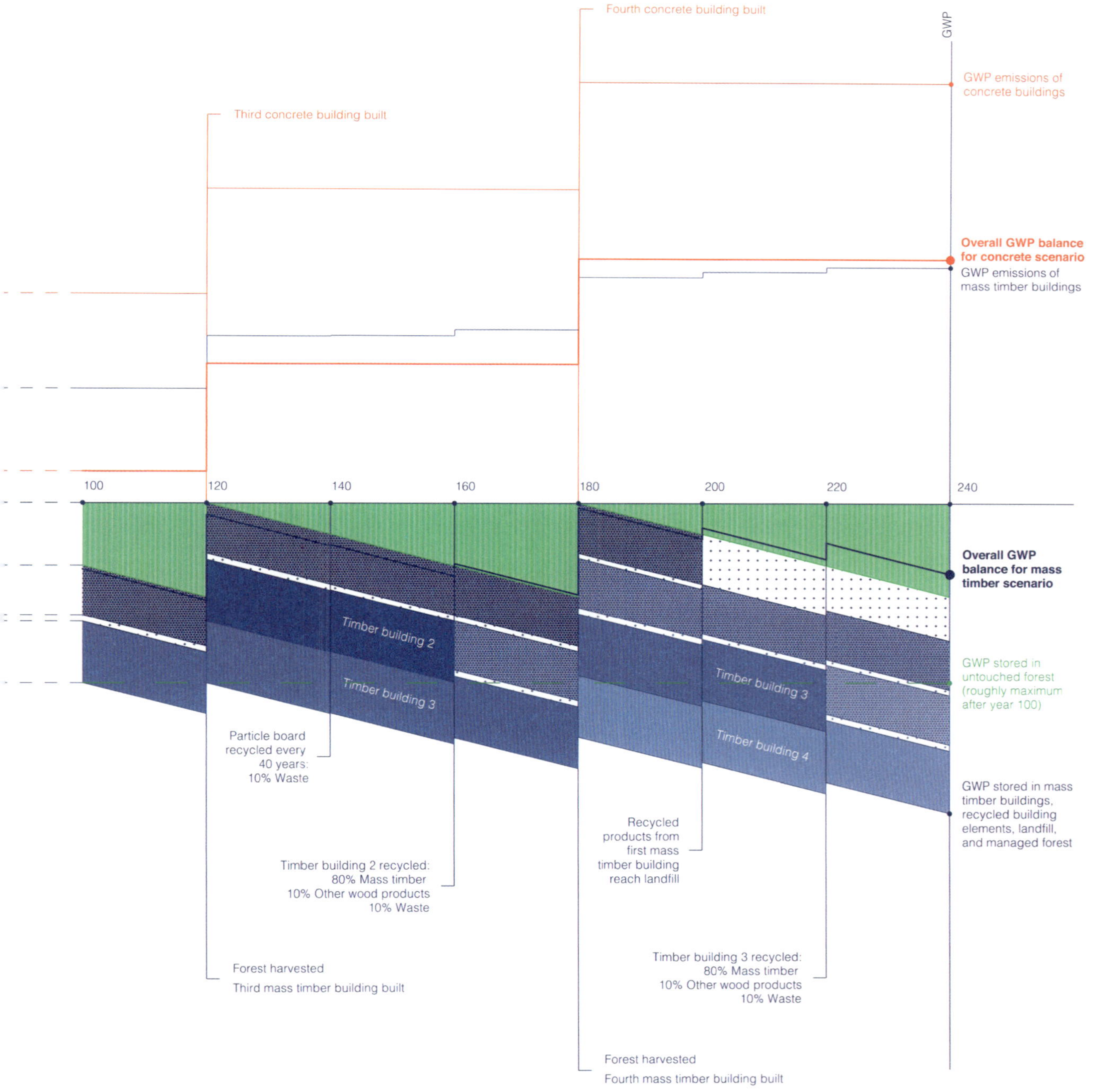

Mass timber fire testing at RISE Sweden, October 2020

Changing Codes, Part II

2019–2022

While the success of the TWB Ad-Hoc Committee in testing, writing, and ratifying new building codes was an immense step forward, many compromises had been made. These included the highly conservative fire protection requirements for types IV-B and IV-A, capping mass timber buildings at 18 stories, the redundant approach to fire protection in concealed spaces, and the strict non-exposure of exterior wood, to name a few.

It was clear there was more progress yet to be made. But to do so would require more tests, more research, and more leadership capable of navigating the ICC process.

The willingness to risk my design practice to collaborate on extensive transdisciplinary research had been driven by a relentless curiosity. How could the *business-as-usual* methods of building be done differently? Could we learn how to build more beautiful buildings with less carbon and the same (or more) durability and safety?

As a community, we had answered those questions. The ICC code ratification in 2019 coincided with the resounding results of the Nature Conservancy LCA studies, demonstrating that mass timber buildings took significantly less upfront carbon to build than their concrete equivalents. Now we were designing Heartwood, putting all that hard-fought work to practice.

But in the back of my mind, questions kept nagging. Three layers of gypsum wallboard encasing every mass timber surface for an 18-story building? And even more extra material to meet acoustic performance. Could anyone even afford to build that? And with every extra layer compromising the carbon performance, would it even be worth it? Perhaps their height could somewhat justify these extreme protections, but what about at the critical 12-story level? Could we at least open up more wood there, at the scale that would be most critical in moving the market forward?

In the TWB committee, we had been designing new building types at a conference table. But as we put them to the test with Heartwood, diving into floor assemblies, acoustical performance, and fire protection details, the questions kept arising. Had the codes and the testing really led to the right buildings?

I had sworn off any more code involvement after the enormous effort of the last cycle, but I was keenly aware that there was more that could, and should, be done.

So, when the opportunity arose to help develop five new fire tests to expand on those we conducted in 2017, I reluctantly found myself saying yes. If we were going to move the market and improve carbon performance for taller mass timber, new tests would be critical to help reduce the overly onerous and conservative fire protection requirements we had be forced to impart on the 12- and 18-story building types.

In agreeing to be on the Steering Committee of this American Wood Council USFS 2019 grant, I sensed that a designer-led research process might be even more successful. During the ICC process, leading as a designer meant navigating tedious committee and sub-committee work, and often embracing compromise. Working directly with the AWC team, however, I could now lead through smaller calls and speak more openly about where and how the fire tests could be most valuable.

The American Wood Council had strategically reached out to the Research Institute of Sweden, RISE, to collaborate on the design and perform the new fire tests. RISE had an outdoor fire test facility in Sweden, with none of the limitations of the ATF's indoor facility. Because of this, the tests could be designed with higher fuel loads, i.e. more exposed timber.

As with the ATF tests, the task was to design and build a mass timber compartment structure, complete with door and window openings, and then try to burn it down five times in a row. Each test would last four hours, with no sprinklers, and no firefighting intervention. Tests were to be conducted in October 2020 with a good chance of fall winds, adding to the real-life fire conditions so critical to credible results.

The tests were designed over the late summer and fall of 2020, with lead international fire researchers from RISE in Sweden and the AWC in Washington, D.C. The AWC would develop the design intent for the test, and RISE would create a digital fire model to test the results. Together, the two institutions would present their strategies and designs to the Steering Committee. At least that was how it started.

Designer-Led Fire Testing

I was standing in the University of Washington Architecture Department's beautiful, 1909 Beaux-Arts building when a call came in on my mobile. Neoclassical wooden trim framed the high, elegantly proportioned windows, and yards and yards of painted molding traced the walls at top and base. Afternoon light was slanting into the studio room, filled with architecture students waiting patiently for my desk crits.

It was Kuma Sumathipala, the lead Grant Coordinator and Program Manager Fire Researcher from the AWC. He had become a key coordinator and trusted ally during the ICC TWB process, and I often would check in with him to help me understand basic terms of fire test protocols and performance metrics. We shared the exciting event of the successful ATF test #2, when I brought my then 16-year-old daughter to join in and watch the four-hour test in Washington, D.C.

Kuma was calling to ask my advice as he worked on the design of the tests. He asked me whether I thought architects would mind having a little strip of drywall between the beams and the ceiling of a mass timber structure. Given the stakes, I took considerable care to confirm that I had understood his question. Was he was really asking what an architect would think if the codes were to require such a detail on every intersection between a beam and ceiling? Yes, that was the question.

Looking up at the tall ceiling of the Beaux-Arts building, I could not answer fast enough. "Kuma, no contemporary architect in their right mind would ever design a mass timber building again if that was the required detail for an exposed mass timber ceiling." I believed I also used the word 'band-aid' several times. He asked me if I was sure. Yes. I think I might also have said that we didn't even need to do the tests if that was what he was going to design.

Eventually, I calmed down. We discussed the perceived risks. The AWC, rightly, was concerned that, if a test was to fail, the foes of mass timber—the well-funded concrete industry lobby, for instance—could eagerly use the failed test as ammunition against all tall mass timber buildings.

Kuma noted that the digital fire modeling had shown that the build-up of heat was the greatest at the right-angle interface between two surfaces. The proposed gypsum wall board strip had started out at 6 inches in depth, but he had negotiated it down to 1.5 inches at the upper edge of the beam. My heartbeat had slowed down as I looked up the ceiling again, looking at the beams.

I took a deep breath.

Test compartment under construction in Stockholm, Sweden

Test 1 interior showing gypsum "band-aid" between beam and ceiling

"Kuma, let's think about this. Why don't we devise a simple test of both conditions? There are two sides of this exposed glulam beam. They both touch the exposed CLT ceiling. Why don't we add your strip on one side and not on the other? Then we set the compartment on fire, per the protocol, and see what happens to both sides. If there is significantly more damage to the unprotected side, or reignition, then we agree the protection would be necessary. But at least we collect real data, and we learn the limits of this material against four hours of unprotected fire."

He said he would run it up the flagpole.

The first RISE test was run to those specifications in the dark early hours well before dawn Pacific Standard Time, on September 16, 2020, in Stockholm.

My phone rang at 3:07 am. It was Kuma. He hardly let me say a sleepy, disoriented hello. "Susan, it worked." "What worked?" "The test, the test you wanted, without the protection strip." My husband, Marco, rolled over in bed next to me, wondering what the emergency was.

"So, you ran the test, Kuma? With one side protected, the other not? What happened?"

"The compartment stood. There was a little more fire outside on the vertical walls than we expected, due to windy conditions, but there was no reignition. It is a big deal, Susan."

"So," I asked again, "the beams and the entire ceiling were exposed?" Yes, except for the 1.5-inch strip.

By then I was sitting straight up in bed, vividly awake.

"Ok, Kuma, here's what we do. We have four more tests. We have four more chances to take risks. We need to use these tests to test the limit of this material in compartment fires." The ATF test facility had limited us, and even though the mass timber performed brilliantly, we all knew the resulting code language was highly conservative. We knew the material could handle more, but we didn't have proof.

"Kuma, we need proof. We want to know how much we can expose and how much we can't. We need the proof of real-life fire tests so that the codes can reflect their results."

He was silent.

"Kuma, let's go further. For Test 2, take it all off. All the GWB, all around the entire compartment, walls, and ceiling. Let's take off the band-aid. If that fails, then we back down on Test 3 until we get it right. We need to find the limits."

He said he would run it up the flagpole.

I tried to go back to sleep. My heart was pounding.

Some five hours later, the phone rang again. Kuma said he had spoken with Daniel Brandon, the Swedish Fire Protection Engineer leading the research for RISE. "He ran a fire model of your suggestion. We have to compromise. We have to cover the front and back walls with three layers of GWB and add a second layer of GWB around the window openings."

I said okay. For multi-family residential, the rear half of the residential compartment would likely be covered with GWB anyway, to accommodate Mechanical, Electrical and Plumbing. We could cover up that much while still pushing the full exposure of the beams, ceilings and side walls.

Two weeks later, the charred panels and beam had been replaced, and the second test was ready.

The phone rang again at 3:00 am. Test 2 was successful. The mass timber compartment had withstood four hours of intense flames, under some of the highest fuel loads ever tested, with no sprinklers, no fire department intervention. As before, the exposed wood had developed a thick layer of char, a little under two inches on average, to withstand the heat. The inner layers of the mass timber were untouched, and, as designed, had withstood the heat. The compartment had not lost its structural integrity. No delamination of the mass timber had occurred. No reignition had occurred. Test 2 had passed.

Sitting up in my bedroom, my voice was clear. "Kuma, let's take it all off. All the GWB. Everywhere. Including that back wall."

He groaned. "Susan, you are making things difficult for me," he said, a polite smile in his voice. I said I knew, I was sorry. "But can we at least have Daniel model it and see what he predicts?"

"Are you sure this exposure is what architects want?" he asked again. It was not only architects, I said, but owners and users - humans. We want to see the wood. The market is demanding it. "Of the entire US?," he asked. Yes, again.

Table 3
Final results for RISE Tests 1,2,4 and 5, noting temperature fail for Test 3.

D. Brandon et al., 2021. "RISE Report - Final Project Report - Fire Safe Implementation of Visible Mass Timber in Tall Buildings - Compartment Fire Testing"

	Test 1	Test 2	Test 3	Test 4	Test 5
Flashover	0:14 h	0:08 h	0:12 h	0:15 h	0:04 h
Start of decay	0:36 h	0:36 h	0:43 h	0:29 h	0:34 h
Duration of fully developed phase	0:22 h	0:28 h	0:31 h	0:14 h	0:30 h
Fall-off of exposed GWB		0:32 h ~1-2 m^2			0:36 h ~1 m^2
Temperature increase during decay phase			3:05 h onward		
Test stop	4:00 h	4:00 h	3:31 h	4:00 h	4:00 h

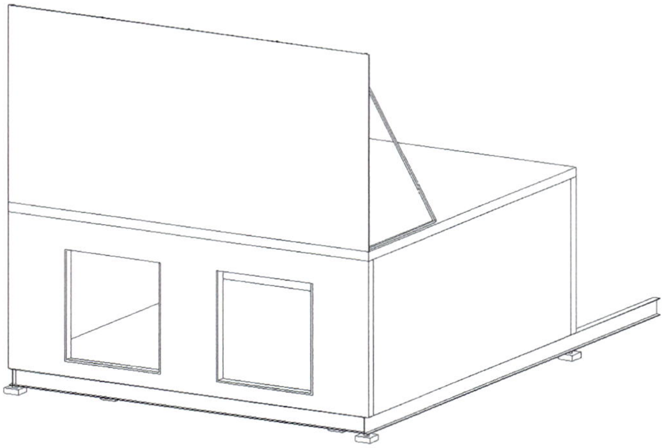

Tests 1-3: Residential configuration

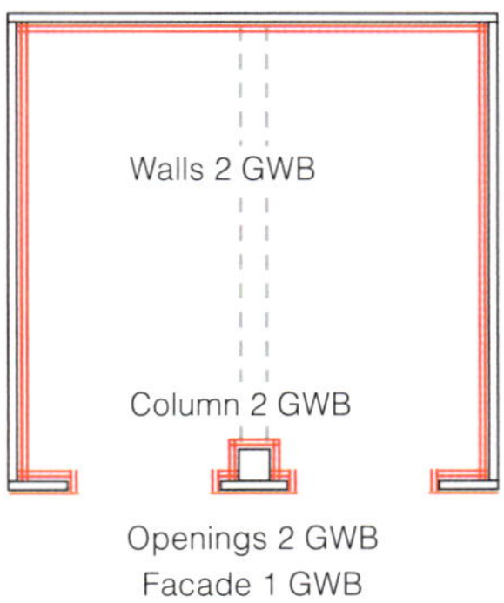

Test 1

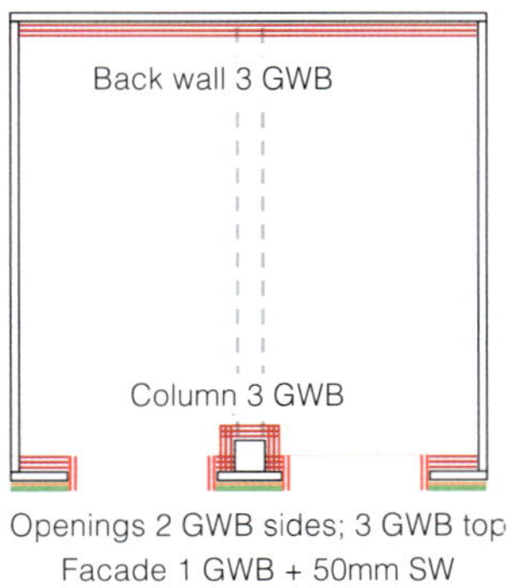

Test 2

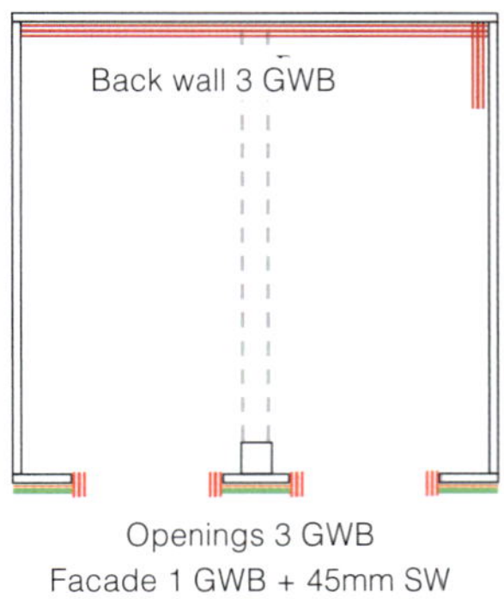

Test 3

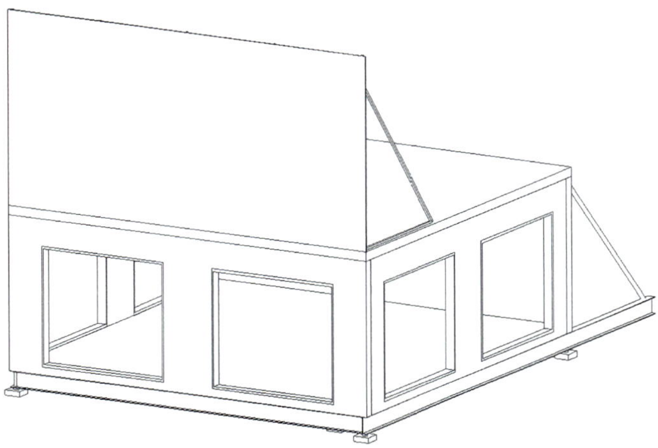

Tests 4-5: Commercial configuration

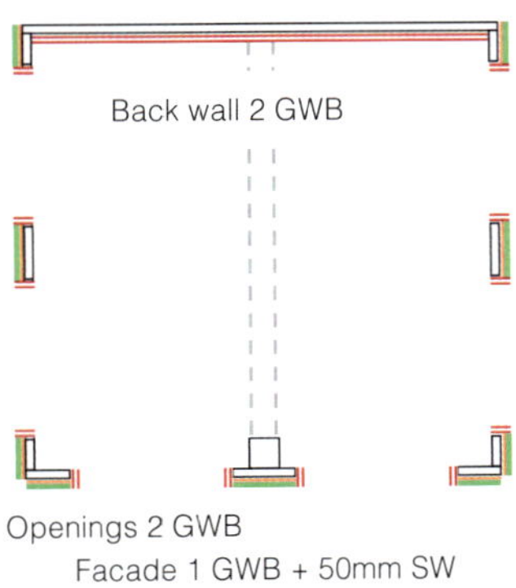

Test 4

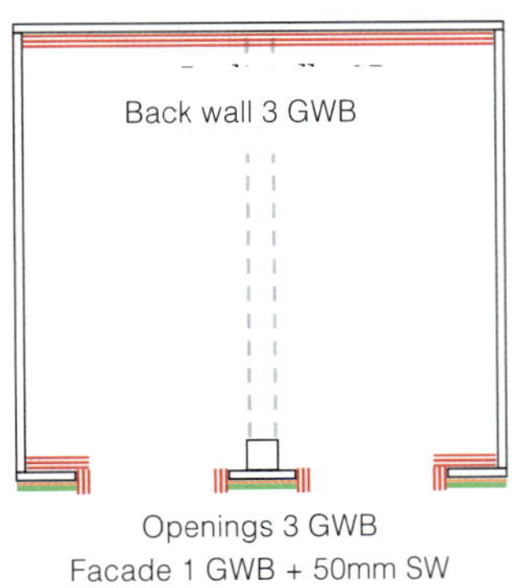

Test 5

He said he would run it up the flagpole.

My heart was pounding. Marco and I tried to go back to sleep.

A week later, Kuma called again. They couldn't get rid of the back wall covering, but Daniel's modeling suggested they could get rid of the front wall interior GWB layers. Critically, this would expose the vulnerable right-angle intersections where the front wall met the left and right walls.

I said okay.

By the end of November all five tests were completed. Each had varying degrees of mass timber exposure, with the ceilings 100% exposed in every case. Tests passed if two conditions were met: no secondary flashover ("reignition") after hour 3, and the exterior wall temperatures below 300 degrees Celsius at the end of the test.

Tests 1, 2, 4, and 5 had passed. Only Test 3, where a floor level right-angle intersection of two CLT walls had been left unprotected, failed due to a slight rise in temperature. In Test 4, two other exposed corner conditions would pass. All tests had passed the original TWB Performance Criteria.

Finally, now, we had established a true limit. These tests represented far more aggressive scenarios than we had been able to test at the ATF, with much more timber exposed. Fed by exterior wind, with no sprinkler activation or firefighting response, mass timber had performed in all but one case. We had modeled and tested both compartments with smaller openings—a residential unit scenario—and then with larger openings simulating an office building.

Working collaboratively, with the best fire protection engineers in the world, we had come far closer to understanding the limits of fire endurance of mass timber than the more conservatively designed ATF tests. It was another spectacular leap forward for tall mass timber buildings.

Pushing Further

By the end of the tests in late October, I was faced with another decision. These tests had been dynamic—led by design rather than facility constraints—and the results had been stunning. Their conclusive outcomes offered a huge opportunity to further push policy. I felt compelled to again take a leadership position.

Yet, during that entire fall, we were undergoing one of the hardest points in Heartwood's design process, with the City of Seattle performing final reviews of Heartwood's Master Use Permit (MUP). This required constant communication and redesign, balancing city review comments with cost and client concerns - all against the looming deadline of the year's end, when investors would consider placing critical private equity into the project… if we had an MUP.

Perhaps hoping to hear a *"No, don't do it, Susan,"* I made calls around the country to people whose voices and wisdom I trusted. People who had also spent years stretching beyond their comfort zones to tackle hard, long-standing policy issues in support of mass timber, from Washington D.C. to Washington State. I spent time talking with former fellow TWB committee members to gauge their support, tacit or otherwise. I began to actively recruit key members.

I knew I couldn't do it alone, even with behind-the scenes backing from the American Wood Council. I would need the support of serious fire protection voices to back up my architect's optimism. Fortunately, former TWB Committee Chair Stephen DiGiovanni and TWB member Carl Baldassara agreed to be co-proponents, lending their serious fire protection engineering credentials to the effort. Their support meant everything, and I reluctantly said yes to leading the process.

The model code language was due in 20 days, before the holiday season begun. While I was still working daily through Heartwood's final MUP Corrections, the three of us, along with key colleagues Sam Francis and Paul Coats from the AWC, held nightly Zoom calls to develop strategies.

We spent many hours crafting two small but highly impactful code proposals, attempting to break through the conservatism of the Type IV-B and Type IV-A code language we had been forced to compromise on three years before.

By December 21st, Heartwood's MUP had been approved, pending a wholly unexpected appeal,[25] and our small group had finalized two proposals to be taken forward: G-146 for Type IV-A, which would allow 40% of the ceilings up to 18 stories to be exposed, and G-147 for Type IV-B, that would allow 100% of the ceilings up to 12 stories to be exposed.

25: City of Seattle, December 4, 2020

Type IV-C
Mass timber elements permitted to be unprotected

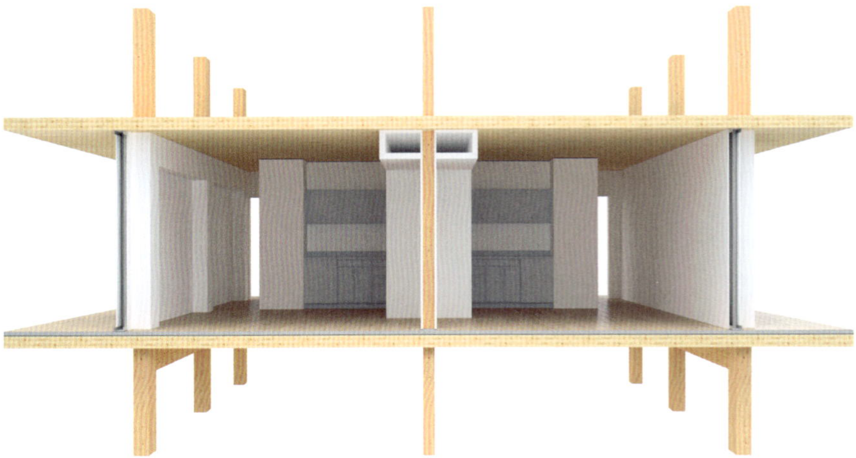

Type IV-B
[after G-147 update]

Ceilings: 100% exposed
or
Columns and walls: 60% exposed
or
Combination of columns, walls, and ceilings: *see 2024 IBC 602.4.2.2.3*

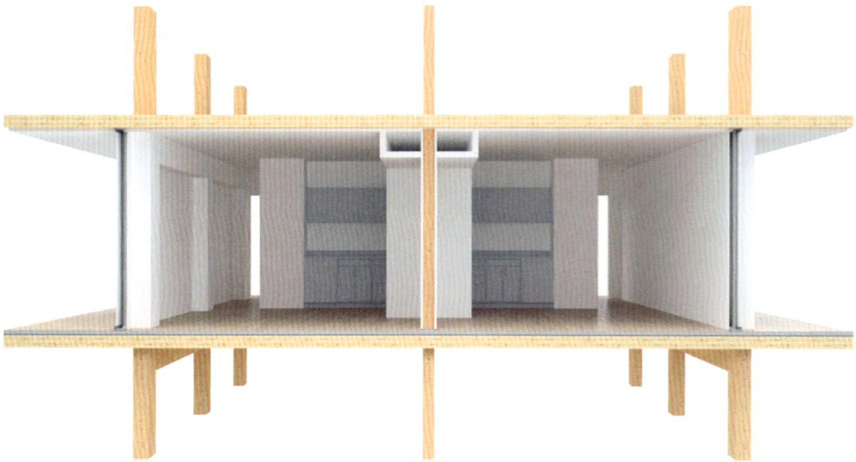

Type IV-A
All mass timber elements protected to an 80-minute rating or greater. This typically includes a gypcrete topping on floor slabs and gypsum wall board wrapping structural members.

Code-permitted mass timber exposure in Type IV buildings, as of IBC 2024

We delivered testimony virtually during the ICC Committee Action Hearing process in April of 2021, just as the Heartwood MUP appeal was denied and the MUP was finally granted. Later, in September, with my friend, Professor Ray Gastil of the Remaking Cities Institute at Carnegie Mellon acting as my proxy, G-146 failed to emerge from the Committee Action Hearings (CAH) process in April, failing by a vote of 5-9. G-147 passed, by a vote of 9-5.

We had mixed feelings. Thrilled that G-147 had passed but keenly disappointed about the G-146 failure, and strongly taken aback by the apparent lack of rigor in the process and lack of rationale behind the negative votes. Few of the committee members, it appeared to us, had read the final 222-page RISE Fire Test Report, or even perused the summary. Their negative commentary appeared to be based on emotion or influenced by competitive industry interests. As a group, as proponents, we remain convinced that even the failed Type IV-A 40% exposed ceilings code proposition is deeply conservative. The RISE tests showed that we could have safely gone much further.

But, even still, G-147 had been successful, and represented a notable change to the ICC tall timber codes. Our continuing collaboration—between designer, fire protection engineering experts, and the AWC—spurred this new code language to increase the amount of exposed mass timber allowed on the beams and ceilings of Type-IV-B, 12-story buildings—from 30% of the floor area to 100%.

This provision was ratified in January 2022 and incorporated into the 2024 International Building Code. Some cities, including Denver, adopted the simple and elegant code language of the Type IV-B changes within days after ratification. As the 2024 IBC is being adopted throughout the United States, this provision for more beautiful, lower carbon, safe, 12-story mass timber buildings will become widely available for designers to put into practice.

Wooden Cities

Heartwood Replication

Heartwood was the first project in the United States to test the limits of the new Type IV-C timber codes. Its design was an intensive and highly collaborative process that spanned four years, and through a comprehensive effort the team developed a design to meet the challenging and specific needs of the project and site.

To us, Heartwood represented not just a bespoke solution for a workforce housing building in Seattle, but the first prototype of a *building system* that could be replicated and adapted to meet a broad variety of other site and program constraints. The hard-won lessons learned in designing, detailing, and constructing this first-of-its-kind building could serve as a starting point for any number of new projects, from deeply affordable multi-family housing to luxury condos, in Portland or Puerto Rico.

Of course, these new projects would come with their own challenges, and we were curious to better understand how our system could adapt to this range of possibilities. In 2022, we were awarded another Wood Innovations Grant from the US Forest Service to devote to these questions, taking Heartwood as a starting point.

Z
Y
X

Heartwood's post-and-beam structure, with its novel all-wood, 2-hour fire-rated joint, provides a versatile framework for new tall timber projects.

With a post-and-beam building, the first thing to determine is the structural grid, in its X, Y, and Z dimensions. Heartwood itself—responding to the dual pressures of its workforce housing proforma and the small lot it shared with its neighbor—was designed with a highly irregular structural grid, with horizontal spans between 7 feet 1 inch and 18 feet 6 inches. While this perhaps sacrificed some material efficiency, it had the advantage of providing us with a proven library of unit designs that fit within this range of spans.

In a new tall wood building (with luck on a less constrained site) we can use these grid spans to optimize for different unit layouts and conditions. A span of 13 feet, 4 inches, for instance, can be used to reduce the production waste when using standard 40-foot CLT panels. Or an 18-foot grid might be used to create larger units in a Type IV-A building, in order to reduce the number of vertical members in need of extensive fireproofing. A 14-foot, 6-inch grid works well for the unit sizes required in affordable housing, and has the added advantage of working well in L-, C-, or E-shaped buildings that include interior corners. Of course, turning corners means that centralized mechanical systems need to be routed under beams, requiring additional floor-to-floor height or optimization for reduced beam depth.

Et cetera.

There is no one-size-fits-all solution to every building. Indeed, the failure of many overly ambitious efforts to "productize" the building industry with all-encompassing modular systems serves to underscore how the messy, diverse realities of construction resist broad-brush answers. But by treating Heartwood as the built prototype for a broad range of unique solutions, we have begun to understand some of the factors that will shape how tall timber can meet the diverse needs of different stakeholders.

Through studies for new tall timber buildings, both real and imagined, we have begun what will hopefully become a long process of refining this new method of construction, which is every bit as versatile as building with steel or concrete. With this work we hope to remove some of the uncertainty our clients feel in taking a leap away from conventional solutions in order to envision a better future.

While mass timber projects face the same macro difficulties as conventional construction in an uncertain economy, we know that, as an industry, adding housing and reducing carbon will be two of our greatest tasks over the next decades. As we have proved with research, testing, and building, mass timber can play an outsized role in meeting these challenges.

It's time for us to build wooden cities.

The Future of Tall Wood

Today, I receive emails and calls from jurisdictions across the country, asking my advice on how to interpret the new code language that we needed to leave vague to help pass the rigorous ICC process. *What is a ceiling?* they ask. *How did you test it? How did you measure how the exposed wood would contribute to fire?*

The codes are constantly evolving, and each new project has the opportunity to expand the body of interpretations that were left open-ended. The codes we developed were prescriptive, but not comprehensive. Opponents, pitting material, against material are still conceiving ways to characterize as ominous well-performed global fire tests that meet the TWB Performance Criteria from around the world.[26]

26: ICC Committee Action Hearings, G128 Proposal, May 2, 2025, Orlando, FL

Ushering in new code language through two different ICC code cycles took some six years of collaboration, writing and shepherding them through the ratification process. The passage of these code proposals opened the door to a lower-carbon built environment at-scale, and for healthier buildings and forests for the United States. They were based on the successful results of the most extensive fire tests ever completed for any building material prior to code adoption in the United States. But they remain conservative, and it's clear that they were only a start. New fire tests will be performed, and policy will continue to evolve to the new data-based findings.

Future fire tests hope to expand the limits of exposed mass timber, especially in 18-story Type IV-A buildings, where the current code restrictions are onerous in mandating extra fireproofing. These layers of fireproofing will themselves be subject to study, to explore less expensive, lower-carbon alternatives to gypsum wallboard.
As new tall timber buildings are built every year, the United States fire community will become more familiar with this material - robust, beautiful, and safe, when properly designed.

The future is bright for lower-carbon tall mass timber buildings.

If this is what the people do when the trees are green,
what will they do when the trees are dry?

Luke 23:31

V.

c h a r

Greenville, California, burning, August 4, 2021

Landscapes on Fire

In June 2017, as the ATF fire tests completed, the impact of the char layer and its fire-protective qualities was resonating within the Tall Wood Building Committee. Transforming the perception of char, from a carbon-packed waste product to a design tool to engineer, protect, and, thus, build tall wood buildings, was a sort of alchemy that I could never have foreseen.

Across the country, that same June, Washington State was in the first weeks of a protracted summer drought that would extend for almost two months, leading to forest fires across Washington State. No rain fell in Seattle for 55 days. In Spokane, no rain was recorded in 80 days. By September, close to 1 million acres were burning on the west coast and winds were blowing smoke into Seattle. Governor Inslee declared an emergency; schools were closed, and people huddled inside to protect their lungs.

Outside the skies were dark orange and ashes from charred wood fell from the sky. We were breathing our forests. A great grief fell upon us all.

In taking charge of my family's forest, the grave responsibility to create firebreaks and reduce understory fuel loads and fire ladders was becoming clearer. In these forests, and millions of acres of others, many overcrowded from human mismanagement, it was critical to act to reduce the risk of fire, before their unnaturally high fuel loads fed vast infernos.

But my small, privately held 144 acres and our Sisyphean efforts to bring them back to health, were only a microcosm of efforts confronting the dry American Western forests, and the huge forests of Canada. The magnitude and magnificence of those forest lands were hard to grasp. As the scale of forest fires grew, millions of carbon-sequestering trees were destroyed, adding volumes of carbon into the atmosphere, often equivalent to a large nation's yearly fossil fuel emissions.[27]

27: Byrne et al., 2024. "Carbon emissions from the 2023 Canadian wildfires." Published in *Nature*.

The problem was thrown into even sharper relief in November 2018, when the Camp Fire came for Paradise. Eighty-five people died, and the west coast froze in horror. Fires were not just a threat to our landscapes, but also to our towns, cities, and neighbors.

It was becoming clear that fire was going to play a large role in our practice.

The Dixie Fire

In August 2021, in the Sierra Nevada Mountains of northeastern California, a fire raged through the high mountain landscape of Ponderosa pines.

When the fires came for Greenville, the town was more prepared than at Paradise. Given the well-known wind patterns of the valley, it had been evacuated for several days, and only a few intrepid residents with press access had stayed, in an effort to keep their scattered and frightened neighbors informed of the fire's progress.[28]

28: Ken Donell, conversation with author, September 26, 2023, Sonoma, California

Greenville had the full attention of CalFire and their associated partners. Encampments were erected for the firefighters, and reinforcements were planned. Preparatory work had been going on for days, with fire breaks cleared in forests and roads widened.

Fighting a fire is a military operation, led by humans. Fires are fueled by enormous natural forces—topography, drought, wind—and by human decisions that accumulate over decades—over-suppression and overstocking of forests, and the design of our homes, buildings, and towns. During the massive fire-fighting operation in the woods around Greenville, there was a legally mandated two-week shift change of leadership. During that shift change, some human intelligence had been lost, and camps were still being pitched when the flames swept through on the night of August 4.[29] Some 1,100 structures were lost, including 660 homes. Seventy-five percent of the town was destroyed.

29: Jason Hodge, conversation with author, October 12, 2024, San Francisco, California

Thankfully, no lives were lost.

The call came in the early spring of 2022. It was Steve Marshall, a friend, comrade, and leader in mass timber. For years, Steve, formerly of the US Forest Service, had devoted his decades of Washington DC expertise to developing a new, higher-value market for timber in the United States. Mass Timber at scale. Could I meet with his long-time friend, Jonathan Kusel, of The Sierra Institute of Community and Environment, next week in Portland?

Of course, Steve.

Jonathan presented as a highly energetic, hyper-focused young 60-year-old. We met at the International Mass Timber Conference, huddled on brightly colored felt cushions beneath the high steel

trusses of the Oregon Convention Center. Although COVID was still in the air, we talked quickly and closely. He told me the story.

August 4, 2021. Dixie Fire. Devastation. PG&E Settlements just coming out now.

Lost homes, lost community.

His quiet, urgent words hung in the vast hall of the convention center, invoking a different world.

How fast could we get building permits to rebuild?

It was the end of March. I told him that if everything went perfectly, we could submit for permits by July and be building by August. If we prefabricated as much as possible, we might get the structures dried in before winter weather hit the Sierras.

Two months later, in May of 2022, we were driving over the Sierra Nevada Mountains to visit Jonathan and his team. We began to understand the enormity of what the fire had meant for this community.

The road wound through high, jagged valleys, carved by rivers carrying water to farms in California's Central Valley, and then to Sacramento and the San Francisco Bay beyond. Above the rivers, we drove through miles and miles of high mountainsides, scraped bare and brown. Sharp black stags of bare burned trunks stood aimless and staggered, clinging to the steep hillsides. Shadows from the late afternoon sun threw down their long, exaggerated alter-egos onto the slopes, multiplying the effect of the blackened trunks by two. Silhouettes of devastation.

Coming the opposite way on the narrow road, logging truck after logging truck lumbered past us in long convoys. Their flat-bed trailers were filled with blackened Ponderosa pine trunks. Huge, sometimes only seven or eight to a truck. As they passed, both heavy and swift, we could see their cut ends. To our city eyes, the pristine purity of the cut logs was astonishing. Inside the charred bark of these burned black hulks, were gigantic logs of pure, clean, beautiful Ponderosa pine wood. Truck after truck of perfect wood.

Inspired, I began to tell myself the story of what I was seeing. Charred, burned trees from the fires. Taken from the hillsides and brought to sawmills. Inside their blackened exteriors, millions of board feet of good lumber. Enough to rebuild, maybe even with CLT. Maybe even enough to sell to the rest of the state and help pay for the entire effort.

What foresight being shown by this rural community!

Soon, we pulled up to Crescent Mills, CA, to meet Jonathan. The Sierra Institute was hosting a ribbon cutting for a new sawmill, to harvest and mill those very logs. Amongst the crowd of state politicians making speeches and locals serving up lunch over barbecues, it looked so easy.

Then, Jonathan shared his reality.

CalTrans is moving those logs. They have to stop the landslides. They are hauling them to landfill.

I had to lobby CalTrans in Sacramento for months to get them to stop here in Crescent Mills to drop the logs here instead.

There are no mills in California that will take Ponderosa pine to make lumber in California. Years ago, it was considered a less efficient structural lumber, so the mills focused on Douglas fir.

We have been working with a local fourth-generation lumber family to reopen this tiny mill on this land to mill these Ponderosa pine logs.

We only have a few months left before the logs will become unstable and unusable.

The layers of troubled, human decisions, by well-intentioned but siloed human bureaucracies in the face of new, human-influenced devastation began to sink in. The scale of waste was staggering. The small mill was heroic, but it was only on its first day, some nine months after the fire. The larger rural mill infrastructure had steadily been depleted over the last 30 years. The clock was ticking against the useful life of the burned logs and there were only intermittent resources available to add further capacity in this remote region.

Implementing a full vision of a circular economy beginning with rebuilding process with wood reclaimed directly from the fire was not yet to be. The first prototype Sierra Houses would be sourced from mass timber some 300 miles away in southern Oregon from DR Johnson.

However, in 2024 and 2025, the highly entrepreneurial Jonathan and his team are working to add local mass timber fabrication through a new startup called Mosaic. This kind of small-scale, rural mass timber production is a new circular model, promoting both healthier forests and communities with homes and jobs. The nimble infrastructure is designed for local species of timber, which are often rejected by larger regional mills, culled from forests in need of healthy forest management.

Today, atelierjones is supporting efforts to help commercialize several different underutilized species of timber, working with leaders in local communities, to promote this thinking. From western hemlock trees, harvested and milled by the Makah tribe on the northwestern tip of Washington State, and then sent to a small startup in Port Angeles, WA, the Composite Recycling Technology Center (CRTC), to the Ponderosa pine to be made into CLT by Mosaic, to thinned, smaller-diameter Douglas fir and Redwood becoming dowel-laminated timber at Mad River Mass Timber in Humboldt County, California, these are complex and multi-year efforts. Each of these entities are moving forward to help prevent forest fires by thinning their forests, bring to market new, under-utilized species of lumber, provide higher-tech jobs for the local workforce, and rebuild fire-hardened homes for their communities from locally sourced wood.

The beauty of witnessing and contributing to this circular economy in action is deeply inspiring.

But why rebuild at all?

Don't people know that fires will come again?

Greenville lies in remote, sparsely populated Plumas County, two hours northwest by car of Reno, Nevada, in the northern Sierra Nevada mountains. Although predominantly white, the Mountain Maidu people who first settled the area make up over 10% of the population. In 2020, before the fire came, Greenville's median income was below $20,000, and the poverty rate more than twice the California average.[30] It is an aging community, with the median resident being a 52-year-old single woman. A majority of the 2,500 residents had lost their homes, as well as the buildings in which they earned a living. Home insurance being a financial luxury, many were uninsured, and had lost their life savings with the destruction of their home. The more-than-century-old community was devastated.

From a distance, it is perhaps easy to say that this tiny community, nestled deep in the forested mountains, should simply be uprooted. That family connections to the land, often going back generations, or even millennia in the case of the Maidu, should be broken in the name of moving away to safety.

30: United States Census Bureau, 2020. *American Community Survey Data.*

Greenville, CA, 2020, Google © 2020

Greenville, CA, 2022, Google / Airbus © 2025

But where to find that safety? Each climate-impacted landscape is different. Each population is impacted differently by climate change. The Sierra Nevadas are not the Gulf Coast, with repetitive waves and water continuing to settle along long low coasts, slowly disintegrating under rising groundwater first, and then, through devasting high tides and hurricane-driven waters.

Fires are random, still. Lightning, winds and humans cannot be predicted as confidently as the daily surges of ocean tides. It is true that the valleys facing the Pacific Coast in the canyons of Los Angeles have perennial fires, powered under the November perennial winds, called the Santa Ana, as if naming them after a female saint might diminish their overwhelming destructive power.

But the wild randomness of the mountains of the Sierra Nevadas are divided by sharp ridges and deep rivers. The towns in their valleys are scattered: 1,000 people here in Greenville. 20 miles over, 2,500 people in Taylorsville, 20 miles over, 4,000 people, in Quincy. Small rural communities, connected by two-lane winding roads along the sides of mountains, hunkered down in the snow-bound winters, going to schools, and running Plumas County, a bank, a regional grocery store or pharmacy to take care of each other as well as possible. Asking people to move over the mountains to a different valley would not only disrupt both communities but, should a fire come to that new valley, it could potentially cause more risk to the now-enlarged population of that neighboring town.

Do we ask them to leave?

The answer of The Sierra Institute for Community and Environment was

No. We do not.

The Sierra Institute envisioned a different tactic, one of resilience rather than retreat. Greenville's location in the midst of a vulnerable landscape could be an asset rather than a drawback. Jonathan and his team envisioned a resilient community, one supporting forest health through thinning and management,[31] while also producing the material to create a fire-hardened built environment. Residents could return home, bolstered by longtime social connections and new economic opportunities.

31: Maidu Summer Consortium+Plumas CAL-TREX, April 30, 2025

For decades, we have seen fire only as an enemy, one to be kept at bay at all costs. But ironically, that attitude of over-suppression has now created fires that burn too large and too intense, decimating both forests and communities.[32] In the past, humans understood fire as one of nature's most important tools for creating healthy forests.

32: Kreider, M.R., Higuera, P.E., Parks, S.A. et al. Fire suppression makes wildfires more severe and accentuates impacts of climate change and fuel accumulation. Nat Commun 15, 2412 (2024)

It is time once again that we learn how to *live with fire.*

WE'RE
REBUILDING

2021–2023
Greenville, California

atelierjones:
Susan Jones, Meghan Doring, Eleanor Lewis, Payton Narancic, Lenore Wan

Developer:
The Sierra Institute for Community and Environment

Structural Engineering:
Harriott Valentine Engineers

Contractor:
Lights Creek Construction

Mass Timber Supplier/Fabricator:
DR Johnson

Modular Fabricator:
Method Homes

Mass Timber Strategy:
Steve Marshall

Photography:
Lara Swimmer

Sierra Houses

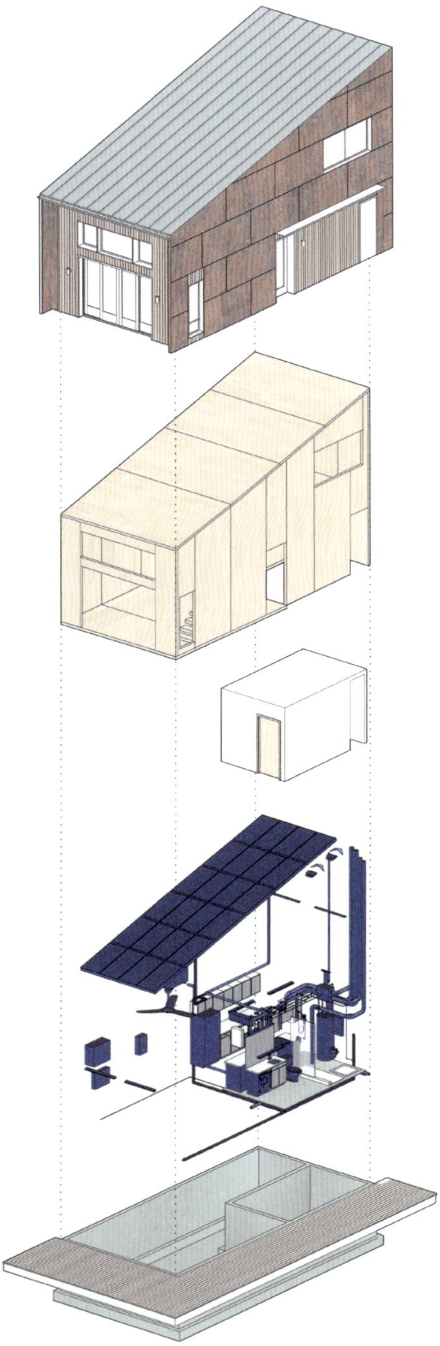

Living with Fire

Working on mission-driven projects focuses the mind intensely. It is an infectious way to practice architecture. The honor of being part of a team trusted to bring life back to a small, devastated town was intensely motivating.

We submitted permit drawings to Plumas County in July of 2022, just four months after meeting Jonathan. We developed three small prototype houses: one, two and three-bedrooms at 558, 652, and 919 square feet, respectively. The houses were permitted both for the three specific sites where they were built, and as master permits that would allow anyone in the county to build to these designs.

To meet the challenge of rapid and affordable rebuilding, the houses were designed to take full advantage of prefabrication. The houses were each designed around a modular wet core containing kitchen, bathroom, mechanical, and electrical systems. After approval of the modular system by the State of California, the cores were fabricated off site, then three were shipped in one piece, arriving in August.

In October, the CLT elements arrived as flat-pack, pre-cut elements to be assembled around these central cores, installed directly on a concrete stem wall foundation. The foundation creates a crawl space below to act as a protective cavity for utility runs and ventilation, and a base for the mass timber, secured by the embedded steel hold-downs required in California's high seismic zone.

The simplicity of this system allowed the houses to be erected rapidly by the local contractor and only a few hands – a valuable efficiency for rebuilding at scale in rural areas where labor availability is minimal. The structures were enclosed before the snow arrived, and, despite supply chain issues, by June of 2023 people were sleeping in their new, rebuilt homes.

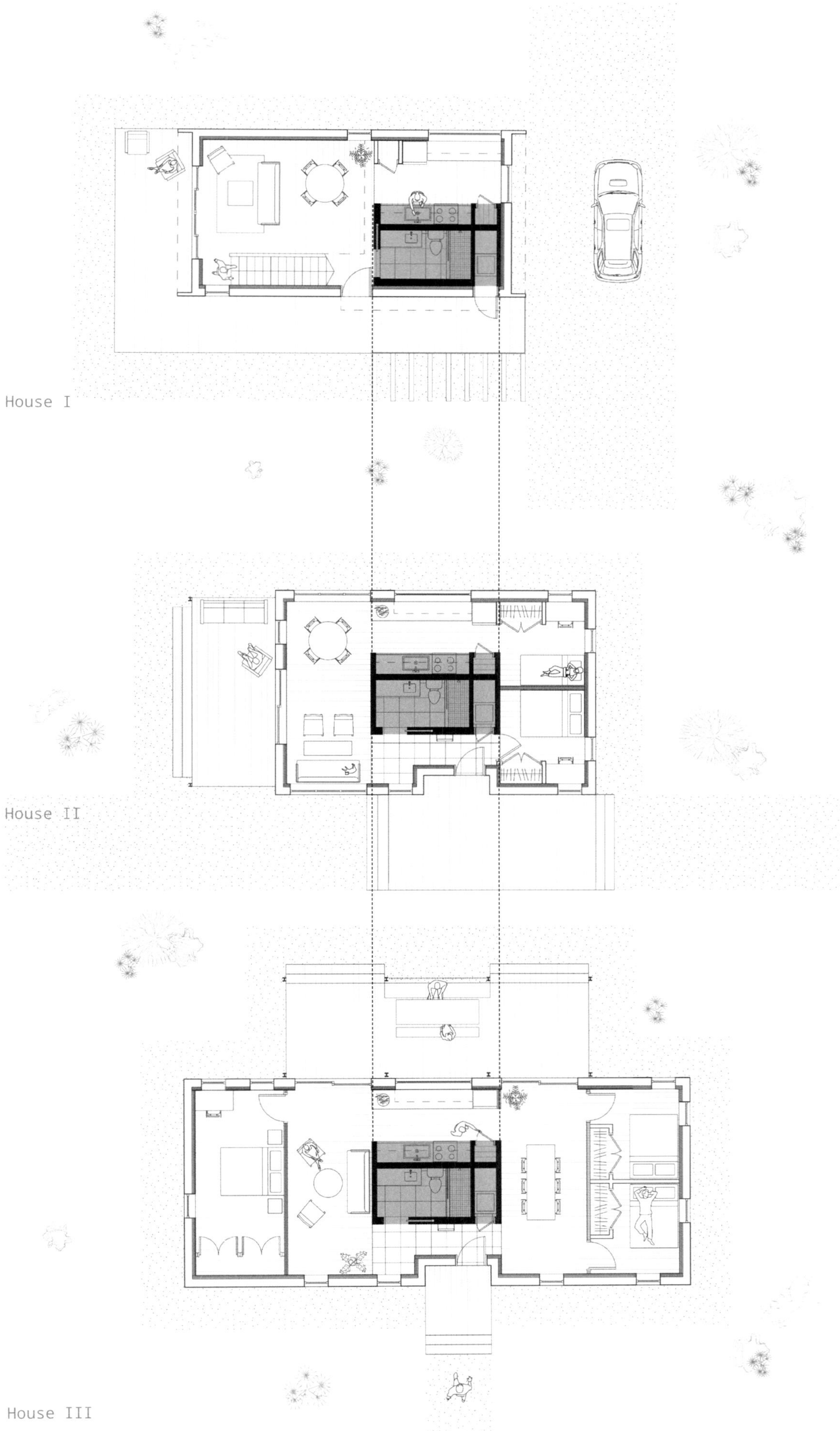
House I
House II
House III

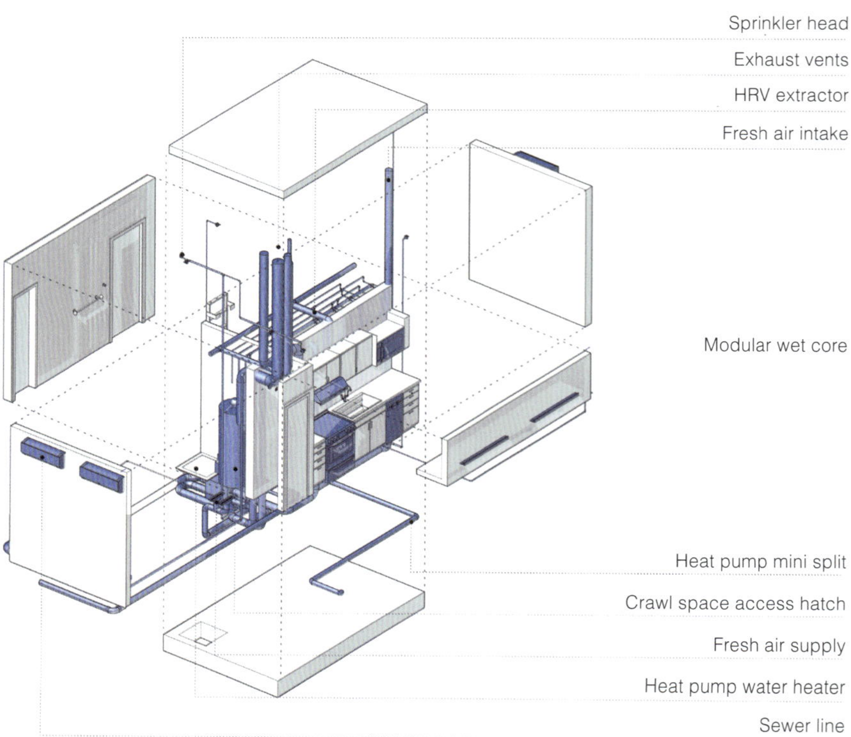
Sprinkler head
Exhaust vents
HRV extractor
Fresh air intake
Modular wet core
Heat pump mini split
Crawl space access hatch
Fresh air supply
Heat pump water heater
Sewer line

JCB
509-42
1-800-UR-RENTS
10420934
CP4F44

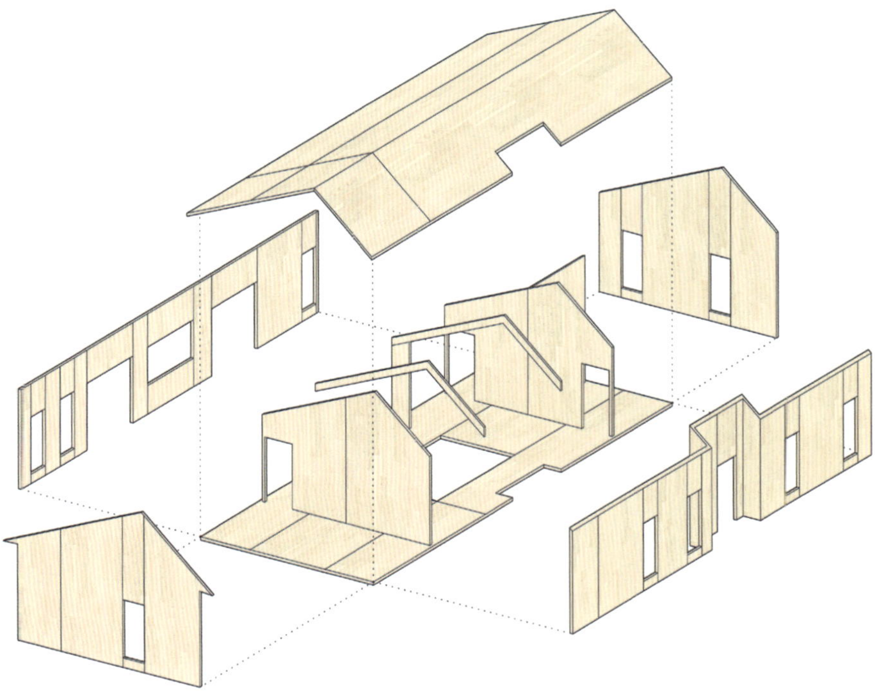

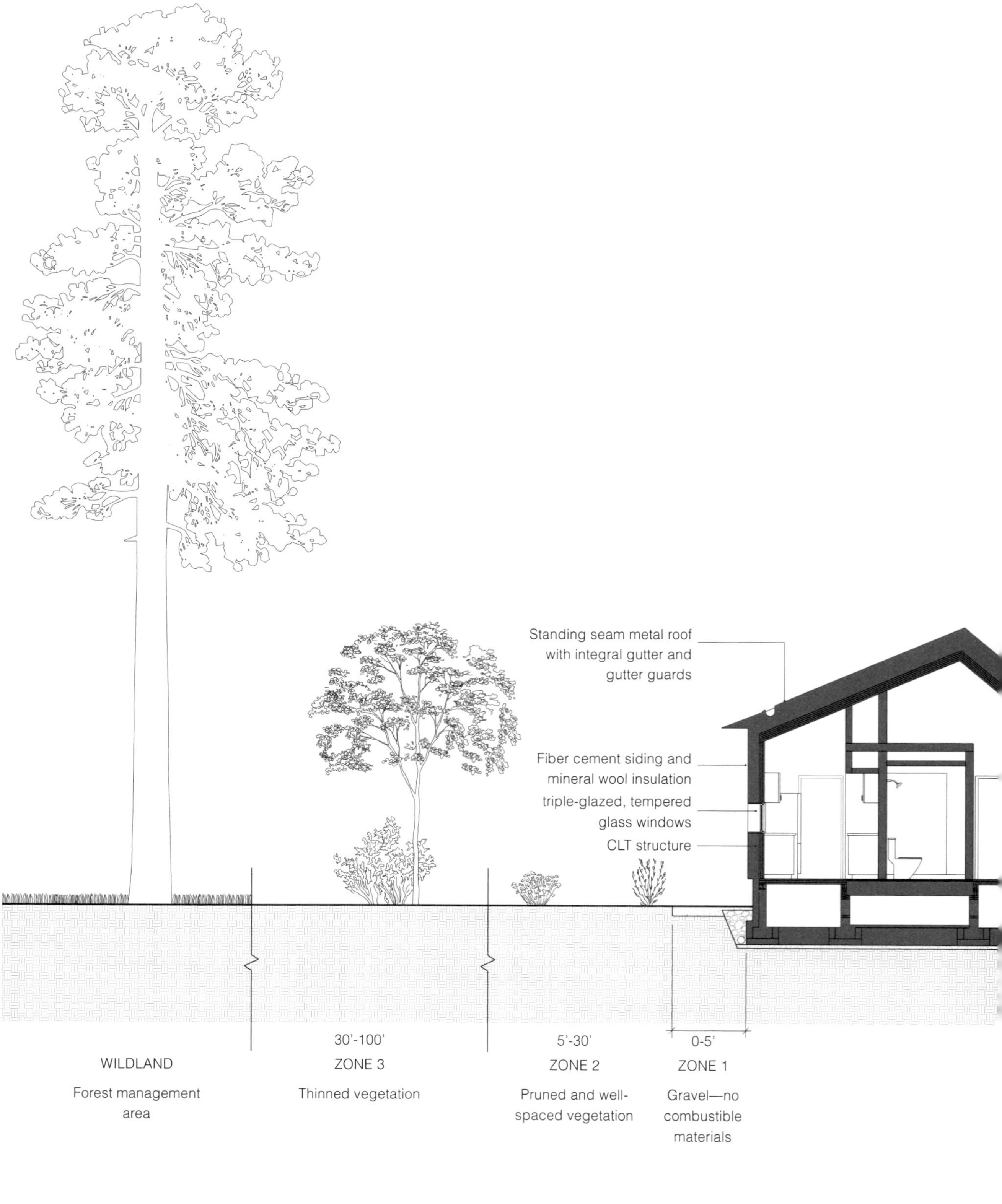
Standing seam metal roof with integral gutter and gutter guards
Fiber cement siding and mineral wool insulation
triple-glazed, tempered glass windows
CLT structure
WILDLAND
Forest management area
30'-100'
ZONE 3
Thinned vegetation
5'-30'
ZONE 2
Pruned and well-spaced vegetation
0-5'
ZONE 1
Gravel—no combustible materials

The homes are virtually airtight, with highly insulated envelopes and high-quality windows. Smoke particulate filters and air-source heat pumps allow for occupant health and comfort even during California's ever-growing fire season. The Sierra systems were based on our own CLTHouse. Gratefully, over the years it has provided a sanctuary of clean air during periods of intense wildfire smoke, and the enclosure and mechanical systems of the Sierra Houses were designed to perform even better.

Of course, chief among the concerns for the rebuilt homes is their safety, if fire, and smoke, return to Greenville. California's Wildlife Urban Interface (WUI) codes guided the designs. The compact forms of the houses—minimizing overhangs and avoiding complex roof forms—are designed so as not to catch loose embers or flammable plant material. Above inches of fire-retardant mineral wool insulation, the house is clad in steel, with a standing-seam roof and walls of hardy, 1/8-inch-thick steel plate. The windows, often a weak point for fire intrusion, are tempered and triple-paned.

Under this exterior armor, the 3-ply CLT provides a final layer of defense against fire. As we know from our work with fire testing, its protective char layer can make the difference between a fire flashing over or burning itself out.

We do not claim that the houses are fire-proof, and with all luck the residents will be able to safely evacuate in the case of another fire. But they are fire-hardened, and if, a raging fire ever passes through again, they are likely to be left standing.

House I

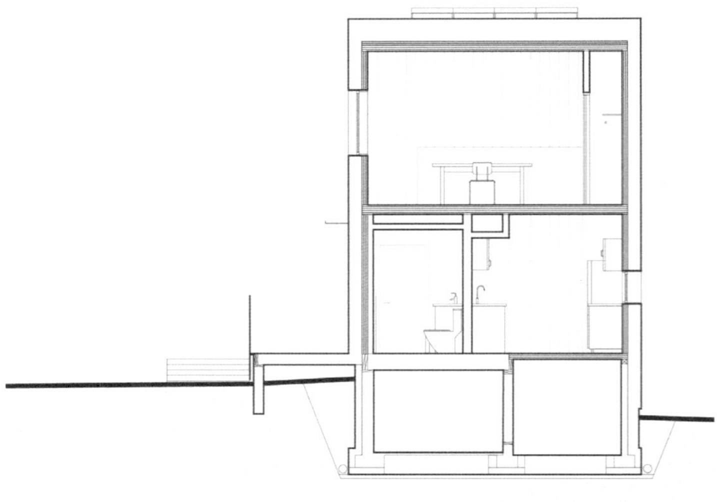

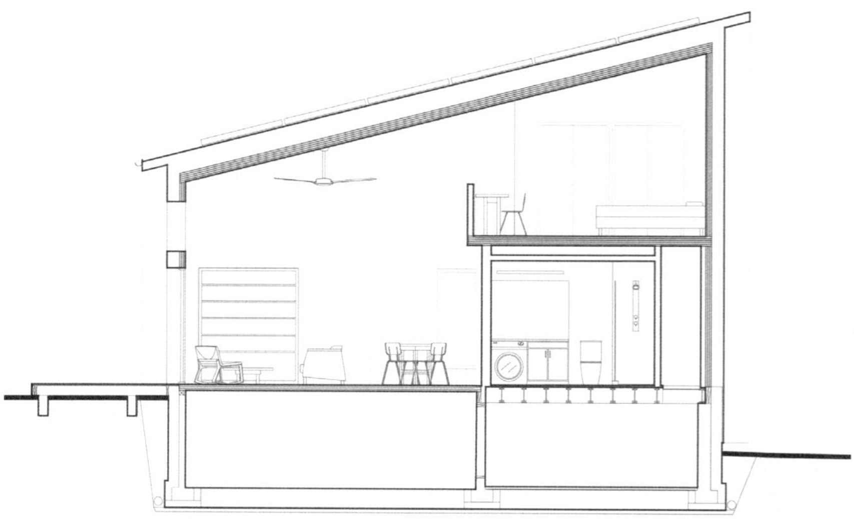

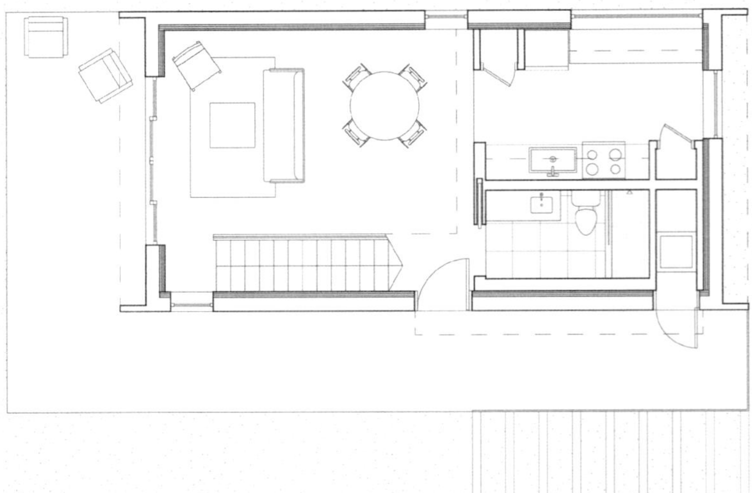

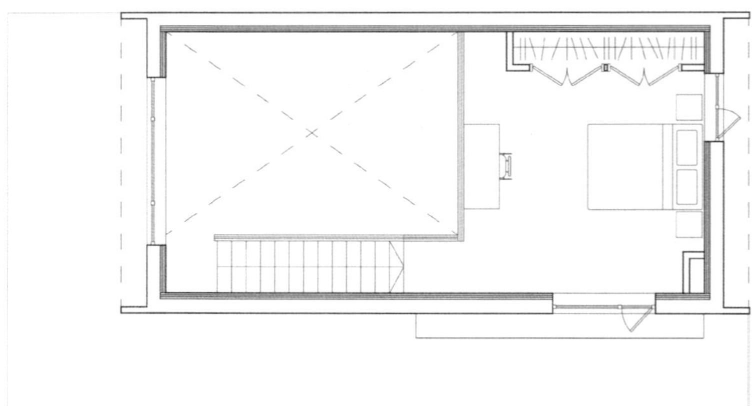

House II & III

House II

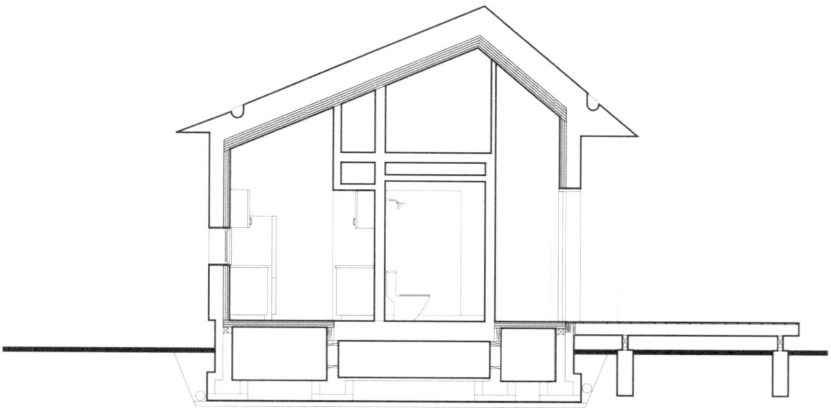

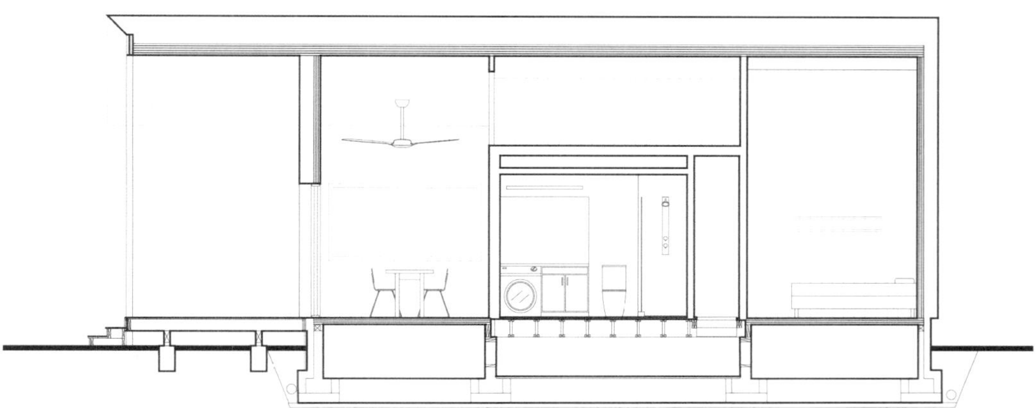

House III

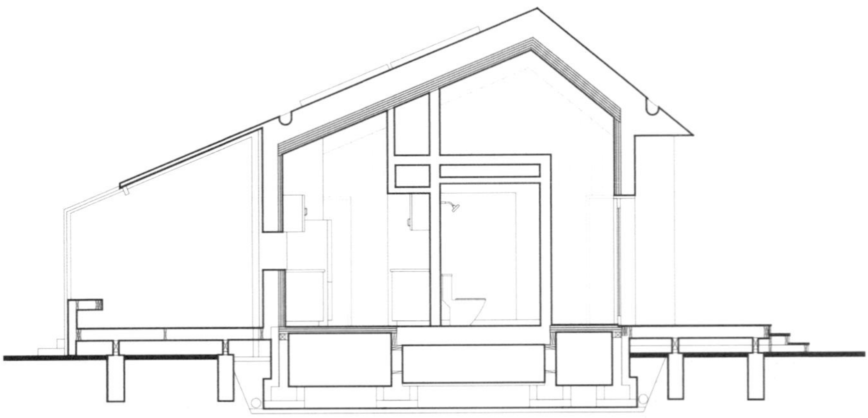

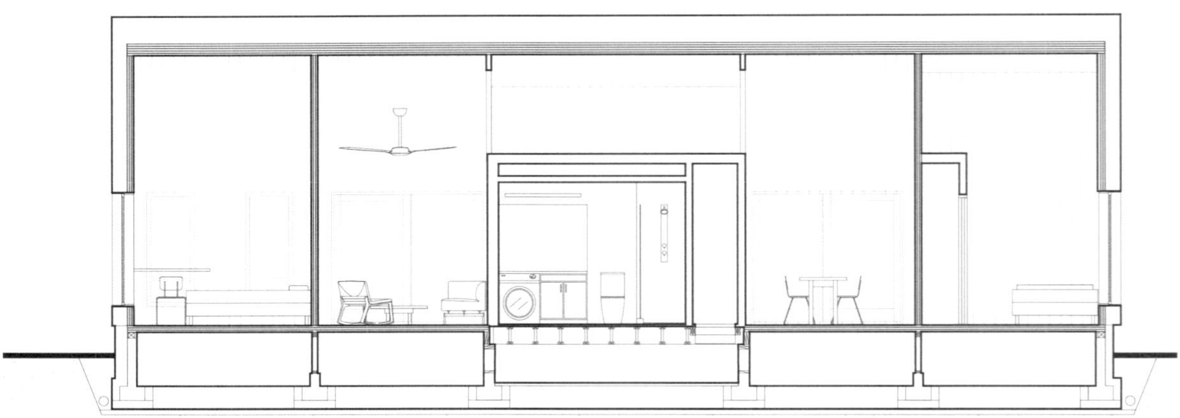

2023–2024
Greenville, California

atelierjones:
Susan Jones, Matt Catrow, Meghan Doring, Eleanor Lewis, Payton Narancic, Jordanna Ebanks, Olivia Champ

Developer:
The Sierra Institute for Community and Environment

Owner:
Roundhouse Council: Mary Joseph, Harvey, Merino, Danny Manning, Charlene Mullen, Shelby Leung, Lorena Gorbet

Structural Engineering:
Harriott Valentine Engineers

Contractor:
Lights Creek Construction

Mass Timber Supplier/Fabricator:
Vaagen Timbers

Venice Biennale Model:
atelierjones and CompanyK

The Roundhouse

Regeneration

One of the many buildings destroyed when the Dixie Fire tore through Greenville was the home of the Greenville Roundhouse Council. A converted 1940s house, it had served as an after-school center for children and a gathering space for the local Maidu Greenville Rancheria. With its loss, not only was an important community space gone, but irreplaceable tribal artifacts and records were lost with it. In early 2023, the Sierra Institute connected us with their leadership council to help them rebuild.

We sat around the kitchen table in a remote house owned by the Sierra Institute, on a cold afternoon in January 2023. The sky was quickly darkening, and there was a sense of urgency in the air as people discussed their plans to travel through the incoming snowstorm. Somewhat impromptu, Jonathan had connected us with the Roundhouse leadership council to discuss ideas about how to rebuild, and we gathered around the kitchen table with slices of lukewarm pizza.

Mary, Harvey, Charlene, and Danny were patient with us. They let us show them our internet-search-collected images of Maidu Roundhouses. They let us explain how round logs were used as vertical columns and horizontal roof beams. We talked about how the opening in the center of the roof let smoke from the fire rise. About how the floors had been dug out from the earth, sunken below the ground outside, allowing people to walk slowly downwards, into the gathering space. They said they appreciated seeing the images and hearing our words.

Then Harvey said, pointing at one image, “And that one is in Chico. I helped build it last year.”

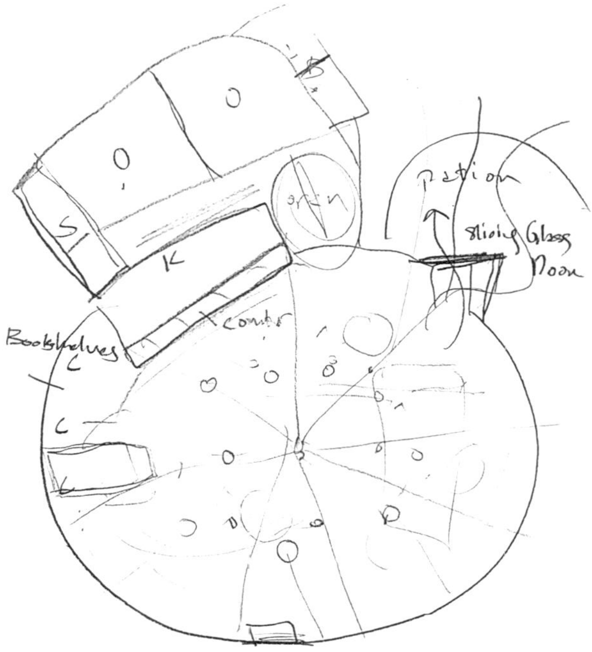

I swallowed hard, deeply humbled at my ignorance.

And then Harvey told us another story. About how the Maidu people would come together to the place where they wanted to build a new roundhouse. They would assemble, hold hands, then move slowly outwards, the circle growing wider and wider, until their arms were completely outstretched. One of them would inscribe the circumference of this circle in the dirt. Then, each person would take a stick or, later, a shovel, and start to excavate this circle, down to knee or waist depth. The dirt would be piled around the outside of the circle, building up the support for the walls. The number of people determined the circumference of the circle of the new roundhouse. Each traditional roundhouse, then, was unique to those who built it, the same people who would go on to use it.

I asked Mary, Executive Director of the Roundhouse Council, if she would draw for us what she wanted. She said she knew exactly what it should look like. She drew a large circle, with a kitchen adjoining the main space, and an office and storage space. And so, the plan was set.

How to translate these simple and profound beginnings into architecture?

How to make construction into architecture? How to make Light on Wood?

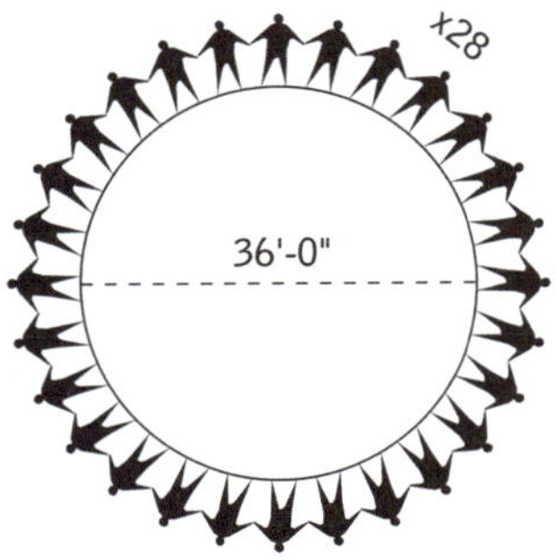

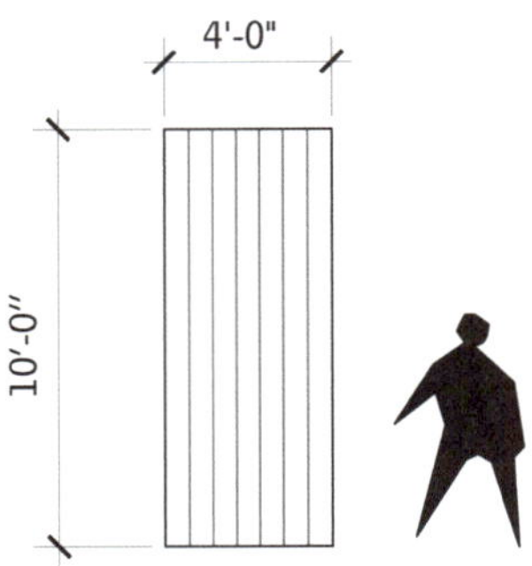

Twenty-eight cross-laminated timber panels define the circle of the central gathering space. Standing side by side at 4 feet wide by 18 feet tall, their proportions are human, creating a community space leave as is. With their soft Douglas fir grain patterns, the panels blend the facets of the polygonal form into an almost seamless, circular drum.

Rising from this base are a series of glulam beams, reaching upward to define an irregular cone above the main space, designed to capture the summer Solstice light. Compound geometries come together at the tops and bottoms of these beams, tilted cone intersecting flat circles. Prefabrication of the mass timber had allowed us to design this geometry with great precision, but, at the last minute, plans for off-site prefabrication of the custom steel compression ring that would join these beams had not come through. Distraught, our team rushed to find a new fabricator, someone with a sophisticated operation who could work precisely from our digital model. Our intrepid contractor, Ed Hammerich, a Greenville local with a small team, assured us that he and his subcontractor could work it out on site. With some hesitation, we agreed.

His team built a wooden formwork, like centering for a Roman arch, and set each custom beam in place. Then, measuring each unique angle, they welded together the steel tension ring that would join them at the top. They raised it up and bolted in the beams. They fit perfectly.

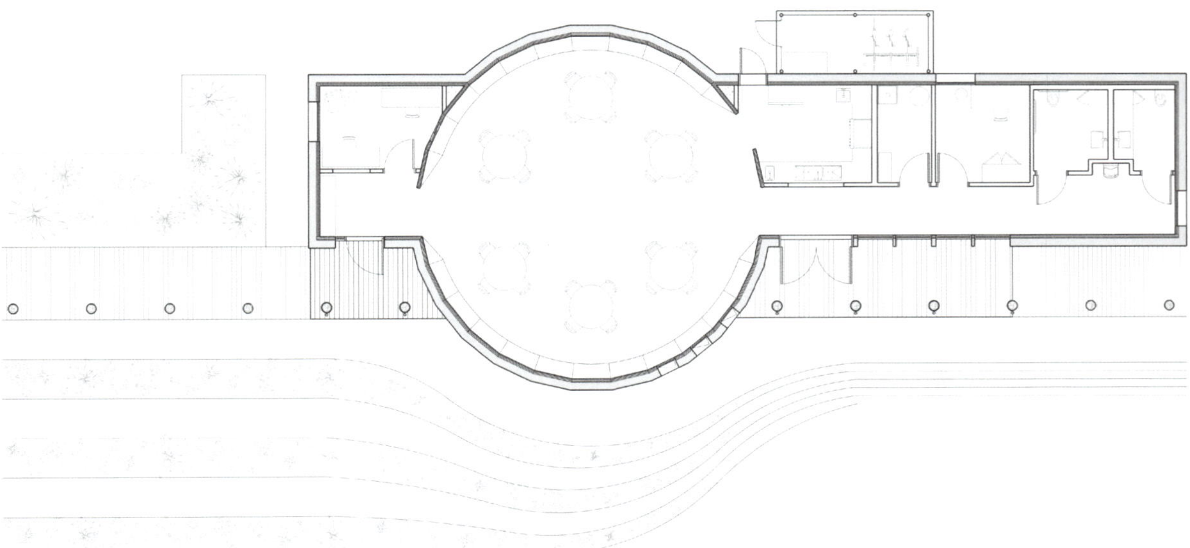

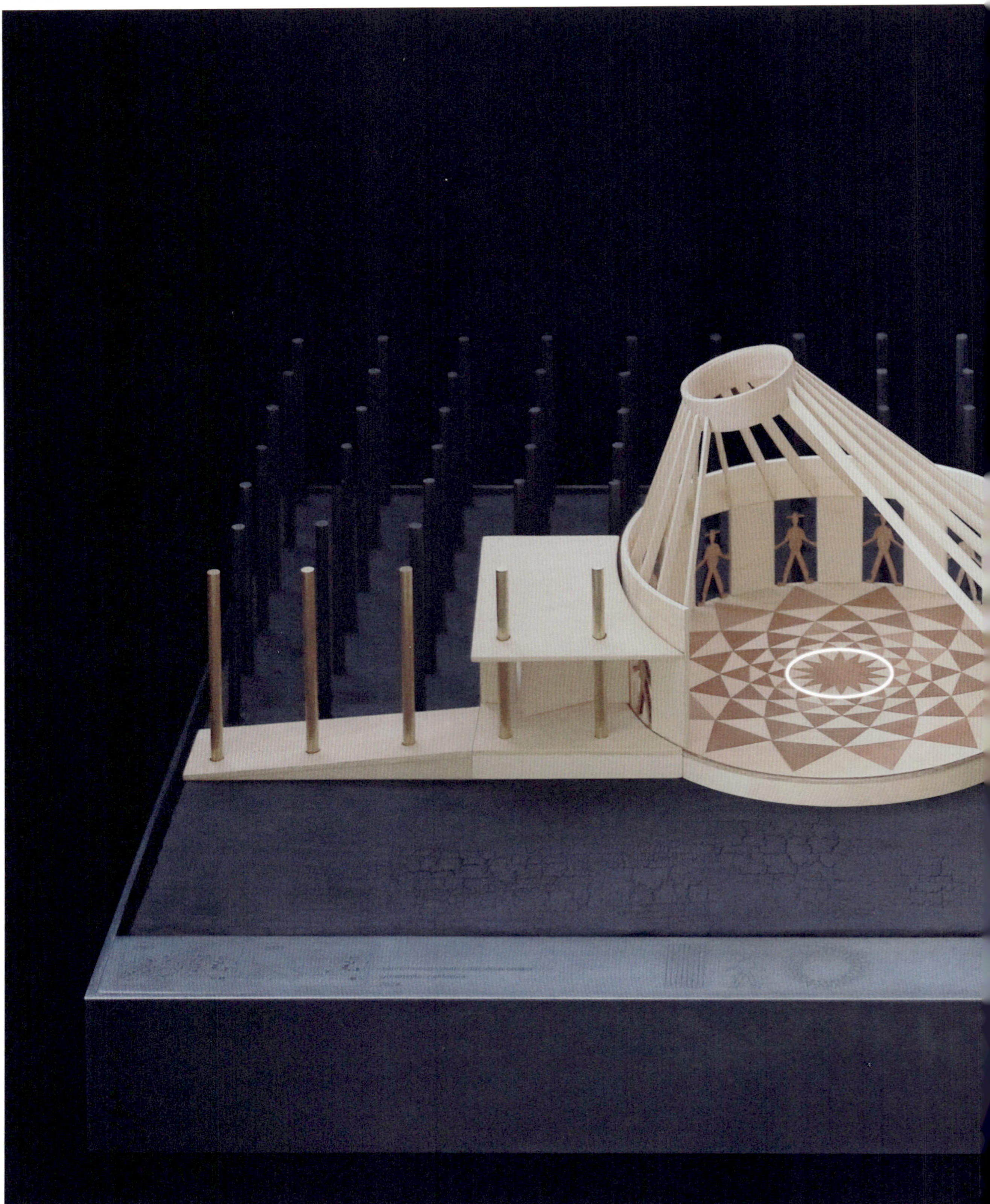

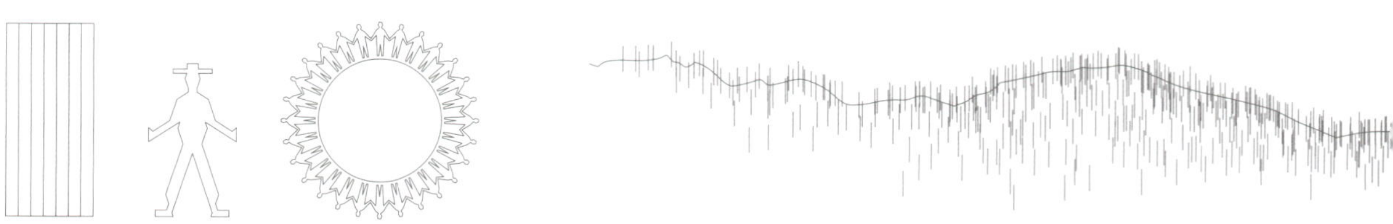

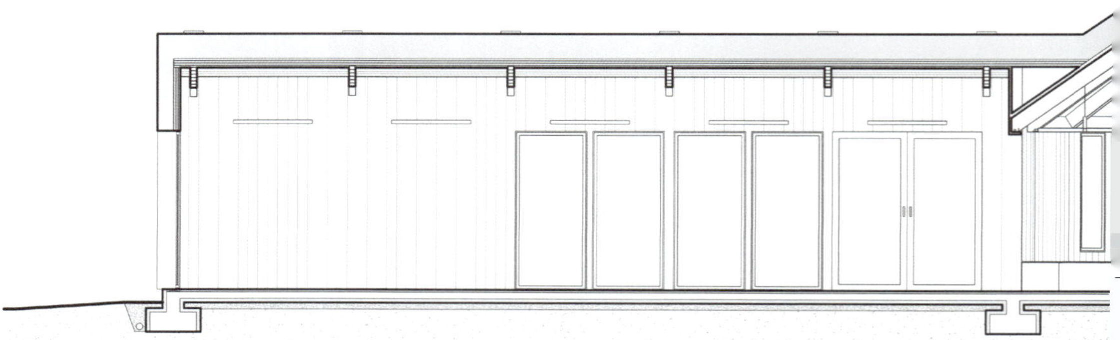

The beams are set off visually against a plywood veneer ceiling, adding to the soft transitions between wooden wall and wooden ceiling. Light falls downward from the central aperture, over the structured beams and down along the faces of the CLT panels. The panels meet a soft plywood bench that rings the space, allowing people to sit with their backs against the walls, with storage space below the seats. Inside some of them are power connections to allow children to charge their laptops when they stop by after school.

The rhythms of the panels are further blurred by the connections of the beams, cascading out from the not-quite-central skylight, off-centered and angled, toward a high-solstice southern light. The steel compression ring supports a round skylight. From this oculus, a disk of light traverses the main space, tracing the wood bench at the base of the drum and illuminating the communal kitchen as the sun travels in the sky.

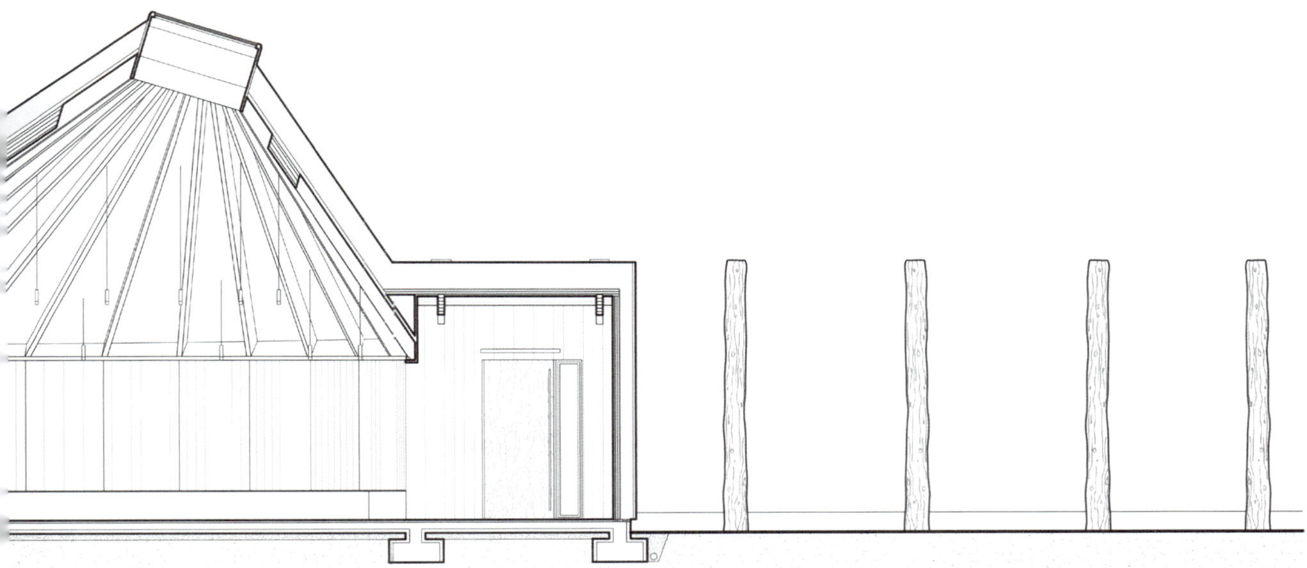

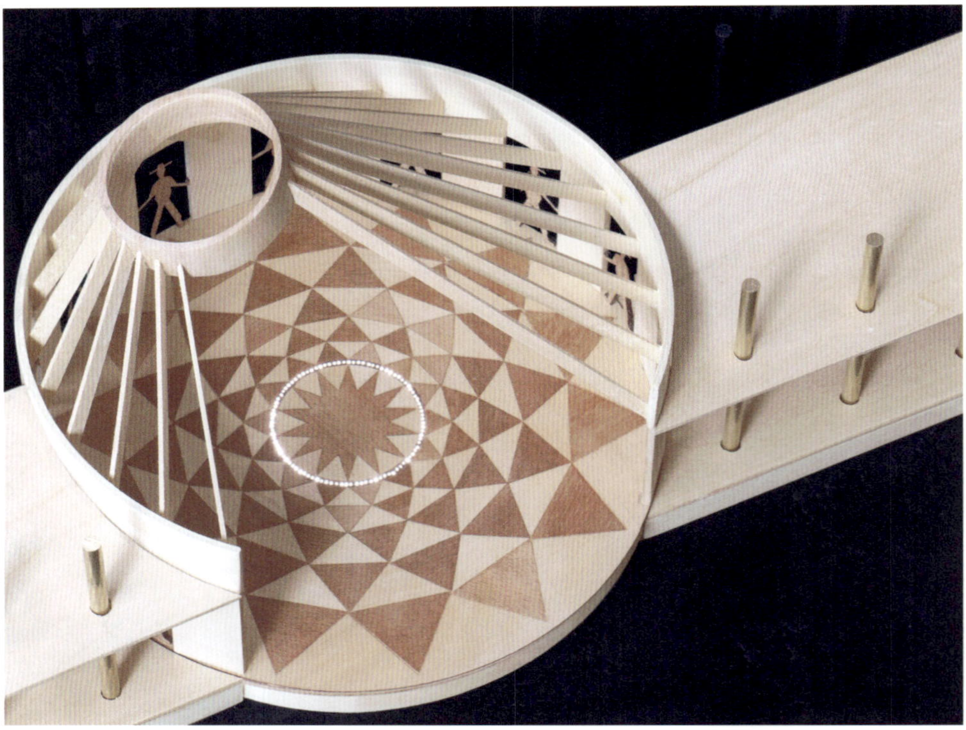

On June 20th, 2024, we joined Mary, Harvey, Danny, Shelby, Jonathan, and others on the porch of the Roundhouse to celebrate its opening. Hundreds of people had gathered from the neighboring communities, and the smell of Charlene's cooking drifted over from across the yard.

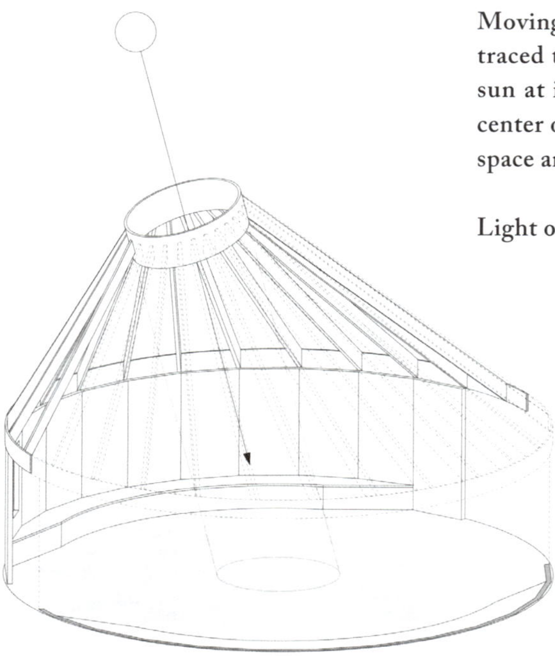

Moving inside to the central space, I watched as the disk of light traced the floor. At the moment of the summer solstice, with the sun at its highest, the angled cone directs the light to the exact center of the round space. The Solstice light falls into the wooden space and becomes a perfect circle at 1:06 pm.

Light on Wood.

EXIT

WIP 300

light
natural light against
natural materials
resonnates with
of our deepest
emotions as
filtering daylight
across, through
deep into spaces
have been created to
hold light, to come
alive in different
to reflect different
times of the day,
the year, reminds
how connected
are to natural
of time and
the words of
kahn, *architectu*
vessel for light.
atelierjones

VI.

True sustainability is going toward an integral way of life, an integral way of thinking

B.V. Doshi

c o d a

Disruption

During the 1990s, the architectural profession and an extended interdisciplinary community was trying to figure out what sustainability would mean for the built environment.

While it would generally coalesce in the early 2000s around lowering buildings' operational energy, early on we were thinking more broadly. The profession was trying to understand where their greatest impact could be made. Emerging out of the crunchy world of the 1970s, where homemade backyard solar panels, living off grid, and the Whole Earth Catalog prevailed, the scale of investigation was generally limited to smaller, individual or academic efforts, often aligned against larger, corporate interests. One of my most exciting projects in high school was designing a solar greenhouse, and later at Stanford I dove into sun angles and kilowatt-hours with renowned Professor Gil Masters.

But design had been somewhat sidelined as a value. It was seen as extraneous, a distraction from the hunt for the more sustainable building. Architecture departments across the county were divided, or worse, staked their grounds firmly, ignoring valuable dialogues from the other perspectives.

As awareness grew in the mid-90s within the world of US corporate architecture, focus on sustainability was often limited to a part-time team member, proudly named "sustainability champion," who could be counted on for information about solar panels, solar vacuum tubes, geothermal pipes, or solar shades. Large carbon-intensive, mechanistic elements that could be easily attached to a project, or detached, as budgets demanded.

As a young architect in the Pacific Northwest, I joined the ranks of those seeking to understand what a more holistic sustainability could mean to the built environment. LEED, PassivHaus, and Built Green standards emerged, along with many others. Learning with and from leaders in the architectural profession, we all stretched to develop a holistic understanding of sustainability, including city planning, mobility, passive solar, water consumption, renewable energy, stormwater, and interior air quality.

Seattle was a hub of energy around sustainability in the built environment, along with Austin, Texas and Portland, Oregon. In 1998, Lucia Athens, after finishing her graduate work in Austin with Pliny Fisk, was hired by the City of Seattle to write the first green building program adopting LEED. Collaborating nationally, Lucia, Tom Paladino, and many others, helped develop and implement early LEED checklists. Led by Margaret Montgomery, we groups of young 30-year-old architects would hold brown bag lunches in corporate meeting rooms to discuss the latest developments in sustainability.

Outside the firm, I had cofounded a little arts non-profit, *space.city*, and in 2002, with the help of Kai-Uwe Bergmann, we raised money to fly over architect Dietmar Eberle of Baumschlager-Eberle to talk PassivHaus at the scale of large commercial and housing buildings. Over my dinner table, Dietmar, Kai and I all encouraged Hamilton Hazlehurst, Development Director at Paul Allen's Vulcan to rebuild Seattle's South Lake Union with LEED Silver buildings. There was energy in the air, and we were all keenly focused on lowering the operational energy that buildings required.

Deepening this broad systems-thinking research by participating in early USGBC Greenbuild conferences in the early 2000s and watching them grow from a few hundred hungry and electrified people in Portland, Oregon in 2004 to massive events in Denver and Chicago with tens of thousands of people, was thrilling.

It was during this time, from 1999-2003, that I became a Design Partner at a large corporate firm in Seattle. In addition to leading design teams, part of my charge was elevating technical design. Broadening my design leadership role to incorporate more sustainability measures, I both mentored teams internally and developed external partnerships with sustainability research institutes, such as the Center for the Built Environment at UC Berkeley. Through these lenses, I led teams designing speculative high-rises and corporate headquarters from Seattle to Sydney to New York City.

But, for me, all that momentum was suddenly challenged one morning, when I was asked to step down from the professional partnership in early 2003. By being asked to leave the formal partnership, one which I had deemed productive, I was personally being characterized as non-essential, indeed, a waste.

In that moment, my personal fear and long-standing lack of confidence in my vision of running an architectural firm, was overwhelmed by the courage to found my own firm, atelierjones. Months later, in the late summer of 2003 in the back room of our home under the Viaduct, I announced a name and email for atelierjones. I assembled a deeply helpful Advisory Board of former mentors and clients from my former firm.

During this deeply introspective period of transition, I purchased a beautifully designed custom edition of William McDonough's seminal book, *Cradle to Cradle*. The complex issues of waste—human-generated waste, from building sites, to food, to water, to wood—began to come into focus. In contrast to the additive modes of sustainability that I was used to, his thinking about the origins of materials and the circularity of waste was catalytic.

Energy from waste. Waste to energy. Certainly, the idea resonated so deeply for me because I had just been deemed inessential, a waste, myself. The concept propelled me forward, and it started to form my vision of what atelierjones could stand for.

I committed atelierjones to understanding deeper, systemic ideas, and bring them to life through design. At the dawn of the 21st century we, the entire community of designers seeking sustainable change, were starting to learn how to both heal and use the waste of the 20th century to rethink our building systems and remake our cities. Bringing design to sustainability, to quote the words of Balkrishna Doshi, became "an inner need, an inner ownership."[33]

33: Balkrishna Doshi, 2023. ECC "Time Space Existence" Interview Series.

But there was work to do.

I committed to an extended research program with I-Sustain, a visionary non-profit founded in Seattle by Patricia Chase and Jayson Antonoff. As a group of public policymakers, private developers, architects, engineers, and contractors, we explored sustainable best practices internationally, and from 2004-2011 we traveled to cities such as Copenhagen, Malmo, Berlin, Curitiba, Rio, Melbourne, and Mexico City. And in 2014, I undertook a similar trip, when I was selected to be a UW Runstad Fellow. Our multi-disciplinary group elected to travel to Columbia, meeting with planners and activists in Bogota and Medellin.

We looked at the intricate relationships between cities, density and transportation, infrastructure and planning policies, and their impacts on our ecological footprints. We looked at green roofs, bioswales, community recycling hubs, waste-to-energy cogeneration plants, walkability, bike infrastructures, bus-rapid transit, open community parks, repurposed landfills, underground thermal cooling, wastewater reuse, and urban agriculture. Exposure to all this opened my eyes to a wide array of design and policy strategies, and we pondered how best to bring them back to the United States.

WES

Waste to Energy

One of the most powerful examples of systems design and policy change was in Curitiba, Brazil. I traveled to the city with I-Sustain in 2006, where the architect-mayor Jaime Lerner had advanced systems of city-making and community in desperately poor neighborhoods. The well-documented story was told to us firsthand, of how bus-rapid-transit systems had sprung up all over the city to provide efficient access to jobs, and public streets and plazas had been made into parks, transforming dangerous neighborhoods.

But the most memorable of these initiatives for me was a community outreach program instituted to deal with waste. Some of the city's poorest neighborhoods were built informally, with streets too narrow for conventional trash collection, and the city lacked the budget for a large-scale recycling plant. Instead, they created a program, aimed at the poorest citizens, to incentivize informal cleanup.

Residents armed with wagons and wheelbarrows could collect garbage and recycling to bring to neighborhood stands. There, they could trade their waste for collection and receive tokens in return. Across the street were trucks, where they could trade these tokens for serious amounts of fresh, healthy produce from the agricultural countryside. The farmers then exchanged the tokens for money, supporting their farms and families.

Local, sustainable farming thrived, families were healthier because of the fresh food, decreasing medical expenses, neighborhoods were cleaner, and the city saved money on waste management. This beautiful system was only possible because the City of Curitiba had started to do something radically different to disrupt the way that waste was perceived. No longer in negative terms, but instead by how much of it could be turned into food and health. Waste had been transformed.

It was also during this time that I began to experiment with different teaching models in my graduate architecture studios at the University of Washington. I taught design research studios on greening our waterfronts, integrating housing and transit networks, managing and cleaning stormwater runoff, designing sustainable homes and hydroponic greenhouses, and how to use landscape to heal our dirty, wasted, post-industrial cities. In these studios, I continually experimented with different models of design and research, including cross-disciplinary collaboration with fellow faculty and students in landscape and urban planning departments.

Our Western Avenue office huddled under the rushing traffic of a 5-story-high concrete viaduct, a veritable billboard for the kind of 20th-century thinking I sought to disrupt. I sought projects that might be able to create change. Not through checklists or labels, but through enduring principles of beauty, delight, and the play of light in space—through desire. We hoped to use this human desire to move hearts and minds (and wallets) toward more sustainable cities and buildings.

Little did I know how long this would take. Especially to make impact at scale. During this torrent of unlearning the destructive practices of the 20th century and relearning new ones, there were many awkward attempts at moving forward.

Of these projects, developed between 2006 and 2011, some were entirely speculative, others connected to real sites and clients. Often honored with design awards, these idea projects became rich vehicles for research, architectural rigor, and developing visual language. The freedom that these projects engendered, along with the underlying technical research required to ensure the design of these systems successfully, was powerful territory for design. All of them sought to disrupt existing ways to design buildings, design cities, design roofs, design with water and with waste. They were vibrant, robust, and thrilling to design.

Below are seven of these idea projects, designed seeking beauty and catalytic change by transforming waste to energy.

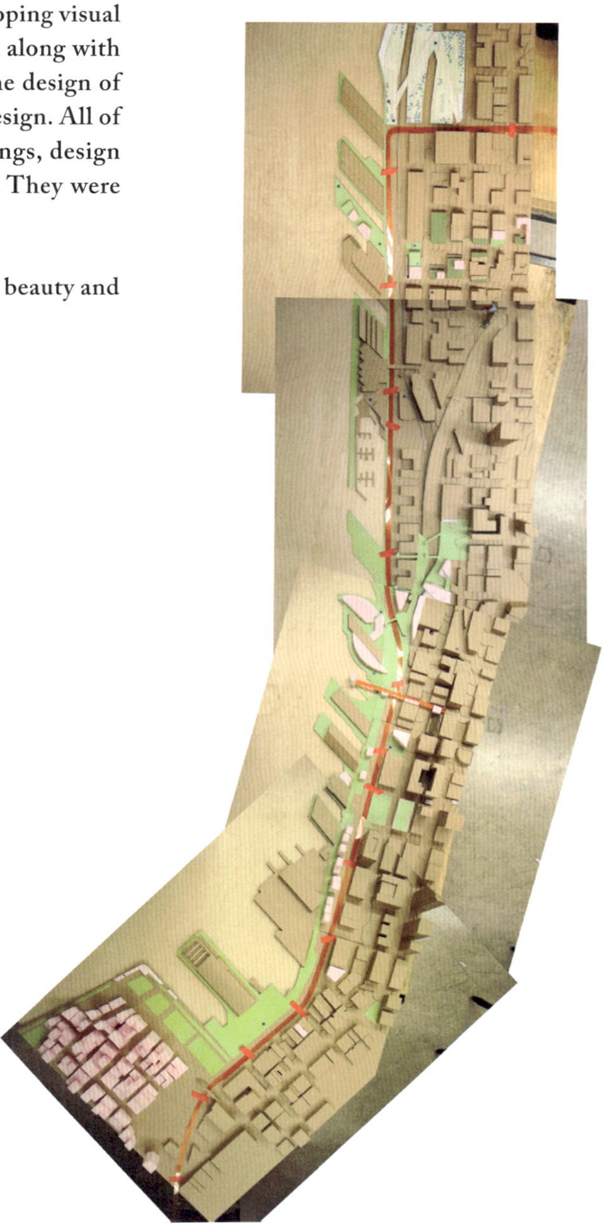

Waste Food: VOShed

Around the time I returned from Brazil, biodiesel was a hot topic. Would we all buy old diesel Mercedes and run them on vegetable oil? Change the world by reusing older, polluting cars, and transforming dirty, wasted fast-food vegetable oil into a substitute for petroleum-based diesel fuels? Cool urban high school kids were starting biodiesel collection stations, and co-ops were springing up all over Seattle.

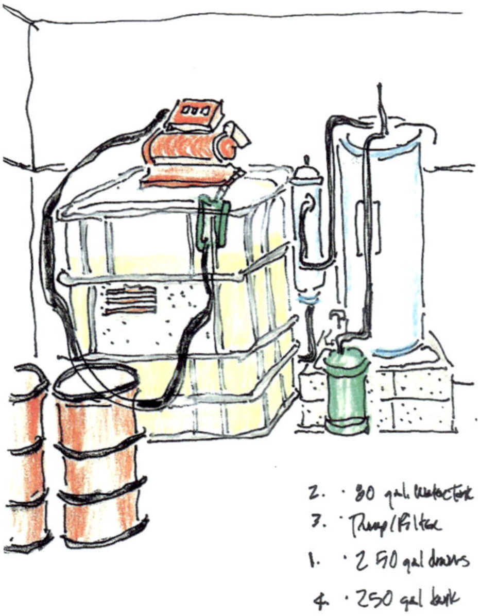

A friend, formerly in tech, owned a bar and hamburger joint. Lots of french fries, lots of vegetable oil. We proposed a small shed for his back alley, to collect and hold the containers to filter the used oil into biodiesel. The VOShed would glow at night when the bar got hopping, a luminous billboard for waste collection, shining on the smokers and cool kids in the alley.

To create this radiant facade, light filtering layers undulated over the containers. These layers themselves carried a deeper message about waste, made from a secondary product from the process of upcycling high-density polyethylene (HDPE) milk jugs. During the manufacturing process of recycling the jugs into furniture, a translucent waste product was emitted and pressed into sheets of lower-grade, recycled HDPE. We built large models made from the waste products of waste products of waste products, to contain more waste, all substituting for one of the most polluting substances on earth – diesel fuel.

The project didn't materialize. Our good client chose not to build it. At least a bit of recognition came our way, when Nader Tehrani and Patricia Patkau gave us an AIASeattle Award for the design. Their confidence gave us momentum, and a bit of publicity, that helped lay the groundwork for a real biodiesel shed.

Propel
Biodiesel
Biodiesel
Customer Parking
COFFEE SHOP

BIODIESEL
Propel
biodiesel

Waste Infrastructure: Propel Biodiesel

Propel, like all startups, was full of dreams, and this one even had capital. Sweden and Norway were investors, and together they had visions of rolling out hundreds of new biodiesel stations all over the United States, taking on the petroleum industry.

Our paths crossed at a CleanTech conference, where I was busy researching waste and biodiesel issues. Those were the early days of tech meeting environmentalism. Connections were made, and we soon had a contract to roll out the first Propel Biodiesel station.

We helped them rebrand, introducing clean white and green into their concepts, and helped them make the whole experience high-tech and user-friendly, without an onsite manager or convenience store. Instead, there was a bed of sunflowers, a reminder of where the biodiesel came from, and a rainwater collection system to keep stormwater from mixing with dirty runoff on the streets. The clean cistern water was used to irrigate the sunflowers, in another virtuous circle of waste – from waste stormwater to the new fuels that could replace petroleum.

For a while I thought we might have a system of royalties in place that would fuel our small firm for decades. I explored patents, we built five more stations locally, fittingly on wasted areas of existing real gas stations. And then, well... They changed leadership, moved their headquarters to Sacramento, and then, even worse, 2008 hit. The Swedes and Norwegians went home. All we had left to keep us going through the dark nights ahead was the luminosity of the beautiful systems diagrams.

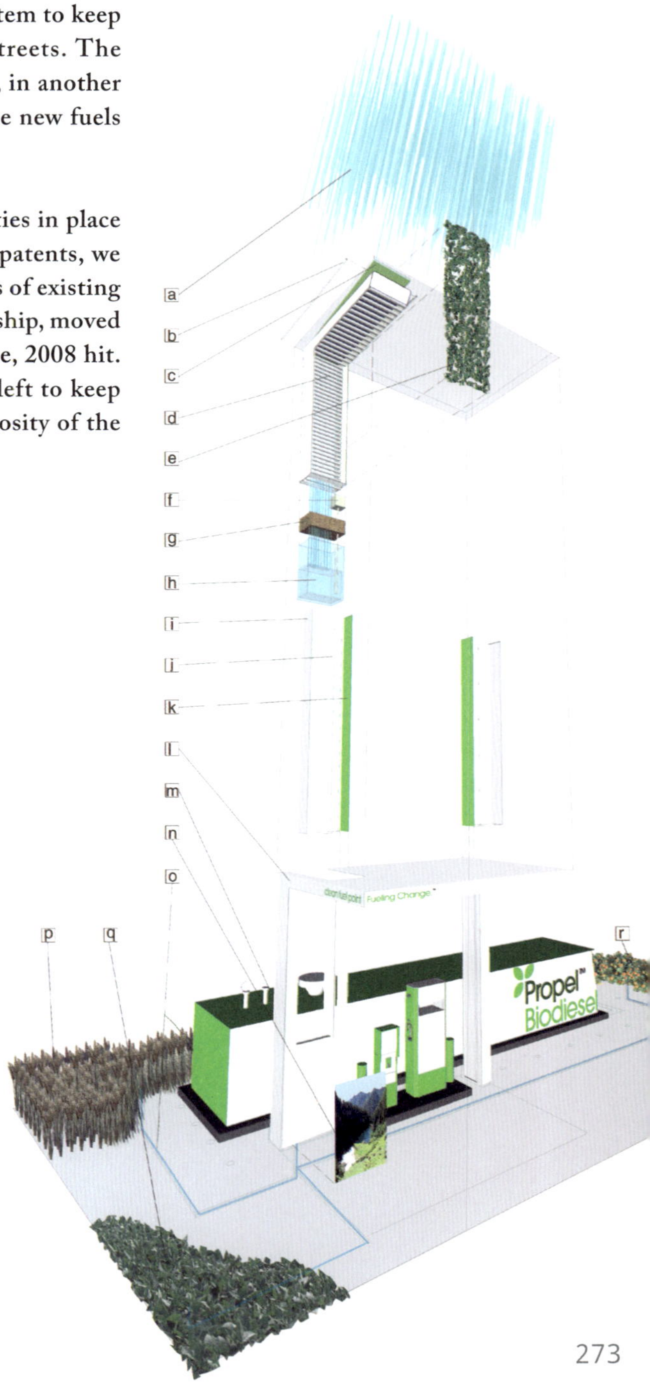

Legend

a. Rainwater
b. LED light fixture
c. Translucent lexon sheet
d. Perforated louvers
e. Plant watered by cistern
f. Water pump
g. Soil
h. Water cistern
i. Steel light box
j. LED fixture
k. Lexon sheet
l. Steel canopy and frame
m. Biofuel tank
n. Local artwork
o. Underground water pipes
p. Wheat
q. Soy
r. Safflower

Waste Roofs: Starbucks Headquarters

Building on the inspiring relationships and research built from the trips with I-Sustain starting in 2004, I continued to explore green roofs and their potential for stormwater use with Kevin Daniels, a brilliant real estate executive who became a good friend. He was part of the company that owned a huge brick building, formerly a Sears warehouse, that housed the headquarters for a local coffee company called Starbucks.

In 2007, Kevin hired atelierjones to do the LEED Existing Building certification on the renovated headquarters. We were grateful for the work, but it was tedious, involving collecting thousands of records of utility bills, water, gas and electricity. We were all thrilled when our team finally obtained a gold-level certification, one of the very first, for one of the largest buildings in the country.

In parallel, Starbucks' CEO Howard Schultz was contemplating another transformation. As the story was told to me, Schultz's tenth-floor office looked down on a 1990s parking garage. Behind the 1-acre rooftop was a stunning view of the Seattle skyline and Elliott Bay, with the crisp Olympic mountains in the background. Schultz's vision was a rooftop garden where his 4,000 employees could have lunch and he could hold all-hands meetings to address the company. So we began, first meeting with the city to secure permission to create a large, outdoor assembly space on top of the garage. The garage had been built on fill—dirt sluiced down from First Hill in the early 1900s—and they were wary of its stability given Seattle's high seismic zone. Patiently, with our structural engineers, we negotiated multiple upgrades to the structure and additional exits for a maximum of 900 employees at a time.

We worked with landscape architects to design four different versions of the 1-acre roof-turned-garden. We were inspired by the beautiful and mysterious "Mima mound" landscapes of the Pacific Northwest, and created a field of 6-foot-high mounds, sheltering fire pits and small outdoor meeting areas. In the center, a paved plaza with a speaking platform could accommodate large events. Solar panels and micro wind turbines would provide electricity. The other schemes were progressively more economical, with the last option being a simple green roof of sedum on four inches of soil.

All the schemes would retain the water during rain events, until the soggy fill around the building could drain it without overwhelming the combined Sewer/Stormwater system. Our research in the 2004 UW Waterfront studio had dived deep into understanding these systems, where rain events commonly flushed copious amounts of raw sewage into Elliott Bay whenever the existing capacity was overwhelmed.

We collaborated with our civil engineers, landscape architects, and Seattle Public Utilities to better understand how to retain stormwater during storm events, for the good of keeping Elliott Bay cleaner. We wrote grants to SPU to trade credit for the reduced runoff and help pay for the system.

Just as we carefully calibrated and priced the menu of options—from the beautiful $4M Mima-Mound scheme to the restrained $1.5M sedum green roof—the recession hit. In early 2009, the project came to a close for lack of funding. Neither scheme would be built.

Waste Sites: Deployable Greenhouses

Just before the recession hit, I had the idea to buy a piece of real estate in Seattle. It was the summer of 2008, everyone was buying real estate and it seemed like soon there might not be any left in Seattle.

The Washington State Department of Transportation had finished spending billions of dollars rebuilding the I-90 floating bridge over Lake Washington, and they had leftover property on the land above the tunnels, which they put up for auction. We entered the auction for a tiny site near Judkins Park and won. Within the next six months, the market value of the site cratered by half.

While balancing mortgage payments, we decided that, in lieu of any immediate economic value, we could at least use it as a community garden. We held a community block party with a local policeman and friend, and, together, we cleared the blackberries and started digging down with our shovels. After just a few inches, we started hearing clangs. More clangs. Turns out, we were hitting asphalt, and we realized that the site had been an abandoned alley, long left to rewild into the city. A waste WSDOT site that had been a waste site.

In digging through the overgrown blackberries, surrounded by accumulated trash, we had to accept that reclaiming of former rights-of-ways, like our former alley turned wildland, might have other urban waste elements, such as toxic soils, dog waste, diesel fumes and a lot of other things that one wouldn't necessarily like in the soil when trying to grow tomatoes. And another questions emerged, common to urban P-Patches everywhere. How would we get water to the plants in dry seasons without an expensive utility connection?

What to do?

The idea of a Deployable Greenhouse was born. Rather than using the thin, polluted soil of the site, we could use recycled plastic bags as raised beds and fill them with soil. We met with the principal of the elementary school across the street and discussed starting a program for the students to plant and nourish the child-sized beds. The greenhouses, polyethylene tents, would capture stormwater for irrigation and shelter the plants throughout the school year, so that kids could plant at the beginning of the school year in the late summer and harvest throughout the fall, winter and spring, literally eating the fruits of their labors.

We also engaged with AIA Seattle and the City of Seattle to consider a change to the land use codes to allow greenhouses in more areas, including in rights-of-way. We built a quarter-scale model and partnered with a local non-profit, AlleyCat Acres, to build a full-sized prototype. We priced it out and started a Kickstarter campaign, hoping to build hundreds of them. It raised $1,300, enough to build just two. While we won another AIA award, this time from Sheila O'Donnell and Giles Saucier, it was clear we needed to move on again.

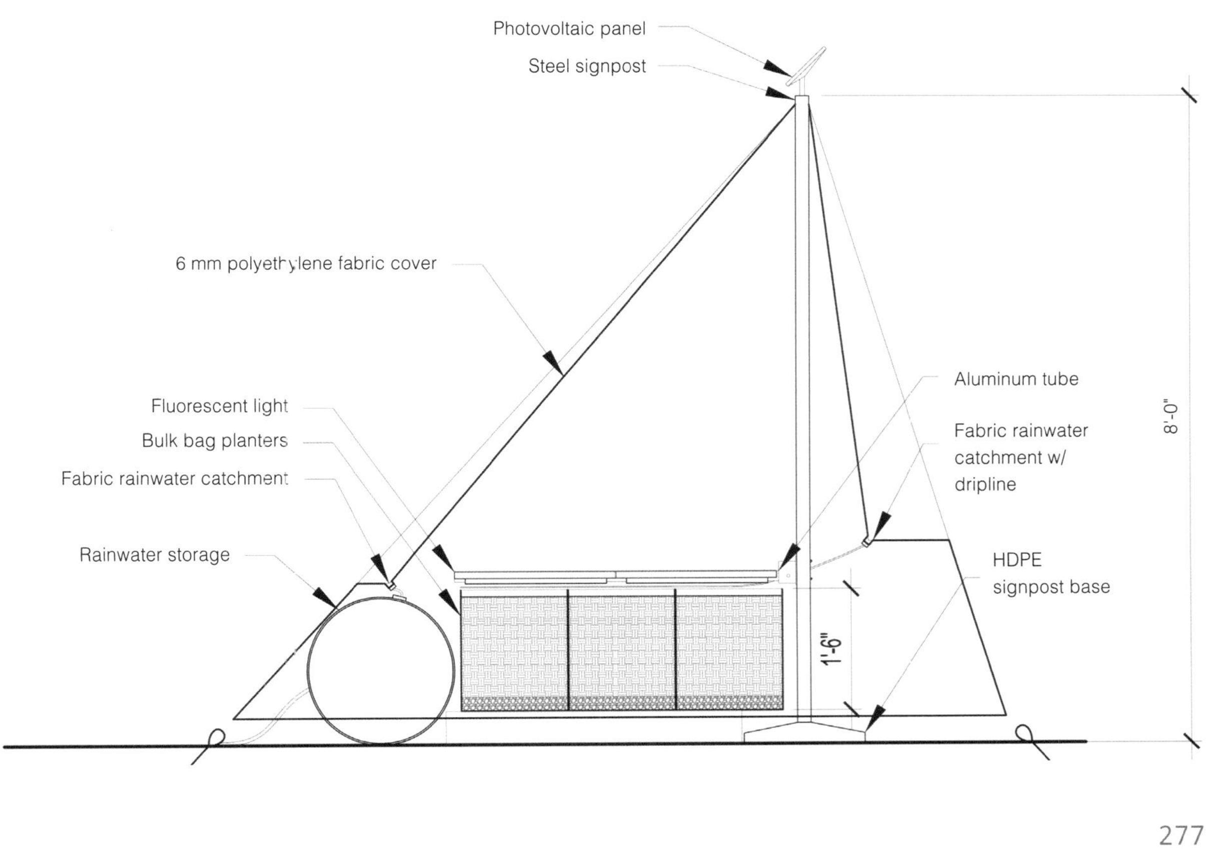

Waste Facades: Vertical Greenhouses

Despite neither project moving ahead, our efforts developing the Deployable Greenhouses and Starbucks Greenroof led to a new collaboration later that year, working again with Kevin Daniels. Now with his own company, he was developing a new mixed-use, high-rise project next to the new Seattle football stadium. Working with a newly created Public Facilities District, led by visionary King County Executive, Dow Constantine he had negotiated an agreement to create a green wall covering up the required six-story parking garage facing the stadium, in exchange for the development rights of the north half of the lot.

But the agreement was not specific about what exactly that "green wall" entailed, and the question intrigued us immensely. We researched emerging explorations into urban agriculture, including technologically advanced projects combining European twin-facade technologies with vertical greenhouses.[34] We thought the idea would work very well, adapted to cover the gaping front of our parking garage. So instead of greening the roof of a parking garage, as we had at Starbucks, we greened the wall of a parking garage to cover up cars with greenery and pull as much of their carbon dioxide from the air as possible, creating a green visual amenity for people in the city.

34: Kiss Cathcart

We researched existing greenhouse hydroponics systems, from the Ebb and Flow technique to the Nutrient-Flow Technique (NFT) system and found this existing rotary technology—originally developed for drycleaners—that a company called Verticrop was using for vertical greenhouses. We adapted this technology for the vertical parking garage facade, altering the system so that the maintenance and harvesting could be done from inside the parking garage, rather than on an independent structure on the exterior. Instead, the dry cleaner motors would rotate the entire stack of planters up, down, and around, giving a person standing in the garage, their back to a level full of cars, access to each plant individually.

Housed in a lightweight translucent enclosure of recycled ETFE, the system would run hydroponically, using the highly efficient NFT system, where a concentrated solution of water and nutrients is pumped through trays. Using eight times less water than conventional agriculture, the crops would grow with bare roots, eliminating the need for soil. The water that was needed could come from stormwater, collected on the roof of the garage.

The waste facade would become a new kind of vertical field, growing bright greens for the restaurant below, covering up the unsightly garage, feeding hungry football fans, and creating a billboard beckoning us to change our disconnected relationship to food in our urban lives.

But then Daniels Development had to execute on other parts of their intricate agreement with King County, and suddenly both capital and an operating management system were lacking. Kevin and his team would go on to be responsible for some very important buildings in Pioneer Square, transforming the historic heart of our city, but this particular vision was not to be.

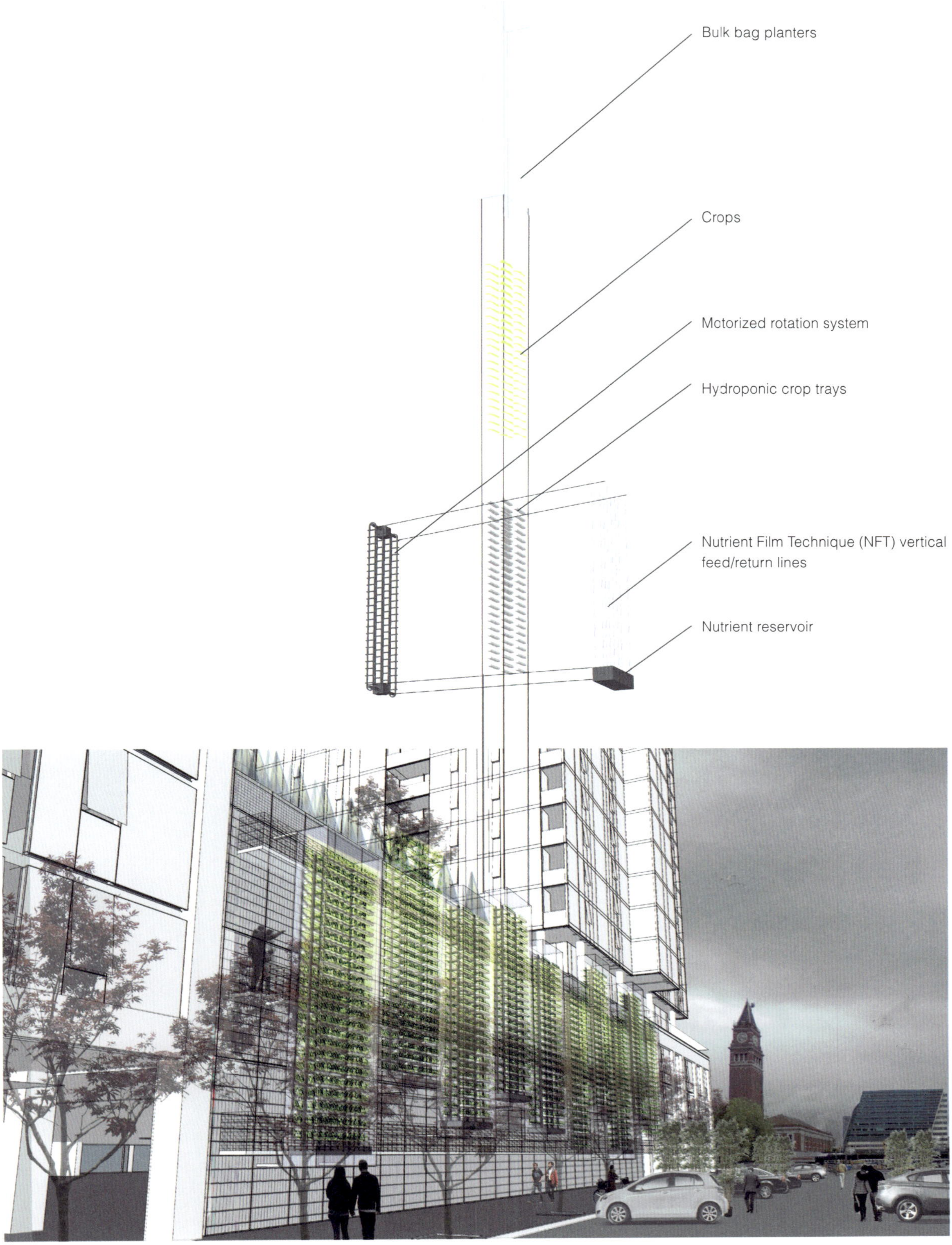

Waste Water: Living City Competition

By 2011, although the Great Recession was ebbing away on the east coast, it was just starting to hit Seattle with full force. In that cold January, I decided that all we could do was enter a competition with some good friends, Lesley Bain of Weinstein AU and Ray Gastil, the former City Planning Director of Manhattan and Seattle and later, Pittsburgh.

The International Living Future Institute, the farsighted organization that had developed the Living Building Challenge (LBC) in 2006, was hosting a Living City Competition. The idea competition was to apply the principles of the building-scaled LBC to the urban scale and envision new ways to lighten the ecological footprints of our cities.

With the momentum of our work exploring water issues in Pioneer Square, we decided to envision the entire historic neighborhood as a giant sponge, absorbing and cleaning wastewater. We proposed upgrading the roofs of hundreds of historic buildings to carry an extra 15 pounds per square foot, creating a carpet of green roofs that would slow down the fall of water. We would excavate existing brick streets to create canals, opening the storied underbelly of historic Seattle to allow stormwater into the bowels of the historic district.

During the six weeks of the Ideas Competition, the dialogue was rich, and the drawings intricate. We ended up winning a Living City Community Award from Jason McLennon, and we left the Vancouver awards ceremony inspired.

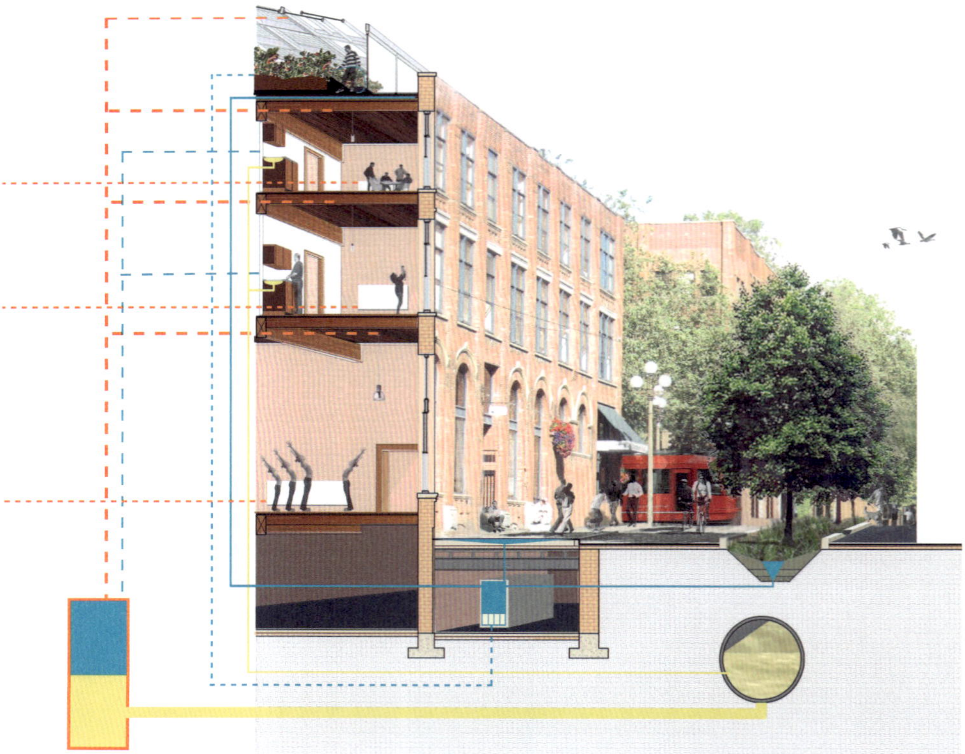

SEAHAWKS
STADIUM

Disruption is a Process

All of these idea projects sought *disruption*. Disruption in our relationships to ecological systems from food, to waste, to water, to transportation, to housing. They aspired to disrupt the way we build and live. While they won awards and kept our spirits high, they were ultimately inert and stayed on the shelves of our architectural firm. None of them went forward. None of them were built.

The term *disruption*, especially when paired with *innovation*, is one that is overly repeated, especially in the technology sector. Clay Christenson, a Harvard Business School professor who originated this usage of the term, cautions about its over-use and potential dilution of meaning.[35] One of his major points is that disruption is not static; disruption is a process that happens over time. And like all thoughtful architects, we get process! Architectural practice is just that—a practice toward getting it right.

35: Clay Christensen, 2015. "What is Disruptive Innovation?" Published in *Harvard Business Review.*

Our idea projects all had disruptive ambitions, and at a research and design level, we learned tremendously from them. They also gave me a sense of how disruption might or might not occur. The success of a design idea is dependent on so many factors beyond the basic merits of its design innovation.

From the timing of the proposal, the cultural, regulatory, professional, or academic landscape at which it arrives, to the appetite of the principals for risk-taking, their access to capital, small scale or global—all of these factors ultimately had more impact on a strategy to succeed at scale than the idea itself.

Only once I focused on mass timber, first at a small scale, designing the experimental CLTHouse for our family of four, putting personal funds at risk to complete it, did the dynamic change considerably. The practice of mass timber was new to the United States, but emerging in North America, and it could be implemented successfully. And even then, it would have stayed just a private house, had I not ventured outwards to collaborate again and again, first with the University of Washington, then our mass timber fabricator and contractors, then with journalists interested in the lower carbon footprint, then with local non-profits, then with their funders, then the State Legislature. The circles grew wider and wider. And that was only in the first year after the house was built.

I learned, again and again, that a broader systemic and clear collaboration with partners outside of architecture helped push aligned goals forward. From the United States Forest Service, University of Washington Department of Architecture, the UW School of Environmental Forest Sciences, the Washington State Legislature, Forterra, the US Endowment for Forestry and Communities, the Nature Conservancy, the International Code Council, the Softwood Lumber Board, the American Wood Council, the Research Institute of Sweden, the American Institute of Architects, to the myriad fabricators, contractors, engineers and consultants specializing in mass timber, and our often miraculous non-profit clients, especially Community Roots Housing, The Sierra Institute for Community and Environment, and the Maidu Greenville Rancheria.

It was not until we all joined hands in a circle and walked outwards together that we were able to create a community of action and impact that was much larger than ourselves.

Disruption is a process.

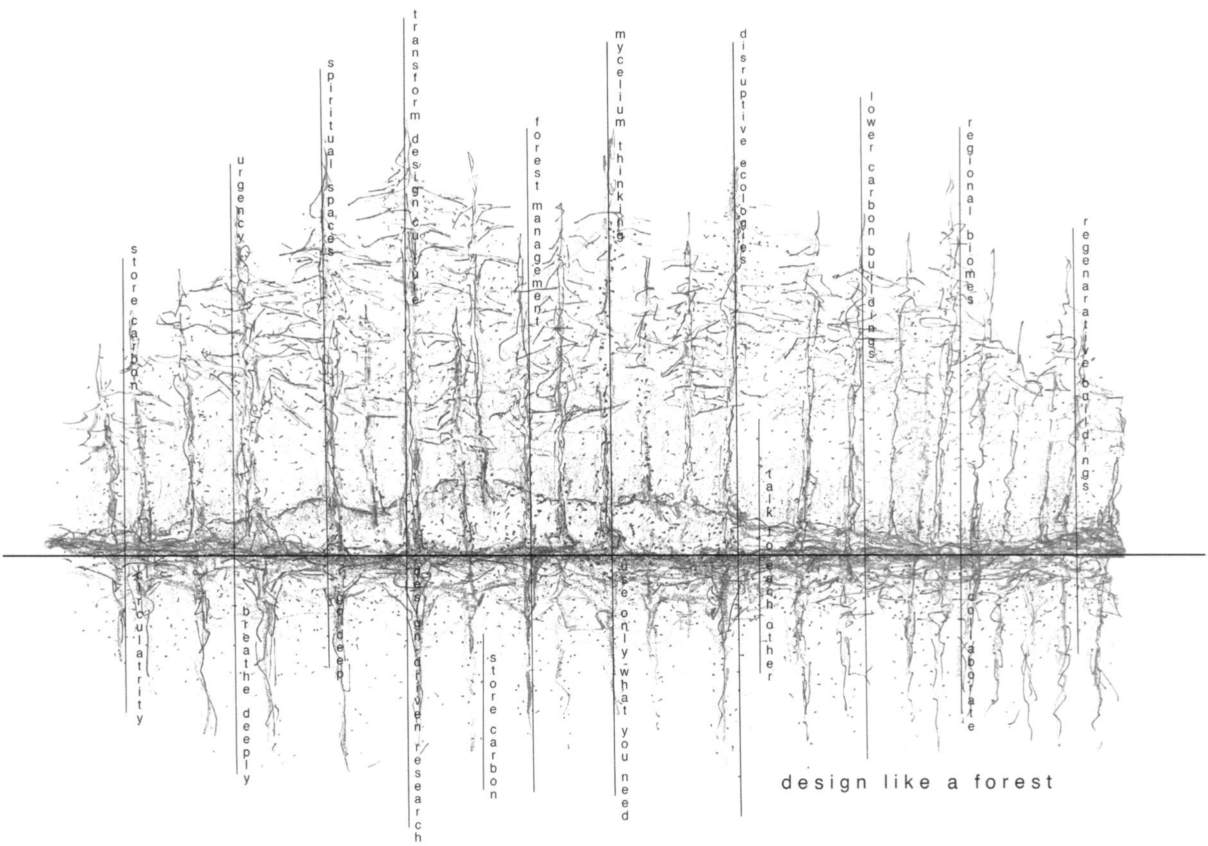

A Livable Future Now

The large, languid curve of the trunk of the Douglas fir tree stirred a memory. Of an earlier photo, snapped in the deep heart of winter. Looking closely at the ridged, deeply incised bark, two series of arcs emerge, arcing upwards. I look more closely. Then back to the Waste Ecologies picture, from ten years before. The same sinuous ridged double arcs.

This grand tree in the center, growing with great health and energy was the same deeply encircled, wasted gray bark of the Douglas Fir I had called my sister in 2015. In March 2025, energetic teams from WADNR came in and created space by clearing the myriad of overstocked, naturally regenerated western hemlocks from around her grand trunk. Standing back, I could see how she soared. Ten years of work had brought light down into the forest.

Against the backdrop of the million acres burning in Canada right now, we believe that forests can become healthier through scalable management, reintroducing the human hand and human-induced fire, following indigenous ways of old. The joy of seeing that vision realized for this glorious, once-trapped 60-year-old tree is thrilling.

What will the next ten years bring?

Architecture must live in the present. We must actively engage with present conditions, adapting to them. Design for *a livable future now.*

Today, on our desks in the office are the traditional stuff of architecture. Modular accessory dwelling units and fire-hardened CLT houses. Custom homes and workforce townhouses. Twelve-story timber apartments that could provide thousands of warm, light-filled units. All using regionally sourced mass timber from well-managed forests.

But more important are the stories these projects tell, and their peripheral impacts.

waste ecologies: 2025

Working in three different regional biomes under three different grants—federal, state, and county, working with two different universities—we help develop supply and demand for workforce housing, designed and built from local local, often underutilized wood. We create demand for small mills healthy, both tribal and enterprise-levels. We create innovative products like DLT, CLT and thermally modified CLT, out of wood species that commercial mills won't accept. From the perennially overstocked western hemlock, milled by the Makah tribe on the very tip of western Washington, to the Ponderosa pine facing drought and fire in the Sierra Nevadas, and the Douglas fir in Humboldt County, which, while commercially viable, could make a higher value, more durable, prefabricated DLT. Design helps drive demand.

Engaging with the present forces us to ask how our cities and homes could become healthier, especially in the wake of the Los Angeles fires in January 2025. How to reintroduce a greater proportion of thoughtfully sourced bio-based materials into their structure, their walls, their ceilings, roofs, and insulation? So that if they burn, a less toxic waste site of plastic and toxins isn't left behind. And, fire-hardened, they are less likely to burn in the first place.

waste ecologies: 2015

We can design buildings today that will last longer than 30-50 years. And we can design today, supplying clues, in the simple way we build them, so that, some 200 years later, during future disassembly, they can be taken apart more easily, reusing their parts to keep their stored carbon out of the atmosphere for hundreds of years more.

Looking back along the path, with its layers and layers of commitment, work, and collaboration, joy, light and space merge seamlessly. Moments of light falling through the structure of a forest, evolve into 40-foot-high walls of wood, and again into hundreds of wooden apartments and homes for people to live within nature, in cities, touching wood when they awake in the morning. Now, through helping write and codify regulations and fire tests, we will be able to build more and more of these homes at all scales. Within the city, small rural towns, people can live within more natural environments, surrounded by healthy materials.

As architects, we can both ameliorate damage and repair the excesses of the 20th century and regenerate hope and beauty for the 21st.

Timeline

The voice that emerged over the course of writing *Light on Wood* was an accessible one, made for people to hear and experience, through a personal lens. The stories I found myself writing about were not meant to be elusive or remarkable, but as clear and simple as possible. They are leaps taken along a primarily professional path, told through a personal voice.

This timeline also presents primarily professional milestones, but, like the writing, the pathway is also interwoven with personal events, facts and photos. It is meant to give depth to the joy, demands and endurance necessary for the emergence of an architect, and to give hope to the talented young architect.

Design

Construction

Research

Susan H Jones

1960 1961 1962 1963 1964 1965 1966 1967 1968 1969

Lafayette Rogan Jones Sr. acquires Mt. Constitution site on Orcas Island

SHJ born, in Chicago, Illinois to Lafayette Rogan Jones Jr. and Ann Catherine Kingsbury

Family moves back to Bellingham, WA

Family builds a home designed by Sid Nesbit, Architect

Viewcrest House, Bellingham, WA
Architect Sid Nesbit

(Herald photo by Don Anderson)

As temperatures dip into the chilly 20s, Susan Jones, a senior at Sehome High School, carefully checks the temperature inside her experimental, solar-heated greenhouse. If the scaled-down version proves to be practical, it is hoped a larger greenhouse can be built at the school.

Sunday Herald, Bellingham, Wash. Nov. 12, 1978 3A

Solar Greenhouse

Solar Greenhouse at Sehome High School

1970 1971 1972 1973 1974 1975 1976 1977 1978 1979

Family builds a home to accomodate Rogan's illness

Lafayette Rogan Jones Jr. dies from multiple sclerosis

Susan works part-time for Sid Nesbit, Architect in Bellingham, WA

Harvard GSD

Fisch Fisch Fisch

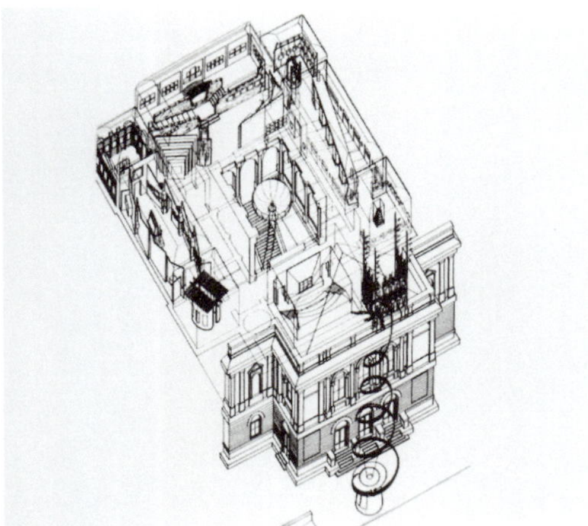

Biedermeier Austellung

Harvard GSD Thesis, thesis advisors Alvaro Siza and Wilfried Wang

Palmers Prototype Shop, Vienna - *Atelier Podrecca*

Fisch Fisch Fisch, Vienna - *with Gerhard Luckner*

Druck Pavilion, Biedermeier Austellung, Vienna - *Atelier Podrecca*

1980 1981 1982 1983 1984 1985 1986 1987 1988 1989

B.A. Philosophy, Stanford University

M.Arch, Harvard GSD

Susan works for The Burdick Group, Industrial Designers in San Francisco, CA

Works for Atelier Podrecca, Vienna, Austria

Berlin Wall falls

Seafirst Art Gallery

Palmers Shop

Paramount Theater Restoration

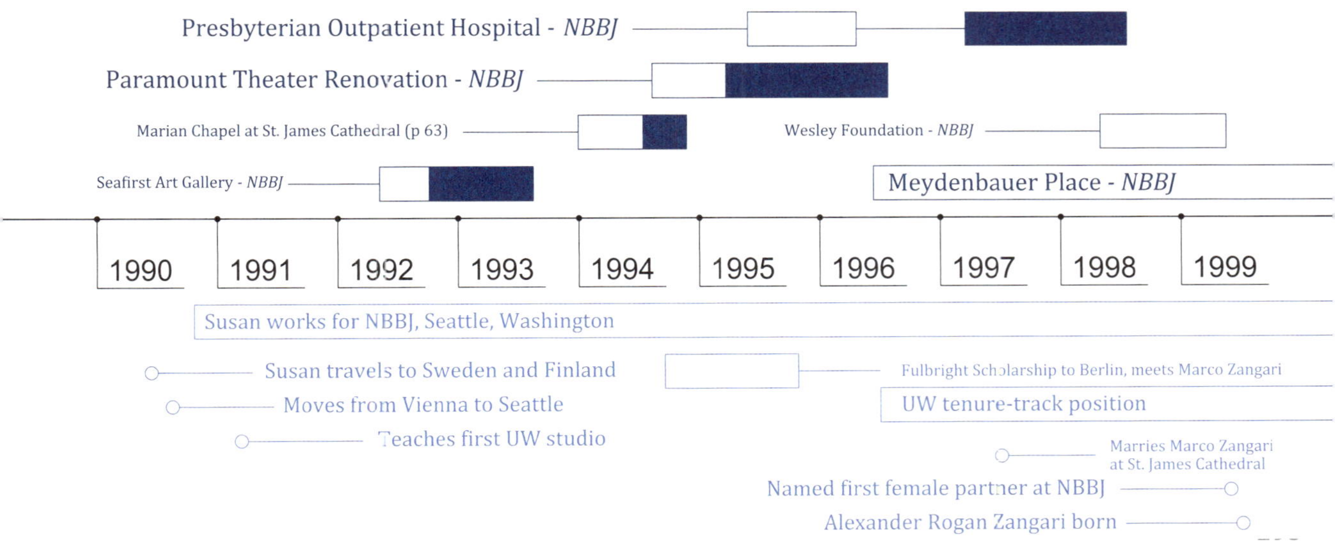

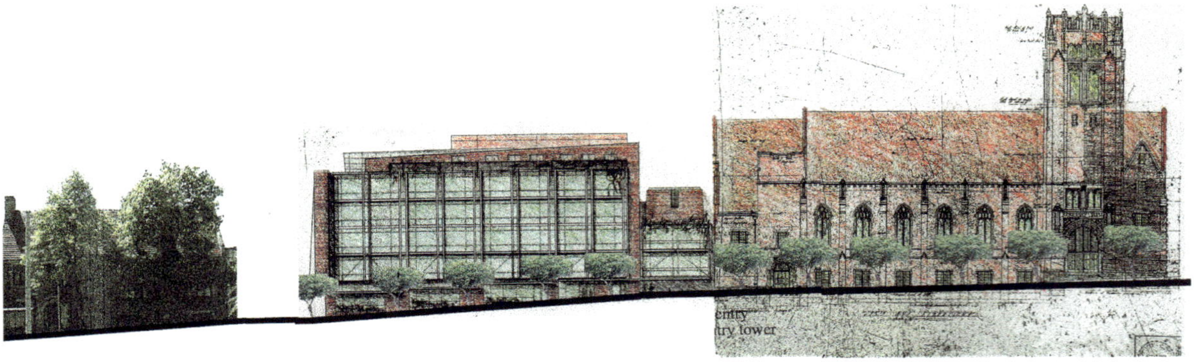

Wesley Foundation Addition

Alley 24

Meydenbauer Place

Mercer Island Prayer Chapel
with Steve McConnell

163 Castlereagh, Sydney Competition - *NBBJ*

Equestrian Center

Spieker Properties Tower - *NBBJ*

Alley 24 - *NBBJ*

Meydenbauer Place - *NBBJ*

Valley Mercer - NBBJ

2000 2001 2002 2003

NBBJ

Anna Domenica Zangari born

Susan Jones leaves
NBBJ partnership

UW tenure-track position

atelierjones founded

Seattle Tower

505 Yale

Dearborn Commons

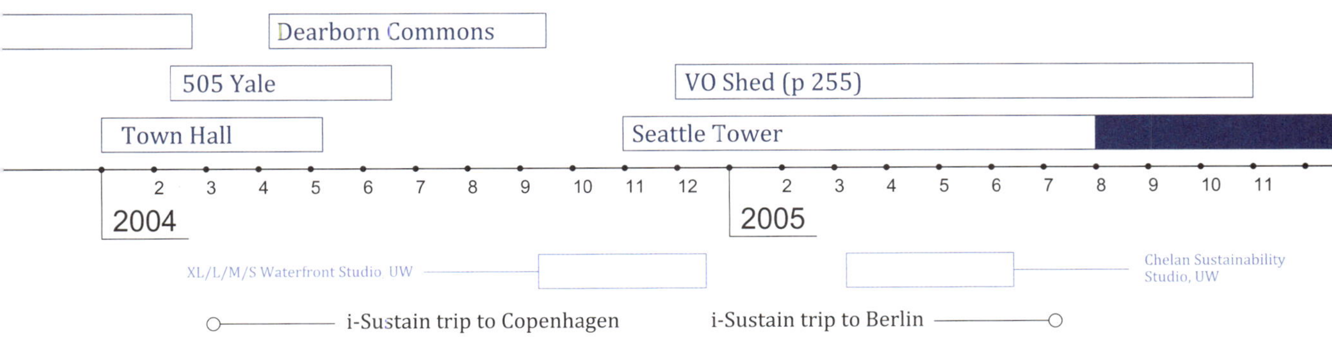

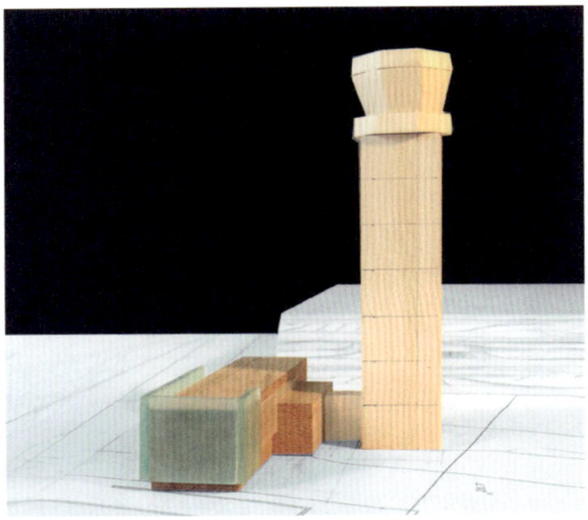

FAA Twin Falls

Wards Cove

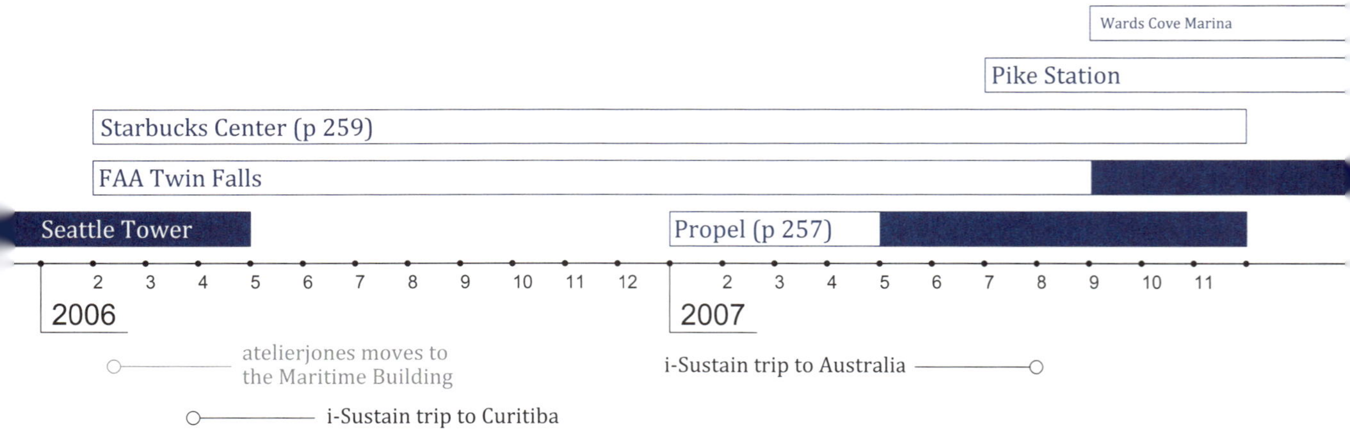

The Residences at Fairview

Paladino

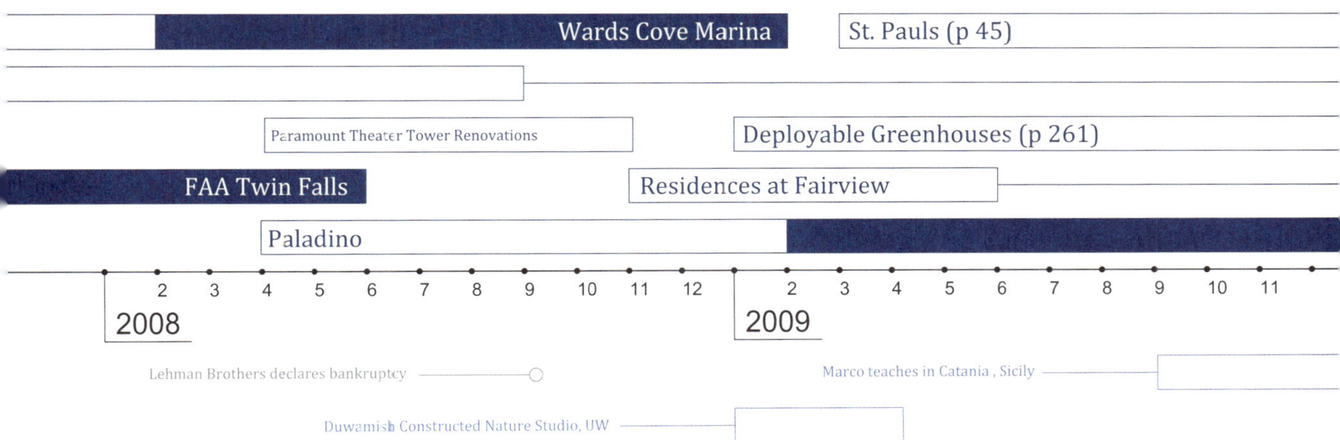

Pike Station

Marlborough House

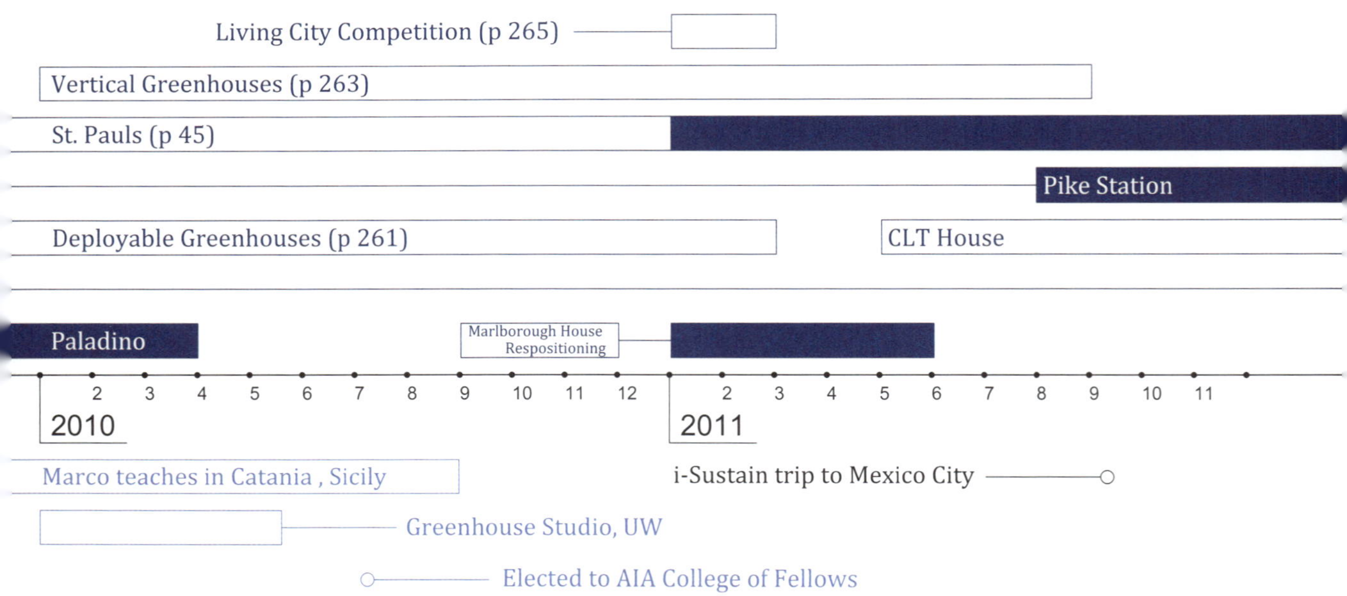

Rock House

UW Classrooms

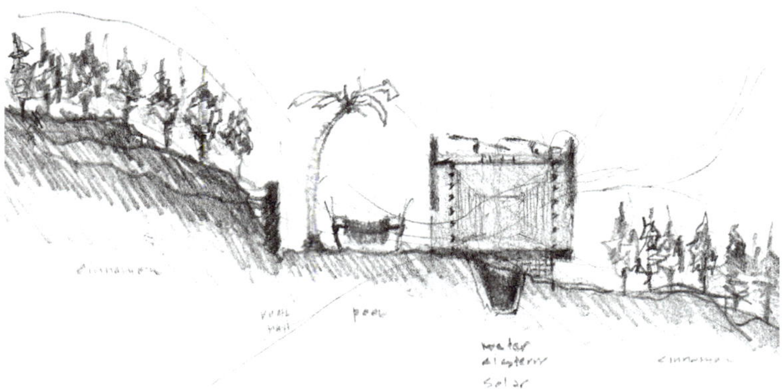

Cinnamon House

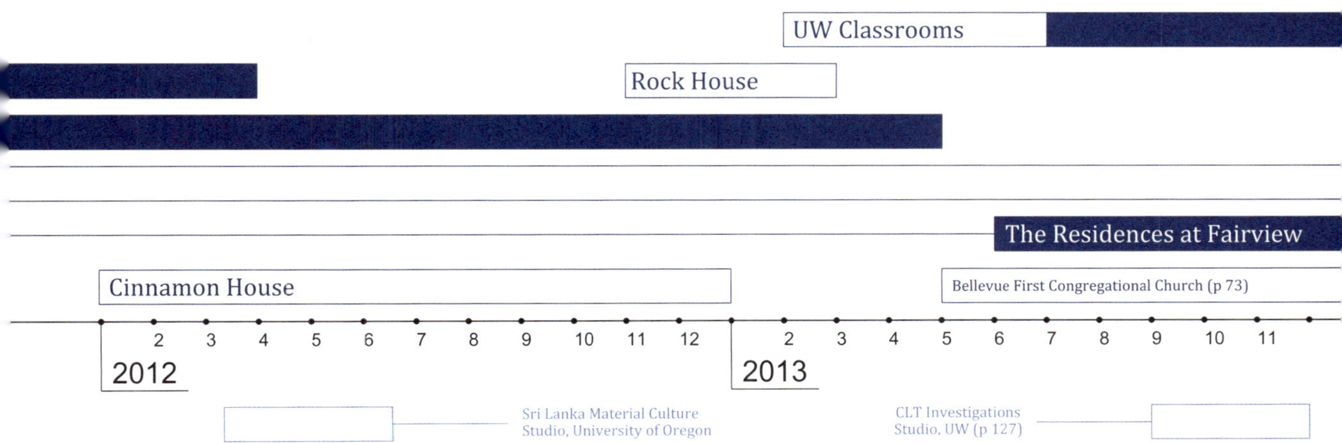

Railhouse

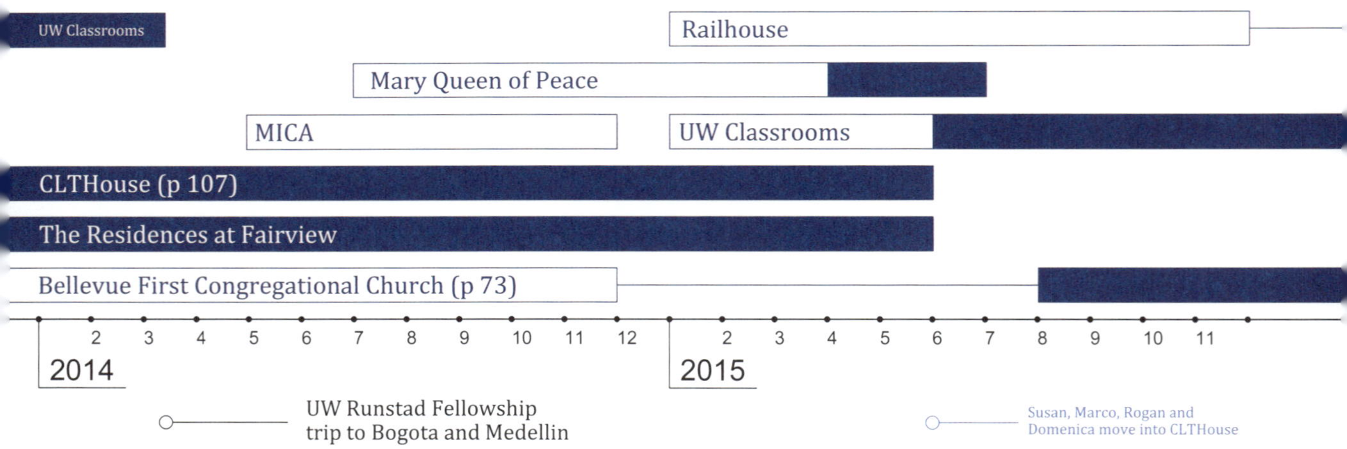
UW Classrooms
Railhouse
Mary Queen of Peace
MICA
UW Classrooms
CLTHouse (p 107)
The Residences at Fairview
Bellevue First Congregational Church (p 73)
2 3 4 5 6 7 8 9 10 11 12
2014
2 3 4 5 6 7 8 9 10 11
2015
UW Runstad Fellowship
trip to Bogota and Medellin
Susan, Marco, Rogan and
Domenica move into CLTHouse

Backcountry Ski Lodge

Mass Timber Ceremonial Hall

CLTSchools

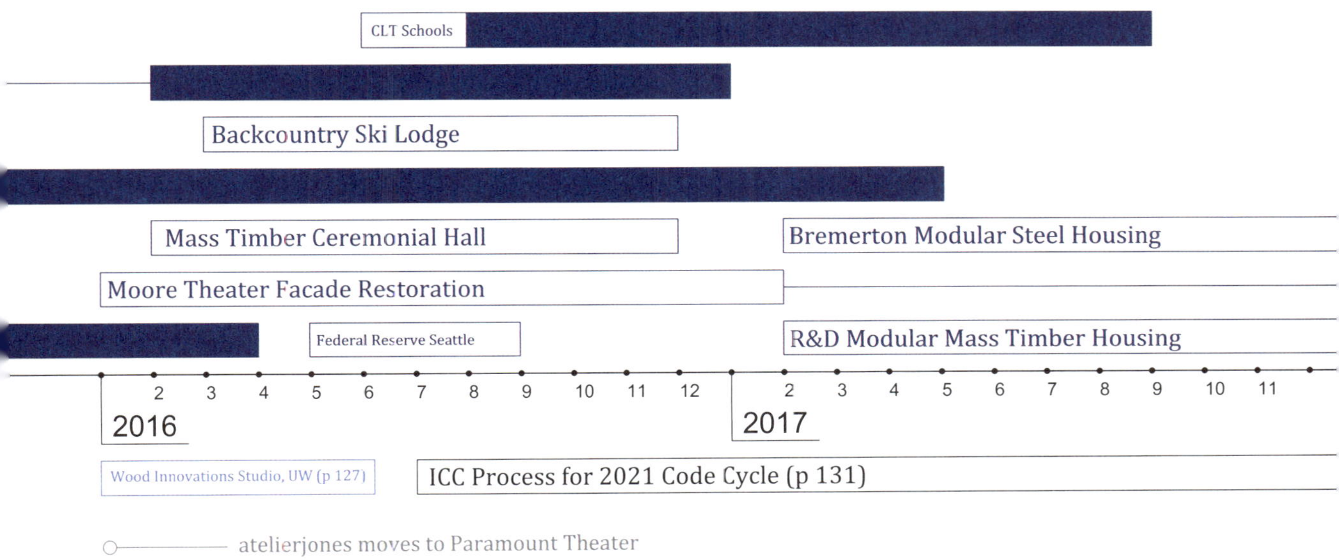

Bremerton Workforce Housing

Forks Timber Museum

Heartwood (p 153)

Forks Timber Museum/ Mass Timber Annex

Constitution Shed (p 23)

Bremerton Modular Steel Housing

Bremerton Light Wood Frame Housing

R&D Modular Mass Timber Housing

2 3 4 5 6 7 8 9 10 11 12

2018

2 3 4 5 6 7 8 9 10 11

2019

ICC Process for 2021 Code Cycle (p 131)

Nature Conservancy LCA study

Thesis Studio, UW

Type IV Codes ratified for 2021 IBC

Mt. Constitution Forest Management Begins

Walton Critic, Catholic University of America

Susan Jones - *MASS TIMBER | Design & Research* published

R&D Modular

Schweitzer Modular Cabins

Methow Modular

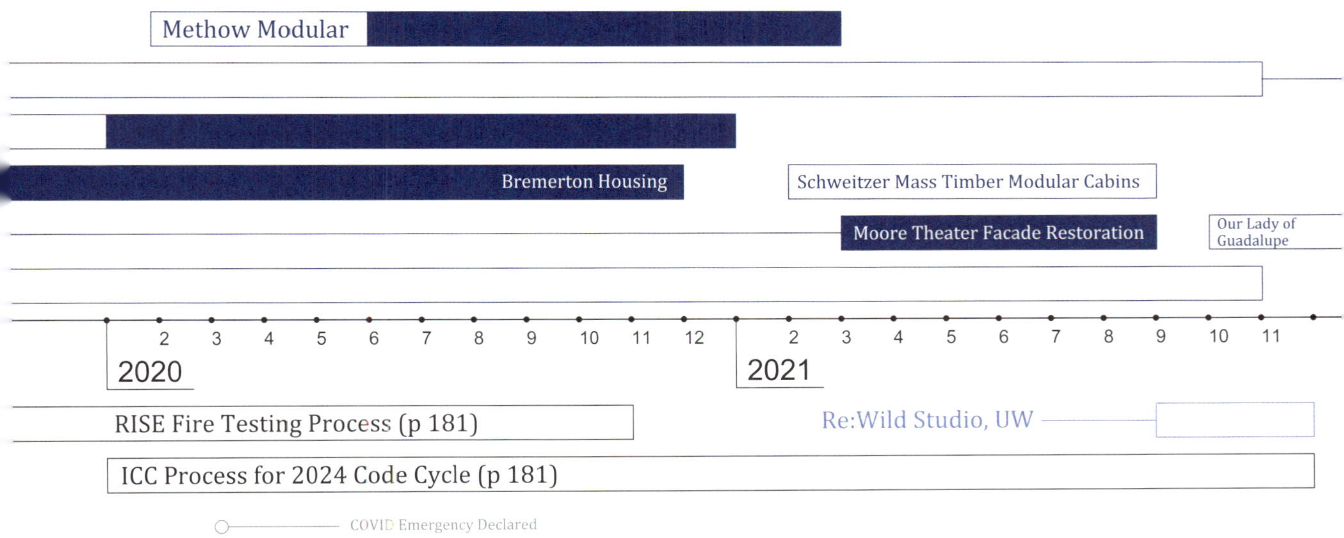

Kenmore CLT House

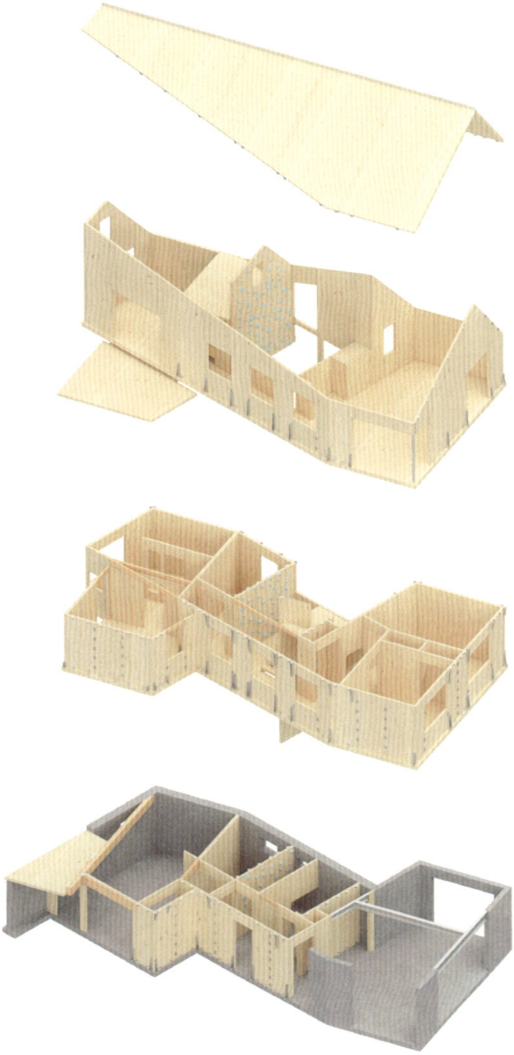

Shoreline CLT House

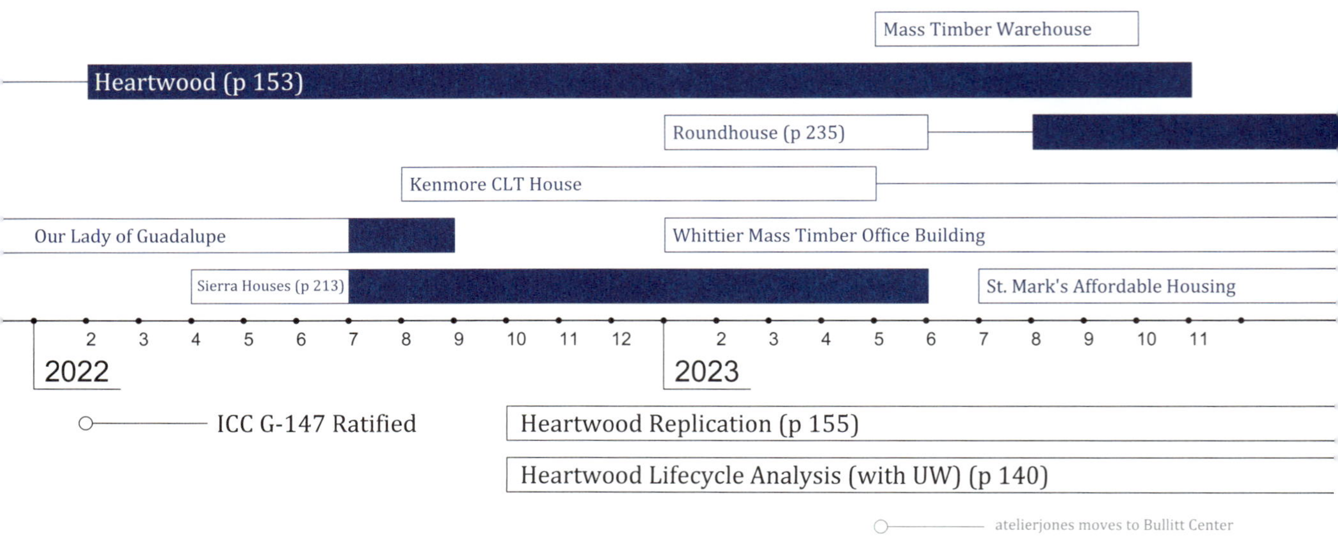

Clallam DADU

Harlem Mass Timber Housing

Green Diamond

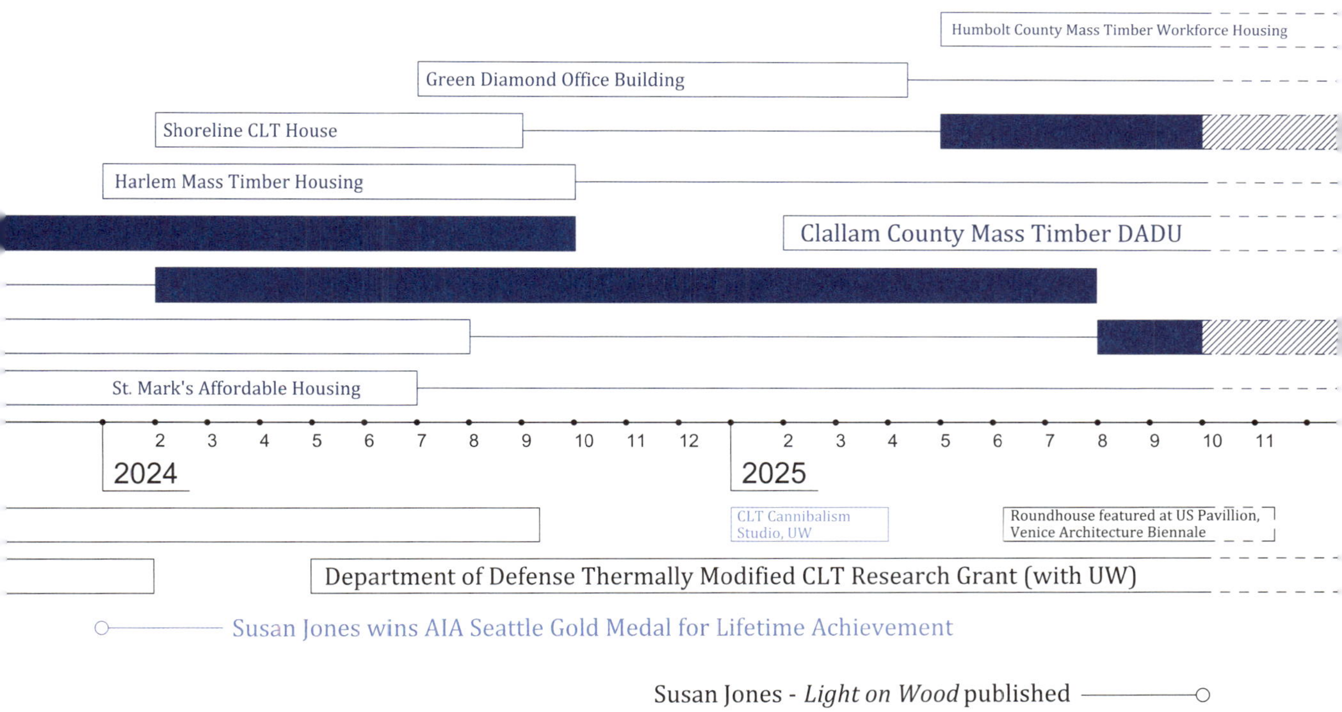

Regular CLT panel

Acknowledgments

While this implacable book wrote itself through the beautiful and inspired summer of 2024, it certainly did not edit itself, nor bring itself into the final form the reader holds today.

I am so grateful to those spectral muses who through distant inspiration, and the colleagues who through direct hard labor, moved me through yet another run-on sentence. They motivated me to, yes, slow down and add a period here and there. I cannot thank them enough.

Thank you to my deeply talented brother and sister-in-law, Gabriel Zangari and Anna Casotti, for their long and patient talks in the spring of 2024, before the torrent of writing began in the summer. Gabe's commitment to the craft of the book and Anna's love of architecture, culture and beauty opened deep pathways of energy and memory, sending this book forth with a voice and force I had never experienced before.

For the yeoman work of my deeply talented colleague, architect Matt Catrow, who lovingly designed each page, balancing image and words, and read through sentence after sentence, patiently editing my torridly paced writing and adding greatly to its clarity—thank you, thank you!

Thank you to Ria Stein at Birkhäuser in Berlin, whom I first encountered on Zoom as a critical and clearheaded editor and who finally materialized in the light and sunshine of the Giardini Marinaressa at the Venice Biennale as a friend I wish I had known far earlier. Thank you!

Deep thanks to Peter MacKeith, Dean and Professor at the Fay Jones School of Architecture, and a friend of many years, for his gifted and imaginative, prescient foreword and his own sylvan leadership.

To Peter Miller, for his friendship and shared love of the book. For his passion for making them, reading them, writing them, selling them, and his encouragement along the way.

To writer Bill Richards of Team Three, thank you for your friendship formed over Zoom, during meals in Portland, and on panels in Venice, and for your reading and encouragement.

To dear friends Anne, Adrian, Ingrid and Pam, whose reading and discussions of how lived experience, identity and personhood is transmitted through the written word, has continually fed this voracious heart for almost two decades.

To the ever-present and inspiring Ray Gastil, the intrepid, visionary leader during the peak years of The Architectural League of New York, and Planning Director of Manhattan. By a quirk of fate, he ended up in Seattle, sharing a desk in my office some 15 years ago, where we became friends, fellow travelers and colleagues of many years—thank you, thank you, for your high calling, cheerful emails, and ever-exacting standards.

To Julio Bermudez, my longtime colleague and friend from Catholic University, for an early, thoughtful and encouraging read in my Seattle office that inspired the final push of polishing and commitment to the edits and images—thank you.

Against the background of our incredible teaching experience at Catholic University in 2018, I am deeply grateful for the friendship of Juhani Pallasmaa, whose devotion to his craft and prodigious twin gifts of writing and friendship greatly inspired this book.

To Marco Zangari, for his constancy and his devotion to the word, the grammar, the precision of how we humans describe the nuances of the lush and the gritty, the glowing and yearning of the exterior and interior worlds we share.

To my mother, for her loving commitment to my comprehension of language from my earliest age, even before I could speak. Her conviction that language can be an extension of our bodies and can express our inner lives and sense of play shaped me indelibly.

Finally, to Domenica and Rogan and Marco. Words cannot express the love and gratitude I feel for having experienced your presence, your love. Your gifts of freedom and challenge, and the boundless crucible of your love guided me through this incredible journey to become an architect, to find my voice and to, eventually, write these words. I love you so much. This book is dedicated to the three of you.

Susan H. Jones
August 28, 2025

Collaborators

While this list is not complete, and the circles of collaboration are ever evolving, below are some of the individuals who have been key in supporting our work and helping expand our understanding of the systems in which we operate. Their knowledge of forestry, policy, fire-testing, and the environmental performance of mass timber has been critical to our work over the past 15 years, and has shaped the ethical imperatives under which we work. I value all of these relationships with the deepest respect and gratitude.

Forestry (2013–present):

United States Forest Service
Steve Marshall
Brian Brashaw, Ph.D.
Kevin Naranjo
Sam Zelinka, Ph.D.

University of Washington College of the Environment, School of Environment and Forest Sciences
Kent Wheiler
Indroneil Ganguly, Ph.D.
Dan Brown, Ph.D.
Bernard Bormann
Teodora Minkova, Ph.D.
Luke Rogers

WA Department of Natural Resources
Hilary Franz
Ken Bevis
Hollis Crapo
Bud Westcott

Orcas Island
Kai Enderlein
Rolf Erickson
Rich Harvey
Carson Sprenger

Yakama Tribe
Tia Beavert
Cristy Fiander
Doug Olney
Phil Rigdon
Ryan Sanchey

Sustainable Northwest
Jacob Dunn
Paul Vanderford

Yale Forest Forum
Gary Dunning
Mark Wishnie
Barbara Reck

Finland
Juhani Pallasmaa
Kirsi Leiman Gullichsen
Mikko Hautala
Petri Heino
Pekka Heikkinen
Mikko Leino
Lauri Linkosalmi
Matti Mikkola
Jenny Muller-Wahlman
Sami Oksa
Johanna Pirinen
Henrik Soderstrom
Anssi Lassila

Sierra Institute for Community and Environment
Amy Hafsrud
Jonathan Kusel
Danny Manning

UNECE, ECE-FAO Forestry
Paula Deda
Eoin O'Driscoll
Florian Steierer

Colville Tribe
Cody Desautel

Forestry (continued)

Karuk Tribe
Bill Tripp

Bill Lane Center for the American West at Stanford University
David Kennedy, Ph.D.
Martha Wyckoff
Peter MacKeith
Jim Hargrove
Edie Sonne-Hall
Russ Vaagen
Rod Fleck
Ara Erickson
Pete Kobelt
Anne Larson
Tyler and Kyle Freres
Chris Kalesnikoff
Gerald Cordeiro
Dwane Sorenson
Kyle Hanson

Life-Cycle Assessments

University of Washington College of the Environment, School of Environment and Forest Sciences (2018-present):
Indroneil Ganguly, Ph.D.
Francesca Pierobon, Ph.D.
Christina Bjarvin, M.S., Ph.D. candidate
Cindy Chen, Ph.D.
Lieke Droog, M.Sc., Ph.D. candidate

CORRIM
Elaine Oneil
Maureen Puettmann, Ph.D.

Forest Products Laboratory
Richard Bergman, Ph.D.
Hongmei Gu, Ph.D.

Carbon Leadership Forum
Kate Simonen
Stephanie Carlisle

Codes and Fire Tests

International Code Council, Initiator (2016–2019):
Mike Pfeiffer, P.E.

Tall Wood Building Ad-Hoc Committee (2016–2019):
Stephen DiGiovanni, Chair
Sam Francis, AWC
Carl F. Baldassarra, P.E.
Kenneth E. Bush
Sean DeCrane
Julie Frappier, P.E.
Jonathan Humble, FAIA
Joe McElvaney, PE
Kelly Nicolello
Paul Shipp, P.E., Ph.D.
Jonathan C. Siu, PE, SE
Stephen V. Skalko, PE
Matthew A. Timmers, S.E.
Andrew Tsay Jacobs, LEED AP, EIT
Felix I. Zemel, CBO

American Wood Council/RISE Fire Tests (2020):
Kenneth Bland, P.E.
Jason Smart, M.S.
Kuma Sumithpala, Ph.D., P.Eng
Sam Zelinka, Ph.D.
Daniel Brandon, PhD., M.Sc.

ICC Codes G146/147 (2019-2022):
Steve DiGiovanni, P.E.
Carl F. Baldassarra, P.E.
Sam Francis

ICC Codes G128 (2025):
Jason Smart, M.S.
Sam Francis
Carl F. Baldassarra, P.E.

Colleagues

I am immensely grateful for all of my colleagues over the 22-year history of atelierjones. The life of an architect is long, passionate and arduous. I have been lucky to intercept these colleagues at various times and places along their professional journeys as they have helped shape my own. Attending weddings and being a steady, empathetic distraction as some of life's most harrowing experiences are unfolding has been one of the privileges of my life. I am deeply grateful for the experiences we have shared, the work we performed, the questions we asked each other, and all of the drawings, models, details and buildings we made together.

It has been one of the joys of my professional life to mentor and be mentored by all of my colleagues.

atelierjones

2025:
Susan Jones
Matt Catrow
Meghan Doring
Eleanor Lewis
Ian Maples
Maia Marshall
Pamela Rhodes

Former:
Todd Afflerbaugh
Olga Amigud
John Bain
Laura Bathke
PJ Bauser
Lelan Bell
Greg Bishop
Madeline Black
Brooks Brainerd
Marlo Brown
Olivia Champ Tremml
Jack Cunard
Ginger Daniel
Graham Day
Jordanna Ebanks
Marisol Foreman
Brian Gerich
Drew Giblin
Dhara Goradia
Sakshi Gupta
Farhana Haque
Bron Heinz
Lucia Herz
Brett Holverstott
Daniel Hoyt
Maria Ibarlucia
Michelle Kang Ha
Abraham Kelso
Haejung Kim
Joyce Lee
Megumi Migita
Kate Murphy
Payton Narancic
Pel Olson
Boyce Postma
Samantha Prouty
Olivia Rodriguez
Mary Rowe
Emily Russell
Kristin Saunders
Justin Schwartzhoff
Roma Shah
Mesa Sherriff
Joe Swain
Sebastian Quinn
Lenore Wan
Chester Weir
Willa Westneat
Simon Woodside
Sophia Wrench
Alex Zink
Weilan Zhang

Image Credits

All images property of atelierjones and/or Susan Jones unless noted below:

Lara Swimmer – Constitution Shed: Front and Back Cover, 23, 32-46; St. Paul's: 54-71; Bellevue First Congregational Church: 48, 88-99; CLTHouse: 115, 117, 123-131; Heartwood: 167,176-185; Sierra Houses: 231, 237-247; Propel: 272
Timberlab – Heartwood: 133, 168, 169, 173, 174, 180
Ian Maples – Mt. Rainier National Park: 14
San Juan County – Mt Constitution Aerial Photo, 1932: 24
Emily Carr – Lone Cedar, 1936: 50
St. Paul's Episcopal Church – St. Paul's under construction, 1962: 56
Fred Hausel - Marian Chapel: 73, 80
Bumgardner Architects – St. James Cathedral Section: 76
Eleanor Kinsel – Marian Chapel: 77
Erika Schultz / The Seattle Times – Marian Chapel: 79
Francisco Lopez Arenosa – Bellevue First Congregational Church: 83
Research Institute of Sweden – RISE fire tests: 194, 198
Justin Sullivan / Getty Images – Greenville Trees: 214
Josh Edelson / AFP via Getty Images – Greenville Fires: 216
Justin Sullivan / Getty Images – Greenville Fires: 219
Ty O'Neil / Sipa USA via AP – Chipped logs: 220
The Sierra Institute / CAL-TREX: 228
Ed Hammerich – Sierra House Construction: 235; Roundhouse Construction: 252

SLOW

Imprint

Author
Susan Jones

On behalf of the publisher
Acquisitions Editor: Ria Stein
Content Editor: Bettina R. Algieri
Production Editor: Heike Strempel-Bevacqua

Proofreading: Matt Catrow, Stephen Roche
Layout and cover design: Matt Catrow
Typography: Heike Strempel-Bevacqua
Image editing: Matt Catrow; Pixelstorm, Vienna, Austria
Printing: Gutenberg Beuys, Langenhagen, Germany
Paper: 115 g/m^2 fine's polar premium Naturpapier
Typeface: Adobe Caslon Pro

Library of Congress Control Number: 2025939314

Bibliographic information published by the German National Library
The German National Library lists this publication in the Deutsche Nationalbibliografie; detailed bibliographic data are available on the Internet at http://dnb.dnb.de.

ISBN 978-3-0356-2990-3
e-ISBN (PDF) 978-3-0356-2991-0

Im Westfeld 8, 4055 Basel, Switzerland
Part of Walter de Gruyter GmbH, Berlin/Boston

Questions about General Product Safety Regulation:
productsafety@degruyterbrill.com
www.birkhauser.com

9 8 7 6 5 4 3 2 1

MIX
Paper | Supporting responsible forestry
FSC® C009051
FSC www.fsc.org

Light on Wood was funded in part by a 2022 Wood Innovation Grant from the United States Forest Service.

Funding to license third party imagery was provided by the Johnston-Hastings Endowment of the University of Washington College of the Built Environments.